From a Dime a Dozen to
Priceless

An Orphan's 70 Year Quest for a Family

The Unbelievable Autobiography of

Steve A. Mizera

This book is dedicated to my extended family: Nick and Marina Klimov and their wonderful children: Yelena, Sergey, Slava and Valeriy. Each brought their special brand of love into my empty and wayward life.

Yelena, who with her warm and loving husband Stas, added the immense and intense pleasure by allowing me to observe Benjamin, Nelly and Timothy become the center of their family. It has been pure joy. My close association with both families is the vicarious fulfillment of my life.

This autobiography is also dedicated to those leaders and to my brothers and sisters of Grace Family Church, Carmichael California, who try daily to keep the second greatest commandment as inspired by God in the bible: to love one another. They have taught me about love.

Cover Photograph - Left to Right Nick, Dad, Steve

Warning

Some readers may find the subject matter and language in this autobiography to be objectionable, especially those readers who have been brought up in a Christian family.

Nevertheless, reading this book may be beneficial to society whose experts claim they do not have the answer to the two very important questions this autobiography raises.

It will also be especially valuable to most Christians as the author relates his personal experiences of being raised in two different Catholic orphanages whose administrators had an excellent opportunity to spread the word of God and to keep His commandments but failed.

Where the author ends up and how he gets there may surprise you.

TABLE OF CONTENTS

FOREWORD

Steve Mizera would not have chosen the childhood he was forced to endure. Nobody would. News reports pop up all the time about figures in positions of leadership using their superiority and power to abuse trusting young children. Boy Scout leaders, Catholic Priests, and even more recently, Penn State coaches have all been stigmatized for their role in the suffering of children under their watch. Unfortunately for Steve, the institution he lived in as a young boy included the stereotypical pedophiliac activity making headlines today.

His journey starts in a very dark place, and brings the reader through his adolescence to his adulthood, including details of the horror he inflicted on victims of his own, eventually finding a new life in Christ, with a loving family that he had been robbed of as a boy. Along the way, the author describes his own theories and insights regarding the choices of those around him, as well as his own.

When the opportunity arose for me to help proofread and edit his initial writings, I found myself intrigued, hoping his words will help reach others and possibly assist them to seek help and/or enlightenment of their own. As it is often said, if this book helps stop one child from being abused, or steers one offender toward rehabilitation, then his goal will have been fulfilled.

Elizabeth McCrory, Citrus Heights, California

PART ONE

Chapter One
Saint Francis Orphan Asylum - 1940

You are standing in a line in your underwear. You are a boy of about eight years of age. It is evening. You are scared. This happens every night. You are awaiting your turn. Along with a dozen or more kids your age, you are focused on a pink butt staring at you. Screams permeate the air. Your butt will soon become pink or red and, you too will soon scream.

This is not my imagination: it was a significant part of my childhood: a sadistic ritual that still haunts me more than sixty years later. In the 1940s this butt-beating was called "discipline". Each Catholic nun at *Saint Francis Orphan Asylum* in Orwigsburg, Pennsylvania routinely carried a note pad and recorded every act that she perceived to be worthy of the nightly punishment. Called "discipline" then, today it would be called "criminal".

(Child abuse and child endangerment are new terms to the twenty-first century: they were non-existent in my childhood. Nevertheless, the discipline (or abuse) had a profound affect on me, and may very well be one of the reasons I lived my life the way I did. I will relive highlights of my journey through this autobiography. Perhaps you will be both entertained and educated on how my life ultimately turned out. Along the way, you may discover *why* it went this way: something I have yet to completely understand myself. Herein lies the need to write this autobiography.)

The oldest boys - about twelve years of age - had the task (or pleasure) of administering the punishment dictated by the nuns. A two foot long, puke green, hickory stick – ½ inch thick and 1½ inch wide - was the instrument of terror. At least one whack for every deed the nuns deemed "bad behavior" was awarded to any child who failed to perform to the nuns' standard during the day.

I often wondered as childless virgins, what could the nuns possibly know about normal versus abnormal child behavior? Some of the young male administrators of the punishment enjoyed their power, perhaps as much as the nuns enjoyed watching and listening to the whacks and screams. But the older boys were only following orders... where has *that* excuse been used before?

It seems to me now that I was always standing in that line. No matter what I did or didn't do I was enrolled in Sister Frances' note book. Numerous times throughout the day I became part of her record-keeping statistics. Was my conduct normal, or outrageous? I think I would still remember if I was behaving irrationally or irresponsibly. But what child knows what either word means at that age. What child can diagnose his or her own behavior at that age? What child deserves this kind of discipline?

I simply accepted my evening destiny. Today what I remember most is the blood that sometimes materialized or oozed from the welts from the butts I watched while awaiting my turn. This did not occur if a child received only one or two or even three whacks. But often a dozen punishing blows turned a child's ass from pink to red to purple before the swelling erupted and the blood appeared. I never got to see mine bleed, but lived it vicariously through the others as I viewed the butts of my young peers.

Later in the evening the other boys would describe my welts to me. Screaming mitigated the pain and fear, a little like it does on a roller-coaster ride. I was always determined to not scream. Although I bottled-up my rage and my pain, I was defenseless against the flow of my tears. Eventually I learned to hold back the tears, too...for almost 50 years.

Although the asylum housed less than two hundred and fifty boys ranging in age from 2 to 12, the nightly discipline line consisted of a mere twenty kids. Slightly less than ten percent of the orphans needed to be disciplined. The rest were probably too scared to misbehave. I was among the repeat offenders. My recidivism rate was one hundred percent. The fear of the discipline did not outweigh the joy of being a child, so I suffered the consequences the effects of which lasted for more than half a century.

The nuns were of a German order. The United States was at war with Germany during my first three years in the orphan asylum. Was this fact significant as a contributing factor for the harsh discipline meted out? Nahhh. Many years later I would reflect on these facts and assumed the ladies in black were just doing their part for their Fatherland's war effort. Clearly, all the nuns' activities (abuse included) were motivated by religion. It had to be so, because after the nightly beatings, we all gathered around to pray! I never understood the connection. I suppose this lack of comprehension precluded me from being a Christian, and planted the seed of anti-religion.

My father was born Nicholas Stefan Mizera on January 4, 1896. At the age of 10, he arrived at Ellis Island in 1905 from Russia via Slovakia. By the time he was 47, due to his job situation and unmarried status, he brought my brother Nick and me to the orphanage. I only recently learned his name and date of birth while doing research. This information was found on his draft registration card signed in 1942 when he was 47 years of age. I suppose he was exempt from World War II because of his age and his employment as a coal miner.

"Mom" (who I do not remember at all) had eleven legitimate children that were older than Nick and me. I was her *thirteenth*! Nick and I were bastards! The word "bastard" had a serious stigma in the forties. Today that has been softened somewhat. In fact, there is apparent pride now from being a single "mom"; a position many teenage girls focus on as a goal.

Of course I don't remember at the tender age of 4 and 2, Nick and I stayed in dad's car while he worked his twelve hour shift in the St. Clair coal mine. Nick told me about this many years later. I heard sketches about Mom's character and behavior from other sources in later years. My mother claimed to want us to live with her, yet she periodically *didn't* want us. At those times, she dropped us off at dad's house in Cressona right at the time he was going to work. We were unknowingly being used as pawns in her personal war with our father.

She would take us when he was not working, but would force him to take care of us while he was heading below ground in the coal mine. She would show up unannounced and drop off both of us to live in his car as he was heading to work. This must have driven Dad nuts! She treated her bastards much differently than she treated her other eleven kids, probably because we were the youngest at not yet 4 and 2 years of age. Being rejected by one's mother has got to be a hard pill to swallow for anyone at any age.

Dad's two bastard kids had neither an ideal childhood nor a normal one. To say we were products of a dysfunctional family is being kind and grossly understated. So at about the age of 4 and 2, Nick and I were deposited in *Saint Francis Orphan Asylum* to be taken care of...and were we ever!

The need for an orphan asylum for Schuylkill and Carbon counties in Pennsylvania was made clear during the influenza epidemic of 1918. That world-wide pandemic often took the lives of both parents (along with close relatives) in many families, creating a large number of orphans. The estimated 186,000 Catholics from both counties were asked to contribute money to build an orphanage.

On October 12, 1921, more than 6,000 people braved the chilly air to attend an open-air mass conducted in connection with the dedication of *St. Francis' Orphan Asylum*. The red and white building was originally a large, old farmhouse together with its 118 acres of ground; it was purchased for $15,000 and was quickly remodeled and converted to a home to accommodate eighteen girls ages 2 to 12. Two nuns were assigned to tend to the orphans.

Right Reverend Monsignor Francis McGovern, Rector of St. Patrick's Church in Pottsville, originally conceived the idea for an orphanage and proposed the idea to Archbishop Dennis Dougherty who presided over the opening ceremony.

The farmhouse was already over one hundred years old by the time it was transformed into a comfortable, attractive home. Over its entrance were engraved the words: **"Suffer the little children to come unto Me, for such is the Kingdom of Heaven."** Also engraved was the golden rule of conduct as laid down on Sinai by the Master Lawgiver of the world: **"Do unto others as you would that they should do unto you."**

By 1923 the Catholic churches began to collect money for the erection of a new orphanage to replace the first one. A goal of $800,000 was established for the building of a structure to house 500 orphans. Ground was broken for the new orphanage on December 10, 1928. The new building was unoccupied until July 3, 1930. By May of 1931, there were 125 orphans in the home.

My brother and I arrived in May of 1942, just as the old orphanage was being taken down. It was an obstruction to traffic on the highway between Orwigsburg and Schuylkill Haven. Neither town had a population of more than 1,500 residents. They sandwiched in the orphanage and were connected by a highway to the south of the orphanage and a railroad track to its north.

St. Francis' Orphan Asylum quickly reached a population of 250 children, including preschoolers. At its peak, the enrollment approached twice that number. The magnificent structure was originally designed to house 500 orphans, so it was quite spacious. The orphanage was a four-story, brick building and cost $815,000 to construct. The Catholics operated their own school with six classrooms. During its history it had also taken in 40 Cuban refugees and a number of orphans created by the Korean Conflict. By 1978 the asylum was down to 11 children.

On February 28, 1978, Monsignor David Thompson, vicar general of the Allentown Catholic Diocese, announced that the orphanage would close in June after 53 years in operation. He said the reasons for closing were the same as those for closing Sacred Heart Home in Coopersburg in June - a decline in the number of children to house and a drop in the ranks of nuns to serve them.

In 1942, along with the population of 270 boys there were also more than two hundred girls in the orphan asylum, but the boys were forbidden to talk to them. There was always a mandatory distance maintained between the genders. On the second floor, in the chapel, boys sat on one side, girls on the other. Meals were served on the first floor in the dining room which was segregated the same way... so were all six classrooms. Even outdoors there was a fence separating the girls from the boys; a 10 foot buffer on each side of the fence kept boys twenty feet away from the girls.

The simple rule was that there would be *absolutely no talking* to each other; not even wordless talk. Looks meant to convey communication were outlawed. My curiosity must have been strong as I often breached the 20 foot buffer. Because I violated these rules, I suffered the consequence of a number of nightly bruises from the puke-green hickory stick.

What has been impossible for me, however, is to imagine the girls standing in a nightly line for a similar dose of discipline. When I was in my early forties I drove from California to Pennsylvania to try to discover my roots. I found a few news articles in the *Pottsville Republic* that told of a "reunion" of the orphans. I was never invited, because I couldn't be found. (Google was not born yet.) I called Sarah Romanick who did attend the reunion. She was mentioned in one of the news article. I asked her: "Did the girls get the same discipline the boys received?" She informed me that there was no nightly green hickory stick line. However, she told me that a playmate at the time and still a friend today was still angry at the nuns four decades later because she was "disciplined." Apparently playing the piano was prohibited conduct. Her seven year old friend was attracted to the piano and thought she would try her hand at it. Big mistake! A nun snuck up on her and whacked her hand with one of those three foot sticks nuns use to point at the blackboard. This resulted in four broken fingers. This child, who was disciplined in 1947, refused to attend the reunion held in 1987.

But the St. Francis' environment was not totally Charles Dickensian. Picnics and parties happened periodically. But excluded from the festivities were those who lined up nightly, less they misbehave. Punishment was piled on top of punishment. At least the general concept of a picnic or party was learned.

There was also an annual May procession. Crucifix and flag were carried by altar boys who were followed by the rest of the boys in two lines, smallest to largest. The girls followed and were trailed by nuns. The march through the countryside was always a pleasant reprieve. There were many white statues at which we would stop to pray.

There were other memories apparently suppressed but awakened later in life. When I went to college in my early thirties, one clear memory surfaced. While taking a psychology course, I learned that a child is naturally curious about his body parts at the age of 5, so that must have been the age I was when I was sitting on a toilet examining my penis, trying to figure out what else it did in addition to pee. A dark shadow interfered with my contemplation. That shadow was cast by Sister Theresa as she peered over the top of the stall's door. She yanked the door open and pulled me off the toilet. This caused me to pee all over her and myself. Yes, I was in that night's line of deviates deserving of at least a few hard whacks. In Sister Theresa's mind, I was masturbating...whatever *that* was.

The Catholic Church has usurped the power of Jesus and bestowed upon its priests the power to forgive sins. The religious organization maintains a confessional booth in its churches where sinners enter so the priest can exercise this power. Sister Theresa had me go immediately to confession in reaction to my bathroom event. "Bless me Father, for I have sinned..." The attending priest must have been amused or perhaps even excited and aroused, as I described my sin.

His assignment of a penance of three Hail Marys was no match for the six welts created by the stick. That I can remember this particular incident *sixty-plus years later* seems to indicate that it very well may have been the start of my wayward journey through life. Perhaps it was that day that led my life to future confusion and conflict.

There were other good times at the asylum. Christmas comes to mind. Each year we received a brown paper bag containing an orange, an apple, a few mixed nuts, some hard candy and a shiny new dime with the current year imprinted on it. We had to sing Christmas carols to our unknown benefactors for this annual gift. Later, the nuns confiscated the money.

Each year we were instructed to write a letter making a request. These letters were read on the local radio station and interested listeners would wrap up a new shirt or socks and deliver them to the orphanage. These were also distributed with the brown paper bag.

I don't recall a tree, or a Santa Claus, or lights. We always enjoyed a turkey dinner on Christmas day. Food at the orphanage was always good and plentiful. But if anyone let any food remain on the plate that was grounds for at least one ass-whack.

One benefit in being raised in the orphanage was the development of a great work ethic. Today, I somehow keep looking back at it as child labor. Child labor laws were relatively new and besides, who would expect nuns to obey them. There was very little accountability from the church administrators to the courts that confined orphans. Today, government exercises much more supervision in its foster care programs which replaced orphanages.

The picturesque orphanage was located in a very rural area. One reason for building such an expensive orphanage in its location was that it was one of the few places where coal was not present underground. Orwigsburg is a borough in Schuylkill County, Pennsylvania. It was named for its found, Peter Orwig. Orwigsburg was the original county seat until the seat was moved to Pottsville. In the 2000 census, the population of Orwigsburg was just over 3,000. It has taken more than fifty years for the population to double.

Farming occupied the countryside between Orwigsburg to the east and Schuylkill Haven to the west: both very tiny towns. There was an active farm attached to the orphanage. In exchange for cheap child labor, the orphanage received food. I can clearly recall the pleasure of pitching hay into a horse-drawn wagon, and picking potatoes from mounds of dirt. This was the kind of "fun" for which we were NOT punished, unless, of course, we harassed the horse or threw dirt or potatoes at each other.

We also fed the pigs the food that was left over from our meals. I can specifically recall feeding hot dogs to the pigs. At that time, I hadn't yet heard of the word cannibalism.

On one occasion, I had the rare pleasure of riding a bike to Schuylkill Haven. One of the kids missed Sunday Mass and I was directed to ride him to Saint Ambrose Catholic Church in Schuylkill Haven so he could attend mass there. (It was considered a mortal sin to miss mass, so as a Catholic, if you die with one of those misdeeds on your soul, you go straight to hell and burn forever.)

Yet even this joyous time turned into a bit of hell on earth. While returning to the orphanage, the mass-misser was sitting on the bike's handlebars. I took a sharp left turn off the highway rather quickly, as I headed down the long driveway to the orphanage. The bike, he and I flew through the air. Both of us suffered wounds and torn clothing, and I earned a place in "the line." The bike was destroyed. I always assumed it was my fault for going too fast. At the age of nine there is no such thing as too fast. Reviewing that accident objectively today I know what really happened. The handlebar-rider must have advertently let his toes stop the forward motion of the front wheel by bringing the spokes to a halt. So I was actually punished for his negligence!

Every kid gets disciplined, some a lot worse than others. One would think, however, that being orphans mentored by purported agents of God, we would have had an exemption from discipline, especially such that crossed the line into abuse. No such luck.

Perhaps the discipline was intended to fill the character void in our personalities left by the lack of bonding. Instead it created resentment and hostility-the opposite effect-and prevented normalcy from ever gaining a foothold.

On the other hand, maybe some discipline - even abuse - is healthy. I also contacted a male who attended the reunion. Louie Domday came to the orphanage in 1945 at the age of four. He and I were the same age. He too was quoted in the September 1987 reunion news story. He told the *Pottsville Republic* that he wouldn't be what he is today if it hadn't been for the discipline he received at the direction of the nuns.

I telephoned him when I returned to California. He picked up the telephone and after I briefly mentioned that I wanted to discuss his discipline statement, he went silent. He did not hang up, but the sound of his breathing let me know he was still on the phone. No matter what I said, he just kept doing his heavy breathing routine. I can only wonder if that is what he really meant by "what he is today." What he was doing was not normal. Was he paranoid? Or rude? Or stupid?

Just about everyone else I talked to who was at that reunion admitted to having one or more obsessive-compulsive behavioral problems: one of mine has always been overeating. In addition, another serious defect in my character has often plagued me: my life-long belief that I had to buy anyone's friendship. Furthermore, as you will learn, another character flaw is something much more horrendous and despicable.

I am sure there are more, but I have not completed an entire self-examination. Underlying most of my problems has been my inability to form "healthy" relationships, probably stemming from the lack of any bonding with "Mom". Some people like and even love me, but it is not because of anything creative on my part. They see something in me that most do not. I have no idea what it is. But would they feel the same if they were aware of my most serious behavioral problem which is both the subject and object of this autobiography?

But let us go back to the fun of growing up.

After the loving discipline, religion was a big priority at *St. Francis' Orphan Asylum.* In retrospect I look back at my first home as a nun and priest factory and at myself as a reject from the assembly line. I was a serious defect not permitted to become a priest. Did that hard, hickory stick cause it?

We started every day off with a visit to the chapel on the second floor where we said our first prayers of the day. This was followed by breakfast prayers, before and after the meal. And the first class of the day was catechism where we must have learned the stories in the bible. We did not learn them directly from the bible because that was written in Latin and we were forbidden to read it!

Recess was usually spent in the chapel, and after the rest of the morning classes, we prayed before and after lunch.

After school we had a treat. The boys lined up in twos with the smallest in the front, like an Alaskan dog sled setup, just like the annual May procession. The nun who accompanied us through the countryside, took up the rear but without a whip. We chanted the rosary. The Catholic rosary consists of repetitious sayings of the Hail Mary prayer- fifty plus of them, interspersed with a number of Our Fathers, or The Lord's Prayer. It took about an hour to complete. My contribution, for which I was always awarded puke points, was in taking an unofficial lead. I would raise my voice just a little louder but loud enough to play leader of the pack. Once my voice dominated, I sped up the chant going ever faster and faster until most chanters tripped over their words. The rosary chant would come apart and halt. The nun, with her lips quivering, exchanged glances with me and did not say a word. She did not have to. She always talked ever so softly because she had underlings who carried her big stick. I knew I was destined to be in the night line anyway, so I may as well have a little fun first.

My brother Nick and I were not close, not even close. I recall a time when Dad came to take us to a county fair where there was a carnival. A nun thought I needed more punishment and prevented me from going. That still hurts today. I was denied one of the rare times I would have participated in a family activity, and I cannot remember why. I do remember that when Nick returned with some souvenirs, he did not bother to share them with me or even share the details how he obtained them at the fair. He added salt to my wound. We were brothers in name only.

Dad did come to visit on occasion. The shout "your people are here" always got everyone's attention, but the adrenalin subsided as soon as you determined that it was not your people, your parents or relatives, that were being announced.

The occasions when Dad did show up, it would be for about an hour. We would sit in his car and talk, I guess. If I would have had told him about the nightly whippings, perhaps he might have done something about it. In retrospect, that is idle hindsight.

I do remember him talking about the Chinese on one of these visits and how they had so many people. I recall that he said if and when we ever went to war with them we would lose because we could not kill enough of them. Was this at the start of the Korean police action? Perhaps it was in 1950 and I was nine or ten years of age.

On his visits, he always brought a bag of potato chips. I think that was my first introduction to foil. Dad had a house in Cressona, Pennsylvania. On the very few visits there I recall picking beetles from plants in the back yard and putting them into a coffee can. I remember that he was making wine in small barrels in the cellar. It seems he was remodeling the house as half of it was not usable. I also recall he would dry mushrooms on newspaper. But for the most part I have very few memories of him. The most vivid memory is of his pending death and subsequent funeral. I was about eleven years of age.

The nuns gave Nick and me brand new brown trousers and informed us that we were to go to the hospital to visit our father because he was dying. I recall being at his bedside. He had a large water-filled blister on one of his thighs. I don't know how or if it was connected but he was dying of miner's asthma or black lung disease as he had worked in the coal mines for a few decades. I recall making three promises: that I would never visit Mom and never drink wine or work in the coal mines. I have no idea what the basis was for any of those promises, but I did not keep two of them.

I only slightly recall the burial, but remember the wake. It was a party and most everyone there spoke a foreign language. I also learned that I had a sister, Anne, much older, who flew in from Seattle, Washington. I do not recall much about her at all as this was probably the first time I learned I had another sibling. She did not share the same mother. Her mother had been committed to an insane asylum. I think this was because she went crazy after witnessing someone dying in an auto accident. Or, maybe that was an excuse used to cover a genetic defect. I came to this conclusion based on what Anne did to Nick and me after the funeral.

Anne apparently got together with the executor of Dad's will, a shyster lawyer. Together they managed to split dad's sizeable assets: the house, a few bank accounts and an insurance policy. I recall pleading with her to take me with her, but she was too focused on "her" inheritance. Another rejection, another wound, and this one hurt much more that the butt busting.

It seemed that within days Nick and I were whisked away to a place and world much different than our safe home for the past decade. We were being driven to *Saint Joseph's House for Homeless and Industrious Boys* in Philadelphia. This was the beginning of my nightmare.

Chapter Two
Saint Joseph's House for Homeless and Industrious Boys - 1953

My new "home" was quite a contrast. All boys, all older than me, and thank God, no nuns. The orphanage was situated in the heart of a black ghetto and its inhabitants were lily white. The large, brick building was noisy, dirty and scary. *Saint Joseph's House for Homeless and Industrious Boys* was located at Sixteenth and Allegheny Avenue. It housed about 400 kids from twelve to eighteen. Freshman and sophomore classes were taught in the orphanage, but juniors and seniors went "outside" to Roman Catholic High, a half dozen miles away on Broad Street.

Shortly after I arrived at the institution an attempt was made to integrate it by introducing a twelve-year old, black orphan. I tried to befriend him as I had never seen a black person before. That was a mistake. I took a lot of punches and insults and it was the first time I heard the words "nigger-lover" uttered.

It seems a wealthy benefactor named Stephen Girard had previously willed the bulk of his fortune to the orphanage on the condition that it would be used to care for white boys. There was an unsuccessful challenge to his will and the Black was sent packing. This was one year before the Supreme Court ruled in Brown vs. Board of Education that separate but equal education was unconstitutional.

A large number of other contrasts overwhelmed me: no girls, instead of nuns there were laymen, and just about everyone was older than me. The sounds and smells of the city were very different than the sweet air and silence of farm country. I was soon to learn to my delight that there was no green hickory stick. In its place and unfortunately there reigned an absence of discipline in an atmosphere of fear. But the most profound contrast was with the adults who were charged with our education and care. Compared to the nuns who guided my first decade, these laymen were as different from each other as they were from the religious females.

One of a half dozen guardians who I fondly recall was a Mr. Goodwin. He was old, thin, gray haired, and funny. At night he played gospel music to put us to sleep. He was quite harmless and perpetually smiling. In a way when he was on duty it was like a sanctuary: fears dissipated, calm prevailed. But he was mostly only around during daylight hours. He would fill in at nights only when other guardians were not present.

Another interesting adult was a Scottish gentleman whose name has long since vanished from my memory banks. His claim to fame was that he coached the soccer team. He was an alcoholic. I guess the alcohol kept him warm on the sidelines as he urged us to "head it" referring to the soccer ball. Other than his slurred speech and wobbly demeanor, he was harmless.

A Mr. Brown taught history and I remember him as a very serious person. I don't recall any time where he caused harm to his charges. He was soft spoken and sincere and took his history seriously even if his students did not. His lack of a smile was haunting. His students were often unruly and I always expected him to explode, but he merely accepted his undisciplined class. It became clear to me quickly that he would not harm me, or anyone else. He kept to himself, a comfortable distance from his charges.

Then there was Bernie Meehan. He taught biology. He wore glasses with a large black frame. They would constantly slip down his nose and he would constantly shove them back up on the bridge of his nose. He had a way of slipping a piece of chewing gum -green Chicklets - into his mouth, believing he was not observed, and taking five minutes to do it. The class focused on his adjusting his glasses and sneaking gum into his mouth while his biology lesson went ignored. He made a lasting impression on me because once I tried to be the class clown and mimic him behind his back. He apparently had eyes in the back of his head hidden in his black bushy hair. He saw me, spun around and knocked me to the ground. This act of violence got a bigger laugh than whatever I tried to do.

Then there was Mr. Whelan. First off, he does not deserve the title "Mister," perhaps "Monster" Whelan would be more appropriate.

Most of these adults took turns watching the kids overnight. There was a very large dormitory where the kids slept and there was a small bedroom where the supervising adult retired to after the orphans went to sleep.

What happened to me and others my age after the kids went to sleep is how Whelan earns his "Monster" designation.

Almost every night he would creep through the aisles of beds and select one of the younger and newer children to accompany him to his room. He often waited until he thought all the kids were sleeping so he could have his privacy and practice his secret.

He selected me one night. He woke me. He took me by the hand without saying anything. He led me to his room and closed the door. He was a huge man. I think it is appropriate to say he was rather fat.

He was mostly bald and had wisps of red hair above his ears. As he sat on the side of his bed he had me kneel down. He was holding both my hands and talking softly. He was mumbling something about praying. He was not a priest and this was my first encounter with an adult male who wanted me to pray.

He had me fold my hands and bow my head. My hands were on the edge of the bed. I followed him as he led the prayer. While praying he put his hands behind my head and applied pressure. With one hand he re-positioned my hands by lifting them and placing them between his legs on his penis. He increased the pressure on the back of my head forcing my face between his legs with one hand and with the other he exposed his penis and pressed it against my mouth. This was a different kind of fear.

I was scared. I had no idea what was happening. He started to tell me how much he liked me and that we were going to be good friends. He had me stand, turned me around and pulled me back so I was sitting on the edge of the bed. He positioned my butt between his legs. He put one hand on my stomach and pulled me back toward him. With his other hand he started to rub my penis.

He was wearing clothes although his pants were unzipped and unbuttoned. All I had on were my underwear or briefs. He reached into my underwear and with the tips of his fingers started to slowly masturbate me. I had recently experienced a nocturnal emission - a wet dream - and now I ejaculated while awake. He squeezed my pulsating penis until I finished. He removed his hand and told me to go to bed.

On my way to my bed I heard snickering in the dark dormitory from a few of the boys who were faking sleep. It took a long time for me to get to sleep. I was angry. I was confused. But mostly I was scared because I did not know what to do.

The next morning was different from previous mornings. I did not like it. As I walked by Whelan to the bathroom he treated me with indifference. Was I dreaming? Was this normal? What happened to me? Would it happen again? What should I do? What *could* I do?

Whelan taught the tenth grade. I was in the ninth. His shift required him to "supervise" his charges for three consecutive nights about twice a month. It was a few months before he selected me to "pray" with him again. I was always aware when he was selecting others. Although I was relieved whenever I was not being selected, I couldn't help but think about what was happening in his room to the boy who was selected.

I never discussed this with any of the other boys. I was really too embarrassed, too confused and too scared. I certainly did not discuss it with the alcoholic Scotsman, the senile Godwin, or the serious Brown. There were no personal relationships between the adults and the kids. It seems they were doing time and would rather be elsewhere.

When it was the Scotsman's turn to watch over us, he sought refuge as soon as possible in his room with his alcohol as his companion, seldom checking on his charges. Mr. Godwin was heavily into music instead of children. No other adult to my knowledge was into sexually abusing my peers.

The priest who ran the orphanage was of the Jesuit order. This type of priest is considered to be the Catholic Church's legal arm. They had spent centuries guiding the church, justifying its position, leadership and authority, while controlling the masses and sharing power with kings.

Although he had an office and was in the orphanage throughout the day, the Jesuit was never present overnight as there was a rectory nearby where he lived. Our supervision was at the hands of the laymen. Was he aware that the orphans were being molested? I have no knowledge or even suspicion that he was aware of Whelan's criminal acts. Were any of the other laymen molesting the kids? Again, I have no firsthand knowledge although vague rumors circulated that this was commonplace.

Father Brown, the Jesuit, had his office on the second floor of the orphanage. It overlooked the enclosed yard where kids hung out. I can only recall one interaction I had with him. Two cats came under the fence into the yard. I was sitting petting both and decided to see their reaction when I held each cat's tail and bent them simultaneously as they faced each other. They screamed, clawed and became the focus of Father Brown who became aware of my act of cruelty. I thought the reaction I got from the cats was funny. Little did I know it had a deeper, sinister, psychological implication. He let me know that he saw what I had done, but he never chastised me or disciplined me. In retrospect, maybe my act of cruelty was my turn to swing the green, hardwood stick.

As a matter of fact, I don't recall any discipline being meted out to anyone during my stay. No hickory stick. No nightly line. Only the apprehension that Monster Whelan would be selecting me to satisfy his sickness substituted as a punishment.

Another aspect of my religious instruction that was missing at *St. Joseph's House for Homeless and Industrious Boys* was visits to the chapel, daily rosaries, and legitimate prayer sessions. I am, of course, not counting Whelan's private prayer sessions. These did continue at random and infrequently. They evolved from masturbation and fondling to oral copulation and attempts at anal sex.

I felt so helpless and hopeless during these unwanted encounters. I was angry, anxious, frustrated and fearful. There was no one to turn to.

After my first year of high school I dreaded entering the tenth grade because I would be taught English by Whelan. I knew I was in for a confrontation and had no idea how I would deal with it. I was turning thirteen years of age in September of 1953. He had to be in his forties. My first molestation by him occurred almost immediately after arriving at St. Joseph's House. It was more than a year later when I finally refused to submit to his sexual desires that he angrily confronted me. He told me I would regret it. So the time for regrets had arrived.

I am not sure if I was a good or bad student. Usually test grades provide this information. I recall one indication that proved I was not stupid. A citywide test was given to all Catholic students in Philadelphia in geometry. The orphans at St. Joseph also participated. I learned that my score was third highest in the Philadelphia Catholic school district.

Whelan gave me Fs in English. That is how he fulfilled the threat that I would regret refusing his sexual advances. He flunked me, and I had to repeat the sophomore year. This took the wind out of my academic sail.

The following school year in 1954 approaching the age of fourteen I started to attend Roman Catholic High. What a rush. Instead of being one of forty-five students in the sophomore year class, I was one of hundreds of students in my junior year. I was drowning in peer pressure. As orphans, a wardrobe was super-minimal, so was knowledge of the real world.

In Saint Francis, we were immune to outside world influences. Most orphans arrived as infants and the nuns defined our knowledge of the real world. In Saint Joseph's, orphans arrived in their teens and brought lots of baggage with them - bags of misinformation - especially about sex. I learned obscene language and fighting. I also learned survival techniques, otherwise known as gang affiliation.

So I was not interested in making friends at Roman Catholic High. I did not know how. Relationships were not my favorite pastime. I did not last long at this high school. A priest taught the first class: catechism. He was arrogant and intimidating. His favorite pastime was threatening and berating the students.

I happened to obtain a starter pistol. It looked like a real gun but only shot blanks. The noise was used to notify runners that they could take off. I took it to class and found another use for it. As the priest came down the aisle, berating my classmates as usual, I jumped up from my desk, took a stand in the aisle, facing him I pulled out the "gun" and fired it at him three times. I then immediately jumped out of the first floor window. That ended my high school education and my term at *St. Joseph's House for Homeless and Industrious Boys.* I was now really homeless, but I was free. I was free from Whelan.

Finding a place to stay was not difficult. A lot of boys ran away from the orphanage. It seems there was an apartment a few blocks away where runaways could seek refuge. That was the airlock that allowed the transition from the orphanage to the real world. A brief education on survival in the real world was freely available. I was a few days from turning fifteen years old. Although we did not get along, my brother Nick had run away a few years earlier. I was following in his footsteps, but I did not bother to locate him.

Chapter Three
Living on the Streets of Philadelphia - 1955

There are a number of considerations a teenaged runaway must deal with once he is free from the shackles of institutionalization. These include housing, food, clothing, medical care, spending money, an informal education, and maybe the short-range goal of socializing. I considered none of these, that is, until the need arose.

Housing, as I mentioned, was initially the easiest. Advice to all potential runaways was the same: "You can stay at the third floor apartment at 15th and Tioga." That is where all orphans desiring a better life start life. So I did.

There was a single adult in his forties who was a bookkeeper by day and a child keeper by night. He paid the apartment rent and in exchange extracted sexual favors from most of the boys who did not mind "getting head," as I later learned what oral sex was called. He was booked solid so initially he did not have time for me on his sex schedule, although I now had a place to stay. Over time, new runaways would show up and others would leave. At times there were as few as three and as many as six others there during my stay. Most runaways yielded willingly to the adult's request for sex-for-shelter. Sexual activity in exchange for housing seemed acceptable to the others. I was getting a free ride.

The next consideration - breakfast - was almost as easy to accomplish.

In the mid-fifties in Philadelphia, milk was still being delivered by horse-drawn wagons. That meant getting up pretty early and walking a few blocks in any direction. Before long, the milk man would be making his deliveries, exchanging full, glass quarts of milk for the empty bottles left on the front doorsteps. Sometimes cartons of eggs and bottles of orange juice were also delivered. Finding them was a bonus. Together with stolen fresh rolls dropped off in front of the area mom and pop store, these stolen groceries provided a nourishing breakfast. And breakfast was generally the only meal eaten. Caution had to be exercised that the same address was not visited too frequently.

Clothing was a little trickier, but clothing wasn't what one called a necessity. Teens are known to wear the same clothes for long periods of time, unless peer pressure dictates that the rules of fashion be followed, or that they be washed. Neither rule applied to me. There was no one to tell me what to do or what to wear. I was free. I was independent. No more butt beatings. No more of Whelan's sexual abuse.

At those times when a half dozen runaways lived at the Tioga apartment, we socialized and plotted. Sometimes when new clothing was on our agenda, we would walk the few miles to a small clothing store in Germantown and make our selection of new jeans and a shirt or two. But instead of paying a visit to the cashier, two of us would create a diversion such as a fake, noisy fight to distract the clerk. The rest of us would race out of the store with our selections as the clerk left the cash register to deal with the distraction. We were never caught. Of the many things we did not have, a health plan was obvious.

I only had a need for medical assistance once. During the day, we often hung out at a local soda shop on Germantown Avenue. Three strangers -kids my age - stopped at the door and motioned to my friend Billy Watson to come outside. He and I were the only two kids in the store. It did not take long for me to figure out they were trying to pick a fight with him. They falsely accused him of making an insulting remark to one of their girlfriends. My friend was not a fighter and definitely would not have committed the insult he was being accused of, so I went to his rescue.

I told him to get inside as I started to challenge the trio by claiming I was the one who said the girl's mother was a whore. Two of the three and me went at it for a few minutes and I was getting the best of them when the third came up behind me a hit me behind my left ear with an iron pipe. Down I went, and off they ran. There was a lot of blood on me, on my clothes and on the ground. I knew I had a medical emergency.

There was a hospital about two blocks away. I walked into the emergency room with blood still dripping from my head. I was told to have a seat with the other dozen or more sick or injured waiting to be examined. After a short wait and observing very little movement of those needing help, I took the initiative. I stood up and started to walk toward the nurse and intentionally fell down. That got their attention and it got me examined in a hurry.

With the bandages still in evidence, I visited the home of one of the trio who caused me to visit the hospital. It does not take long to obtain this kind of information, because kids love to brag about their exploits and conquests.

Before I visited his home, I borrowed a 38 caliber pistol. I barged through their front door waving it while demanding everyone come to the living room. I did not intend to shoot anyone, but they did not know that. Maybe it was the "thou shalt not kill" commandment that echoed in my mind. I announced my threat by stating that their teenager caused my head wound and that he would be getting his payback in the near future. His mother and father were terrified. So I guess that made me a teenage terrorist.

I was beginning to understand that my bark could be more effective than my bite. I wanted the entire family to know that I was wronged and for them to anticipate his injury in their future. I can still hear my performance: "It may not be tomorrow or next week, but he is going to suffer just as much as I did." I gave him a nasty look and departed just as quickly as I arrived. I never followed up believing that the threat was sufficient payback. I was sure he would relay this incident to his cohorts and that would be enough to keep them out of my life. It was.

For months I did what any irresponsible runaway would do. What took up a lot of my time was joyriding in stolen cars. The Philadelphia subway system has parking lots in the suburbs to benefit the commuters. They drive from their homes to a parking lot, leave their gas-filled cars and then subway it to work for at least eight hours. My friends and I did the reverse. We would sneak onto the subway by squeezing thru the exit turnstiles and exit the last subway stop in the suburbs. Taking our choice of cars for the day was a little like shopping. There were always so many to choose from. Starting cars in those days was rather simple. Behind the keyhole were four connections for wires. One connection was for accessories such as the radio and one was for the starter. Two others connected to the power and the distributor. It was simply a matter of using the silver foil that came with packs of cigarettes and wedge it in amongst the four wires. After the engine started, removing the foil from the starter wire was necessary. The "key" was on.

We were never caught. Often we brought the car back to the parking lot, unless we ran out of gas first, in which case we would abandon it.

Most of the former orphans living at the Tioga apartment eventually got jobs and found their own places. After a few months I found myself the only runaway left. It was just me and the book/child keeper.

He decided to have a man-to-boy talk with me. He explained that he was gay, (called queer in the fifties) but did not explain what gay meant. Whelan never did either. I suppose he was making an attempt to seduce me. I was 185 pounds and almost six foot tall. He was thin and kind of feminine. I did not contribute to his conversation and he did not try to force himself on me or make any further sex-based suggestions. Perhaps I had come across to him as someone who could get violent. Perhaps it was my recollection of Whalen's sexual advances that caused me to project a look that he feared. In spite of my limited knowledge of sex, I was as naive as they come, but content to continue living there.

Although my knowledge of sex could fill most of a tea-cup, I was soon to get an education. And my cup would soon runneth over!

I spent most of the day swimming in the Delaware River drinking Coke. We did not use alcohol because it cost money which we did not have. I came "home" to find everything gone! I guess the bookkeeper concluded that he would not get to first base with me, and feared he might get a beating instead. So while I was out, he moved out. Another different surprise was in store for me before the night was out.

The apartment was on the third floor. There were two apartments on that floor. In the other apartment lived an older married couple. The man was absent a lot and

29

his wife sought refuge in the proverbial bottle. She came home rather drunk one night and like a gentleman I helped her into her apartment. She was so drunk she did not know who I was and for once, neither did I.

I carried her to the sofa and plopped her onto it. She inadvertently spread her legs; her dress fell back exposing most of her privacy. I had never seen a naked woman before and my curiosity tugged at my morality.

Here was my opportunity to experience sex with a woman first hand. I popped my belt, dropped my jeans, leaned over her, put one hand under one of her thighs and prematurely ejaculated!

Wow. Oops. Geezz. What just happened? I had to get out of there before she sobered up or woke up, or before her old man showed up. The morality issue along with other nagging questions -like how are you supposed to have sex - would have to be dealt with later.

Days earlier I found myself hanging out at a restaurant and the waitress took a liking to me. She was plying me with free coffee and a sandwich or two. She had asked enough questions to determine I was a runaway. On the verge of being homeless again, I found myself at that restaurant again. I managed to mention that I was looking for a place to stay because the bookkeeper moved. I was oozing with confidence. I supposed that now that I had my first piece of ass I could go in search of my next.

Did I hit the jackpot!

The twenty-six year old lady gave me the key to her apartment on Broad Street, two blocks away from the dinner, and told me to make myself at home. Wow. I would have a home at last. She said she would be there after work.

When she arrived, I don't think she waited ten minutes before she had me in bed with her. I guess my ego was as big and hard as my penis. This classy lady wanted me! No premature ejaculation with her. They were all premeditated ejaculations. One right after the other. Sex was fun. I had just turned fifteen and now I had an "old lady".

She - I honestly cannot recall her name - had plans for me. She insisted that her apartment was my home. "Just be here when I get off work" she warned with the nicest smile. "Who wouldn't be" was my attempt to be conversational. Even more than fifty years later I can remember that happened on a Monday. On Tuesday, after she returned home from work, she gave me what she called an energy pill. It was such a tiny white pill. Unknowingly, I had my first bout with speed. And she had an exceptional bout with me for much of the rest of that night.

Wednesday, Thursday and Friday were repeats. Pills were followed by sex. But Friday concluded much differently than with she and I falling asleep.

St. Joseph's, which was less than three blocks away, conducted a dance every Friday. It was one of the ways the orphanage raised money. I had a number of acquaintances, both orphans and girls who attended the dance. I wanted to see them after the dance broke up at eleven that evening.

As I started to leave, my lover turned into Mrs. Hyde. Although I tried to convince her that I would be back after visiting friends at the dance, she was not buying it.

I was determined to go. She was still naked as I opened her apartment door to leave. She came running toward me. I ran away from her. I was actually a bit scared. She followed me out the door and chased me for twenty feet down Broad Street. Broad Street is a main thoroughfare in Philadelphia. There was a lot of traffic even at eleven at night. Horn-honking added sound to this nude woman chase scene. I raced around the corner of Allegheny Avenue and dashed up to 16th Street. Although I continued to look over my shoulder, she did not follow me.

Fortunately I was able to outrun her. Unfortunately, I was homeless again.

The dance let out at eleven o'clock. Twenty minutes later everyone was gone. I found myself hanging out on the corner of Broad Street and Allegheny Avenue, just two blocks from St. Joseph's and one block from my previous home. I was not about to return to her, not even for sex. I found myself hanging with someone I barely knew and let him know that I needed a place to crash. He said I could stay at his place and we walked about five blocks and entered a two story apartment building. As I walked into his apartment out of the corner of my right eye I observed a guy, fully clothed and a naked girl on her knees. They were in the kitchen and I was being led into the living room.

Although I was curious I turned away as I walked away into the living room. Perhaps I was too afraid to ask what that was all about. My immediate need for a place to sleep was my only concern. I found a place on the couch and started to watch TV.

Amid lots of noise and yelling I was awakened by someone who grabbed me and yanked me off the couch. I became aware that I was being dragged across the room and then down the flight of stairs. Except for a few flashlight beams bouncing off the walls, it was dark. I was being dragged down the stairway by two cops. I was shoved into the back of a patrol car. I was not told what was happening or where I was going, but within ten minutes I found myself being deposited into what apparently was Juvenile Hall. I was locked in a small room...a really small room. There were no furnishings and the walls were covered with padding. A sink and toilet shared the room with me. There were no windows. A light bulb burned constantly. Time drifted by slowly. What had I gotten myself into, and why?

What seemed like hours later - I could not tell whether it was day or still night - a bowl of what appeared to be oatmeal was shoved into the room and the door was slammed shut.

Where was I? Why was I here? I could not understand what was happening to me or what *would* happen to me. I was really angry and the longer I was held there the angrier I got. I could not communicate with anyone. There was no one to talk to. Periodically food on a tray was shoved past the opened door and it was slammed shut after the empty bowl or dish was removed.

The person who brought the food would not talk to me. He would not answer my questions. He just took the empty dinnerware and spoon and replaced it with one with food and another spoon.

I spent a very long time in that room. I had no way of knowing the time or if it was day or night. The food deliverer would not even give me the time of day. I thought I was losing my mind. Sometimes I had oatmeal for three consecutive meals. It was easy to loose track of day and night.

The room was opened again a short time after yet another oatmeal meal had been shoved in. Two big men ordered me out of the room and motioned for me to go down a hallway. They would not answer my questions either. At the end of the hallway was a door. Before I reached it I vented my anger by putting my right fist through the wall. It hurt me but I got my message across without saying a word.

I was ushered through the door into the room which turned out to be a courtroom. The naked girl, now clothed, was sitting on a chair next to a guy in a black dress - a judge as it turned out. She was asked a few questions only one of which got my complete attention: "Was this one of the guys who raped you?" she was asked. She looked at me and then she looked back at the person who asked the question and said softly: "No, he was not." Had I really known how to pray, I would have prayed to God to thank Him for her telling the truth.

Rape? What was that? Was that what was happening when I entered the apartment? Was I a coward or simply ignorant that night? I have often revisited that scene in my mind and have yet to be able to answer my question.

I was whisked out of the court room by the same men who brought me in and within minutes found myself alone on the courtroom steps. I was free to go, but to go where? I had no idea what I would do or where I would go. I knew I was homeless once again and all alone and had to deal with both very soon.

Because I was told I was free to go, I went back to my old neighborhood. I soon learned what happened after I went to sleep on the couch. The girl who was being forced to give oral sex had asked to go to the bathroom. She had locked the door and slipped out the window and jumped to the ground below. She was naked.

Two different naked girls in my life in one night. One was a crazy criminal. (Having sex with a fifteen year old boy and being ten years older is called child-molestation today.) The other was a victim of crime having sex forced on her. And I was a fledgling actor in one and a victim of circumstances in the other.

Looking back at my unusual past, I noted that when I was raised in *St. Francis Orphan Asylum* I was protected from outside influences. In *St. Joseph's House for Homeless and Industrious Boys* that was not the case. Words like rape, gay, or other words dealing with sex were either not used or not explained. Instead, substitute words like getting laid, blowjob, gang-bang, faggot or queer were uttered. There was no such thing as sex-education. To date, my informal sex education came from Sister Penis Peeper, Monster Whelan, child-bookkeeper, an old, drunk lady, a young, crazy, naked lady, and most recently, an honest rape victim.

I was not in the loop anyway as those kids who were snickering pegged me as a "faggot" because I ended up in Whelan's web a few times. Only one time did any of them have the balls to make a direct comment.

That happened about ten o'clock one night before the lights were turned off. Our dormitory was on the third floor. Five blocks away was Connie Mack Stadium where a night baseball game was being played by the Philadelphia Phillies. Every time there was a home run the noise from the crowd would erupt. Kids hung around by the window to see if they could see the ball flying through the air. Three kids were sitting on one bed near the window and one made reference to me as Whelan's punk. I did not know what a punk was but I knew what he said was an insult.

I slowly walked over to them, leaned over and took one punch at the kid who made the remark. I broke his nose. He was taken to the hospital. I was not disciplined. And, the insults stopped, at least publicly. I was not a violent person, but from somewhere I found the courage to take a stand in my defense. Why wasn't this courage part of my character later when the young girl was being sexually abused?

Now I found myself about to enter another phase of my unusual life. After I left the courtroom, I headed back to North Philadelphia to my old neighborhood. I was told that I made the newspaper. I never read a newspaper so I did not know the significance of being the subject of a news article. I was not interested in finding out. I had to find a place to live before nightfall.

Finding places to stay was easy enough but boy did they end up in weird ways. I flashed on the Tioga apartment, the naked lady's apartment, the rapist's apartment. What lie ahead for me? Should I sneak back to *St. Joseph's House for Homeless and Industrious Boys*? Would they even know I ran away? Nahhhh. Whalen would certainly know. I would take my chances on the street.

I am not sure how but I found myself in South Philadelphia and had both a place to stay and a job! The place to stay was a room in the cellar of a "mom and pop" store owned and operated by three Italian brothers. The job was to be their employee, their only employee. The entrance to the cellar or their warehouse was a flight of stairs three feet wide upon which were nailed 2 twelve inch wide boards. This made it easy to slide boxes down to the "warehouse". It also made it difficult to retrieve inventory or to climb back up with boxes.

I was told I could have the room rent-free, could eat what they had for sale in the store, and would be paid fifty cents an hour. I worked ten or more hours each day. No one kept track. I started on a Friday and was told I would be paid the following Friday.

I worked seven days and when I asked for my pay I was told: "Next Friday".

I suspected I was being exploited and might never see a pay day. I was angry but hid it well. I slid down the ramp and found boxes that contained five-pound containers of coffee. Maxwell House, the coffee company, was running a promotion. They had put a coin in each can. There was at least a quarter in every can and some cans contained a silver dollar.

No one else ever came to the cellar so I was free to open all the cans, dump out the coffee and collect the coins. I went through thirty-six cans and collected two silver dollars, three half-dollars and 19 quarters for a total of $8.25. The sixty hours I had already worked would have paid me $30 so I was still short. Pocketing the loot and brushing off the coffee, I went upstairs.

I waited until only one of the brothers was in the store. I waited until he opened the cash register. Then I grabbed all the twenties and tens and raced out the store. I did not stop running until I reached the subway station five blocks away. I had outrun him and outwitted him. And after counting the money, my payday amounted to $230 plus the $8.25 in change. I headed back to the only neighborhood I knew, that which surrounded *St. Joseph's House for Homeless and Industrious Boys*. I wondered if what I just did was what the word *industrious* meant.

I ran into Bill Pegliaro. He had also run away from the orphanage. But now he had a job and he had a very small one-bedroom apartment. After a short discussion, I became his roommate and was able to split the rent and pay for groceries. He turned me on to a job at Gimble's Department store in downtown Philadelphia. He worked in the record department at John Wannamaker's Department store two blocks from Gimble's. My job was supposed to be for the Christmas season only and although I worked full-time, it was to be a temporary job. I worked in the clothing department.

A home. A job. I made it!

Having had a great work ethic, I caught the attention of supervisors who kept me in the employ of Gimble's after Christmas. I was assigned to work in the automotive department. This was not actually a part of Gimble's but was a New York company that had sublet space in Gimble's. They sold tires and auto parts, and used the Gimble's name in their advertisements.

I worked for a fellow named Robbie Robins. Somehow I learned he was Jewish and in his early forties. We got along just fine. He was a father-figure. He was kind and always lent me a buck or two before pay day so I could buy lunch. I was being paid $37.50 a week for only 48 hours work. The government was keeping some of my pay check for taxes and social security, whatever they were. I was only interested in the cash I was given when I cashed my paycheck. Every week I had more than $32. I worked hard for this money. I did not mind hard work. Robbie really appreciated my hard work. I appreciated having him for a boss and a mentor. My life was beginning to take the shape of normalcy.

Chapter Four
A Dime A Dozen - 1957

About three months into this job I arrived one morning and Robbie was not there. He had been replaced by a twenty-one year old college graduate who was related to one of the owners from New York. I was both devastated and apprehensive. How could this happen? Robbie was such a good person and a hard worker and my friend.

Other employees on the second floor, where the auto department was located, told me about Robbie being replaced. And moments later I met his replacement.

A short, skinny guy popped up in front of me and announced: "You're a dime a dozen..." He said this with a look of disgust on his face and a sneer, and added: "... and don't you forget it."

Now I was dumfounded, and pissed. This was my new boss? I didn't think he should be talking to me that way. He doesn't know me. What had I done to deserve this insult? Surely Robbie must have told him what a hard and dedicated worker I was. What happened to Robbie?

My mind was spinning. My world was upset. Would I be fired next? I kept hearing his insult: "You're a dime a dozen" echoing in my ears. I knew what I had to do. I simply had to prove that I was worth much more than a twelfth of a dime. But how? I had very, low self-esteem for most of my life. This was the first time someone told me how low it should be. Although I had never had an appraisal of my self-worth before, the value had to be much more than the dime a dozen he thought I was worth. I was totally focused on him, on my survival, and on developing a plan to prove my worth.

My duties included keeping the shelves stocked with wax, light bulbs, seat covers, batteries, and everything else one would expect to find in an automotive department of a store like Gimble's or Wannamaker's or Macy's. They were the big three and their only competition was Pep Boys. Stores like NAPA and AutoZone and other specialized stores were not yet on the drawing boards. But the big item for sale was tires. Ours were kept in a warehouse on the tenth floor of Gimble's. Periodically the company ran a full page newspaper ad on a Sunday, and that meant the following Monday would be very busy. The ad drew lots of housewives in from the suburbs.

I would wait for a call from the sales floor and grab two or four tires and race down to accompany the buyer - usually a woman - to the parking lot and load the tires into her car. Often I was offered a tip, but I refused them saying I am already being well-paid. My $37.50 gross paycheck usually lasted until the following payday so I really had no need for additional money.

It was from the sale of tires that my big opportunity to get even with Mr. You'reADimeADozen surfaced.

Some customers did not want to take the tires with them either in their car, or sometimes they took public transportation to the store, so we would ship them by United Parcel Service. I would ship these orders because I was the shipping clerk. Shipping entailed tying the tires together with twine and affixing a portion of the sales slip to the string. Once a day, UPS would take a pallet or two or three away. They would check the slip on each bundle of tires. This was the only security in place to remove tires from the store.

On the sales floor, when there was a tire sale on, the five part sales slip was often not inserted correctly into the cash register because of the number of sales. The part of the sales slip designed for UPS would not print and the sales person would have to use a blue pencil to write the one line of information that would have been printed had the sales slip been inserted all the way. That was the only security and the only way tires could be shipped. And this was the way that I would get "my" tires out of the store. There was no accounting of the invoice slips. A new book of invoices was used when the old books still had a few invoices remaining. Those remnants were tossed into a box. I rescued them for my marketing plan.

I was also the inventory clerk in addition to the stock boy. I had to keep a record of all tires unloaded from the trucks and deduct those which sold. Each Friday, the owners of this sublet business would drive in from New York, and visit the tenth floor. They were content to count by noting how many tires high multiplied by how many columns wide multiplied by how many rows deep. They would compare it with their cash register inventory.

That number would also match one of the two sets of books I kept after my theft of their tires started. New tires had a coating of graphite that migrated on to whoever handled the tires. Dressed in expensive suits, the New Yorkers never handled the tires. If they had bothered to get a little dirty, they would have uncovered my plan as the numbers would not have matched when they discovered my method of displaying their inventory.

The first pair of tires I stole I sent to my friend Ronnie Gibson who had an apartment in West Philly. He was also an industrious boy who ran away from St. Joseph's but was no longer homeless. I told him that if the driver asked any weird questions to deny the tires were ordered by "his father" and refuse to take them. If, on the other hand, they were merely dropped off, or he had to sign for them, to call me when the driver left.

I waited nervously for that call. When it came and he reported success, I was overjoyed. Mr. You'reADimeADozen would owe me a re-appraisal one day soon.

There actually is honor among thieves. I soon had four "salesmen" selling pairs of brand-new, white-wall tires - even snow tires - wrapped in paper for $20. Ten bucks due immediately and ten after the tires were delivered. The salesperson kept $5 and got another $5 upon delivery. My commission was $10, more than a day's wages for "selling" a pair of tires.

I kept a good set of dual-books. According to my records I sold 1,250 tires in two and a half months or about 20 tires a day on average. My take was more than $3,000 or an average of $200 a day. The tires sold for about $20 each from Gimble's or four times as much as I was selling them for. (I did not charge sales tax, as I did not know what that was.) Gimble's lost about $25,000 which represented the cost of the tires and the lost profit. What really impressed me was that my plan made Mr. You'reADimeADozen look like he was really managing a profitable business.

I had one potential buyer - a good Catholic - who changed his mind before I had a chance to ship his tires. I returned his $10 and hoped he wouldn't upset my apple cart. He didn't. He took his money back and presumably confessed his attempted theft to his parish priest and not to Gimble's.

To keep the New Yorkers at bay and in the dark and to protect my plan as I implemented it, I would take the freight elevator to the eight floor where large furniture was sold, and retrieve large, empty, cardboard boxes. I put these in the center of the tire inventory and covered them with the appropriate height of tires, and they occupied the appropriate number of columns and rows. The number matched the cash register report used by the New York owners and matched one set of my books.

All good things really must come to an end.

I was rather loose with my new-found wealth. I would put my tail between my legs and even though I would have pockets filled with tens and twenties, I would appeal to Mr. You'reADimeADozen for a dollar on Wednesday, the day before payday, so I could buy lunch because I was "broke." I enjoyed my inward chuckle as he made me eat shit while getting out his fat wallet. I now enjoyed his insults. I planned to have the last laugh.

If you knew me then you made a buck out of our "friendship." I gave anyone money for any reason. I had two cars, both 1941 Plymouths. One was a white convertible and the other a black coupe. But I took the subway to work. I did not want to risk driving to work and parking at the indoor lot across from Gimble's.

With my newly found wealth, I started to do a lot of dating and partying, which now included drinking.

One Monday morning I showed up with a serious hangover. I was not paying attention to the fact that Gimble's had a full-page ad and a big tire sale underway. The phone must have rung for twenty minutes. I was sleeping off my hangover on the tenth floor. My sleep was interrupted as I noticed Mr. You'reADimeADozen wagging his finger and screaming something about I would be fired. I eased out of the couch - borrowed from the furniture department - and stood up to face my skinny, obnoxious boss. It only took one punch to put him out of his misery - temporarily. And rather than suffer the humility of being fired. I quit!

I had to get out of town fast. And I knew where I was headed.

St. Joseph's maintained a summer home in Sea Isle City, ten miles south of Atlantic City in New Jersey. Each week in the summer a number of orphans were bussed down for a vacation week. The previous winter, Albie Schmidt and I took off from the orphanage in the winter, and broke into the summer house. We spent a few days there and hitch-hiked back to St. Joseph's. No one was the wiser. We were not missed. We enjoyed our little adventure. Now I was about to go on another adventure but not as an orphan. And Sea Isle City was my destination.

(I had heard that Albie, who also ran away from St. Joe's, tried to rob someone with a gun which went off accidentally. He was sent to prison. I wish he had contacted me. We could have shared my tire business adventure.)

I arrived in Sea Isle City and spent the first night in the back seat of my car.

Lady luck was on my side in the morning. While having coffee in a small café, I learned that the owners had a small trailer for rent. I had plenty of cash so we were a match. So for much of the summer I would not be homeless. I would be a beach bum.

I soon learned what cash flow meant. Rent, meals and recreation made mine flow away. It would take a job to replenish it. And Ben Alexander had a job he needed to fill.

Ben owned and operated - by himself - Sea Isle City Automatic Transmission Service. In 1956 most new cars were offered with a standard transmission. Automatic transmissions were an option. Sea Isle City had a population of about 10,000 year-round residents, but in the summer it swelled to more than 100,000 people, most of whom were wealthy folks from Philadelphia or New York City who maintained summer homes in this vacation town on the Atlantic coast.

There was plenty of work for Ben. He had three or four cars with automatic transmission problems. My job would be to remove the transmission and replace it when it was either rebuilt or repaired. I learned to do this very quickly and I had plenty of time to watch as Ben took a transmission apart, replaced the worn parts and re-assembled it. He was kind enough to explain what the parts did.

I long ago stopped looking over my shoulder for whomever Mr. You'reADimeADozen might have sent to try to find me. Thoughts of him discovering my furniture boxes substituting for stacks of tires always produced a smile on my face. I was enjoying weekends and evenings on the beach. I didn't bother making friends or developing relationships. I guess I just did not know how to do either.

Accidentally, I did meet and enjoyed puppy love with Joyce Kitchens. She just turned sixteen, was from North Philadelphia and must have had an impact on me. After fifty years I still remember her telephone number: Livingston 9-3196.

She owned a bike and I took her for a ride one evening. She was on the handlebars and I was singing the Elvis Presley song "I want you... I need you... I" crashed into a pole and she broke her watch. I memorized her number hoping to have a date with her one day in the future, if I ever returned to Philadelphia. My only memory of her now is her phone number and her broken-watch-bike-ride. Apparently I did not have much of an impact on her as she later went on to marry and moved to Oklahoma.

Summer ended rather abruptly as it always does after Labor Day. Ben's business dropped off dramatically and consequently so did his income. By early November he was concerned about having enough money to pay the rent. He got lucky.

A fellow who owned a funeral business in Pittsburg, Pennsylvania was on vacation with his wife. She had been driving on the beach and got stuck in the sand. She tried rocking the car back and forth by using low and reverse gears. She managed to get unstuck but ended up with only low gear. She left the engine running and her husband brought the car to the Chevrolet dealer in town but they did not have anyone who could fix automatic transmissions. Because business dropped for them too, they had laid-off their automatic transmission specialist, but referred the funeral director to Ben.

When he showed up, I jacked-up the car and noticed the problem immediately. It would be a very simple fix. An "L" shaped piece of metal about four inches long that connected the shifting rod to the transmission had snapped. I figured it would cost less than a buck and take five minutes to fix.

Out of ear range of the customer I informed Ben as to the problem and solution. He had the biggest grin on his face as he went back to the counter and pulled out a large, cardboard box of parts from below the counter. He switched his grin to a grimace and started to sadly tell the soon-to-be screwed funeral director that it would take two or three days to fix his car and that he should book a motel room in town.

After the funeral director left to book his room, Ben told me take a rag and a bucket of gas and make sure I cleaned the transmission so that it looked like it had been removed.

Three days later he called the owner of the 1957 Pontiac station wagon with the good news. "We fixed it and you are ready to go." The bill was for slightly more than $500. It was more than enough to pay the rent and to pay my wages.

I made a mental note to myself: so *this* is the business world.

A few weeks later a package arrived from Detroit. It was from General Motors. The letter that accompanied the plaque thanked Ben for helping one of GM's good customers in his hour of distress. At sixteen years of age I was learning that, contrary to popular belief, crime did pay. Being in business and being a criminal were the same thing!

But that was the last of the good business. Ben started to date the daughter of the owner of the building. She was in her late twenties and heading for spinsterhood. She was rather plain looking and easily a virgin. Ben would become a member of the family where rent would no longer be an issue.

He must have professed his love for her in such a way to sweep her off her feet and cause her to accept a wedding date in early December. I was asked to be Ben's best man.

Ben had a 1948 Hudson Hornet, a fine car that he spent more time with than with his bride-to-be. I also think he *loved* the car much more than he loved her. On the wedding day, he gave me the keys to his pride and joy and told me to park it outside the church and wait for him and his bride to exit the church. I was then to chauffer them to a local motel for their honeymoon. He was driven to the church with his landlord and future father -in-law.

I ran back to the shop, threw the garage door up, cranked up the Hudson and started to back out of the garage. Those '48 Hudson Hornets had such small, narrow slits as windows in the rear. What looked clear to me was not enough clearance for the roof of the Hudson. I became aware of this only after I heard the roof screech as the bottom of the door carved grooves into the roof and then splintered the wood as is likely to happen when wood meets steel.

Ben was not happy to see me drive up in his modified pride and joy. It would not have done Ben much good to chastise or berate me. He knew I did not have the money to fix it. He couldn't take it out of my pay as there would be no more paydays. I always admired Ben's method of getting out of tight spots, but I was a little confused about his ethics. His honeymoon was over and so was mine.

As there was no work, I left for greener pastures. I went north to Westfield, New Jersey. There was a really nice, large shop specializing in automatic transmission repairs. It was owned and operated by a father and son. I dropped in on a Friday, noted they had lots of cars and proceeded to pass myself off as an automatic transmission expert.

The son pointed to a 1954 Chrysler and said it had no reverse. "If you fix it, Monday you have a job." he proclaimed.

The Westfield library had a Chilton Motor Manual, a thick book that describes how to trouble-shoot and repair any car, so I checked the book out for the weekend. I also found a room for rent almost across the street from the transmission shop. I buried myself into those parts of the book that discussed and illustrated troubleshooting and replacement of parts for the Chrysler transmission.

From what I read I could simply remove the pan at the bottom of the transmission and replace a strut: a piece of metal the size of a postage stamp but much thicker. The strut normally fit between a servo or hydraulic oil pump and the band or metal belt that wrapped around the clutch assembly. When oil pressure squeezed the band, it stopped the direction of the car.

According to the troubleshooting guide, this part generally broke if a driver tried to go into reverse gear from drive without stopping the car. Chrysler products in 1957 had pushbuttons to change gears, like the Edsel which had them in the center of the steering wheel. The broken strut was a common problem.

On Monday I put the car on jacks, drained the transmission fluid and removed the pan. I drove to the local parts house and obtained a new seal for the pan along with a replacement strut. When I returned to the shop I used a long screw driver to compress the band while I slipped the strut in place with a pair of needle nose pliers.

Both men were surprised when I removed the car from the jacks and backed it out of the garage before ten o'clock. They charged the customer almost three hundred dollars for my two hours of work and offered me a job at $75 for a five day week.

I actually made a few friends in Westfield. I also found time to drive back to Philly to see if I could score with Joyce Kitchens, my first love, but no luck. Maybe she remembered how destructive I was to her bike and her watch.

Mondays were bummers for an unusual reason. I worked hard and smart and would earn my $75 for the transmission shop well before lunch. The next four and a half days I was working for the owners for free. After a few weeks I decided to ask for a $25 a week raise.

The owners told me they could not afford it and finally offered me $10. I accepted but decided to open my own business. I had already turned 17 years old before leaving Ben's employ.

I had cheap ball point pens imprinted with my name, phone number and *Steve's Automatic Transmission Specialist*. I called in sick and started to distribute them to every car lot and gas station in Westfield. One of my newfound friends had a business rebuilding automobile starters and generators and had lots of extra space. I made a deal with him. I would give him ten percent of any money I was able to make. If I made none, he got ten percent of nothing. He agreed.

On a Monday a few weeks later I quit the father-and-son shop when one of my cards produced my first job. I had the car lot tow the car to "my" garage. I was on my way to success.

It took two more weeks before I received my next call as I transitioned from employee to self-employed. My first job was very easy. A leaking transmission did not command a lot of money as it required simply removing the transmission from the torque converter and replacing a seal. It took three hours. I charged $35 plus the cost of the seal. I did not know that you could charge a customer more than what you paid for the seal, or more than $10 an hour.

But soon the phone was ringing constantly. Within two months I "hired" my first employee, whose job it was to remove and replace the transmission. I was now doing the rebuilding. Ben would be proud of me, except he might disagree with my integrity.

Somehow I found myself getting involved with SPEBSQA, the Society for the Preservation and Encouragement of Barbershop Quartet Singers of America. I was beginning to get the hang of socializing. Even met a young lady and we dated. Estelle Zinger was from a rich family in Wynnewood, Pennsylvania. She was attending a fancy private school and singing was one of her interests. I was tagging along.

Unfortunately I was not good at cementing relationships. I guess after being deprived of relating to females (other than nuns at St. Francis) and their absence at both St. Joseph's and at my one week at Roman Catholic High, curiosity and caution were my guides. I suppose I always expected a little bit of Crazy, Naked Lady to surface.

Estelle had a real mothering instinct about her. She invited me to her home to meet her parents one weekend. This was really awkward for me. Her mom took a liking to me and her dad took to pitying me. He had a sense of humor I did not understand. He was a lawyer and I suppose he looked at Estelle and I as the mismatch of the century.

She took me to her prom and instead of attempting to get a little sex afterward, I fell asleep, to the relief of her parents. She was such a moral young lady that I would not have scored had I tried.

As I now recall, I must have had a normal but boring existence for the next few years. Although I was "in business for myself" that was really not normal. I was not yet eighteen. I did not have a driver's license or insurance. I did not have a bank account, or a business license. I had a few relationships and fewer friendships and they were not close. I seemed to be drifting aimlessly. Nothing outrageous or even exciting happened in my life now. So I decided to join the United States Air Force.

PART TWO

Chapter Five
Patriotism and Politics - 1960

There were so many things I had not done by my nineteenth birthday. Flying in an airplane as a passenger was among them. Choosing the Air Force was an easy decision: I was a bit of a coward so I did not consider the Marines. I did not want to get shot so the Army was out. I did manage to get out on the Atlantic Ocean once, but got sea sick so the Navy was also out. That left the Air Force. I was not interested in airplanes but was interested in doing something other than getting oily working with automatic transmissions. I viewed my enlistment as a vacation.

Although my formal schooling was completion of the tenth grade or my sophomore year in high school (twice - thanks to Whelan's revenge) I managed to score high enough on the entrance exam administered by the USAF even though I did not have a complete high school education. My scores were on a scale of 0-100: Mechanical 80, Administrative 80, General 75, Electronic 60, and Radio Operator 80. So I guess I was not a dummy.

I was told by the recruiter that I would be flying to Texas. I showed up at the office where I joined other recruits in a bus ride to the airport at Newark, New Jersey. One nervous kid expressed his fear of flying so I suggested he sit next to me on the plane. I lied when I told him there was nothing to fear. I bragged that I had flown many times.

It was dark outside when the plane took off. As I tried to re-assure him there was nothing to be afraid of, I realized we were no longer on the runway although it felt like we were still bouncing on concrete. The plane shook and my fear must have showed and stripped him of any confidence I lent him earlier.

We made a quick stop in Washington D.C. at night to pick up other recruits, and then we were off to Lackland Air Force Base near San Antonio, Texas. It would be a ten hour flight. The stewardess was handing out sleeping pills and although I never heard of sleeping pills before, I took a few. They appeared not to work so I asked other guys to get me a few more. During the flight I took at least eight pills. I had no idea there were consequences for taking too many. Forgive me for trying to sell myself as naive, but it is the truth.

After we landed at Lackland the sleeping pills finally kicked in. I struggled to stay awake while we received an orientation speech, received uniforms, and got a free haircut. We ended up at a barracks where I quickly lost the battle to the pills by falling asleep. The sergeant's screaming could not overcome the affect the pills had on me. His voice was no match for the pills. I tried getting up but to no avail. I got off to a poor start in my four year career with the USAF.

I spent five weeks at Lackland Air Force Base, doing physical exercises, jogging, rifle-practice, cleaning toilets and a variety of other exciting activities. I also took a number of tests. Although we were close to San Antonio,

Texas, and we had free time, I chose to explore the base and take in a movie instead of visiting the Alamo.

One additional test determined that I would be a good radio operator so I was ordered to Biloxi, Mississippi after basic training. A long bus-ride across Texas was my introduction to boredom.

Kessler Air Force Base in Biloxi, Mississippi would be my home for the next ten months. Radio operator school taught me two things: the Morse code which was useless and typing which was useful. Both were good learning experiences, as was the camaraderie. I was even introduced to a little culture when volunteers were sought to travel to New Orleans to hear Isaac Stern (the violinist) in concert.

But just as I did in Texas, I avoided going into town and felt comfortable staying on base. Perhaps I would have added to my culture and learned firsthand of the southern gentlemen's discrimination against Blacks. But I missed that historic opportunity.

The ten months were mostly uneventful. One morning I was a little lazy and did not feel like shaving before falling out for an inspection. The drill sergeant noticed my stubble and demanded to know what my problem was. I responded quickly - like a smart ass – and told him someone stole me radio. "What's a radio have to do with your unshaven face?" he barked. My reply: "My razor was on top of it, Sir!" did not go over well. After ordering me to do twenty-five pushups, he ordered me to visit the base psychiatrist. I have no recollection of that interview, but he must have confirmed the sergeant's opinion that I was just trying to be funny. A more accurate appraisal would have been that I was trying to get attention: something obviously absent in most of my life.

While I was at Kessler, Estelle had gone to the trouble to write to the Base Commander at Lackland AFB to find me. She wrote a letter to me at Biloxi and informed me that she was going to the University of Pennsylvania and invited me to visit after my tour at Biloxi was over. One of the dumbest things I did in my life was to ignore her and not take her up on her invitation. I was not aware then of my many inadequacies. Now, fifty years later, I am still learning of more of them.

After radio school was completed I was enrolled in something called a Channel and Technical Control Operator class. Turned out it was a bit like being an old fashion telephone switchboard operator. In addition to making people connections we also replaced transmitters, radio receivers, and telex machines that were not working with spares that did work using the same patch panels. My first assignment was to report to McClellan Air Force Base near Sacramento, California.

Just before leaving Mississippi for California I met Lane Missamore. He was a troubled airman, a super delinquent, and that was probably the reason we hit it off so well. I stopped him from throwing a brick through the window of a bar on our last night in Mississippi. He too was being sent to California, but to Beale Air Force Base in Marysville, just forty miles north of Sacramento. We used the money the Air Force gave us to fly to California and bought a 1949 Ford to drive there. I still did not have a driver's license and of course we did not have insurance. We found another airman who lived in Flagstaff, Arizona and talked him into going west with us and to chip in for gas.

I have always liked driving, so it was me behind the wheel until the first problem occurred: a water pump went out when we were 420 miles into our trip. We had that fixed in Shreveport, Louisiana and proceeded across the border to the boring ride across Texas. It was almost midnight when we arrived in Albuquerque, New Mexico. It was very hot, almost eighty degrees. It was only February. I curled up in the front seat to try to get some sleep. Lane had gotten sick and was sprawled out in the back seat. The youngster from Flagstaff took over the driver's duties.

We had just driven more than 1,200 miles from Biloxi, or more than 800 miles non-stop, except for gas, from Louisiana. I was tired but could not get to sleep, especially not in half a front seat. After a short time I found myself using the driver's leg as a pillow. My right hand reached inadvertently between his legs and rested on his penis. He did nothing. Neither did I. I felt him getting hard. So did I. I kept my hand on his hard cock. Before I drifted off to sleep, I did not question why or what I was doing.

I awoke to hear a conversation about snow, that it was a foot deep, that we had gone off the highway, and that we were stuck. I then learned we were out of gas and not quite to Flagstaff. We were fortunate in hearing a voice via bullhorn of an Arizona Highway Patrolman asking if there were any children in the car. I hollered back through the dark there were three, and as if by magic, a tow-truck materialized and pulled us back onto the highway and gave us enough gas to get to Flagstaff. In 1960 gas was less than twenty cents a gallon. It cost $5 for the towing service. Our passenger's mom owned a Chinese restaurant, although neither she nor he was Chinese, so we had a free chow mein breakfast. He and I did not make mention of our strange sexual encounter, but it did bother me for quite a while after. Sex was sure confusing.

There was a blizzard in Flagstaff, Lane had developed a nasty cold, and we had no chains. That may not have made a difference as I had never driven in snow before. We were heading south to Yuma, Arizona. It was an exciting and scary long ride downhill and only after the snow disappeared did I get to relax. By late afternoon it was more than 90 degrees when we arrived in Yuma. Our compass was pointed west toward San Diego, where my "sister" Anne Morgan lived. When she came to our father's funeral, she lived with her husband in Seattle, Washington. Shortly after returning from the funeral, her husband was killed on the job. He was a steel worker. She moved to San Diego with her two kids and my inheritance.

I did not know that she had ripped-off Nick and me of our inheritance when she came across country for the funeral. It seems Dad had a number of bank accounts which she drained while she mourned. Dad owned a house in Cressona, Pennsylvania. His executor - a local shyster lawyer - conspired with Anne. She ended up with cash. He got the house. I did not learn of this until years later. I had long ago forgotten that she could have gotten Nick and me out of the asylum when Dad died and did not. So the overnight visit was relatively pleasant. She had two young daughters and she was grooming both to become nuns. What a fine Catholic she was. Little bit of a hypocrite and thief but offering her kids up as nuns was probably designed to offset her immoral and dysfunctional behavior.

The end of our cross-country adventure found us going north to San Francisco where Lane lived with his parents. I can still recall racing across the Bay Bridge. Lane was driving. Believe it or not, the famous song "I Left My Heart in San Francisco" was playing and being sung by Tony Bennett on the radio. I noticed the very large sign that read BUMP and which required our speed to be 10 MPH because of construction. It was night and raining. When our car hit the bump my head hit the roof. It really hurt. Lane thought it was funny.

Lane's dad owned a bar in the Mission district, real close to what is now the gay district in San Francisco. Lane's mom was an alcoholic and she immediately reminded me of the lady who was my first attempt at intercourse.

We stayed at his home for a week. He was off visiting his friends. I preferred to stay by myself. I did not mind that Lane's mom came home loaded one night. She climbed into my bed and had her way with me. I think this is the first time that I considered myself a mother-fucker, and a good one at that. It had been a long-time since I had been laid. I put into practice what the "old" crazy, naked waitress had taught me.

Lane was not aware of my relationship with his mom, but because he did not have much of a relationship with her either, it probably would not have made much of a difference to him. We remained good friends for the next few years. He would come down to McClellan AFB in North Highlands from Beale AFB in Marysville and we would head off to San Francisco. He enjoyed drinking, and booze was always available at his dad's bar - free! I was now getting drunk on a regular basis. It was 1962 and I was 21 years of age.

During my early and short career as a car thief when I ran away from St. Joseph's House, I took a fancy to a 1953 Lincoln. I took it for a joy ride and vowed one day I would own one. (Lane got to keep the 1949 Ford that made it 2,341 miles from Biloxi)

I found a 1953 Mercury that looked a lot like the 1953 Lincoln at a car lot in San Francisco. My experience gained under the guidance of silver-tongued Ben Alexander in the transmission business came in handy. I took the car for a test-ride. Out of site of the lot, I managed to tighten the adjustment between the gas pedal and the transmission's valve body assembly so that the car would stay in low gear. It would not shift to drive which meant the car was racing at twenty miles per hour.

When I returned it to the lot I was able to get a significant reduction in the price for the car because the transmission was "broke." But what goes around comes around, and I was about to learn this for the first of many times.

I had the oil changed a few months later at a gas station in Sacramento. On my way to San Francisco, the oil plug, which was not tightened by the "mechanic," loosened enough to allow oil to leak. I almost made it to Davis twenty miles to the west, when the engine seized up.

I had to have my 1953 Mercury towed back to McClellan AFB. I could not take it onto the base because I did not have insurance or a driver's license. Insurance was not mandatory then as it is today. My car was parked just outside the gate with other cars airmen owned who also did not have insurance. I could see it from the barracks.

Lane had the brilliant idea to take the car to San Francisco where we could install a re-built engine in the garage of his parent's home. So on a weekday after midnight, he showed up with his Ford and did what readers of this autobiography may find unbelievable. We removed the driveshaft and put it in the back seat of my Mercury with the front of it stuck out ten inches from the driver's side window. He, behind the wheel of his Ford pushed me in the Mercury, bumper to bumper. We would get up to fifty miles per hour, then he would back off and I would coast. We did this for the entire 93 miles right down what is now Highway 80, across Highway 37 known as the Black Point Cutoff, south on the Redwood Highway or Highway 101 and over the Golden Gate Bridge. At the toll booth, I made believe my car wouldn't start and hung my head out the window and shouted to Lane behind me: "Mister, can you give me a push?" God had to be watching over us during that trip.

His home was at 19th and Santiago, a mere five miles from the San Francisco side of the bridge. At three in the morning, there was no one paying attention to this incredible (and stupid) journey. In retrospect, I guess I was rather irresponsible and maybe I did deserve a few of the butt-beatings in my youth. Today it is unlikely that anyone could go five miles, doing what Lane and I did in 1962, without being stopped by the California Highway Patrol. Actually, with the ubiquitous cell phones today, no one could go *one mile* before getting busted.

My military career was like going to summer camp. Our barracks at McClellan AFB was next door to the Air Police barracks. To keep them on their toes, we periodically played practical jokes. For example, we would tie a wire from the door to the fire alarm box so the first person who entered would wake everyone from the three floors and we would be entertained by how quickly they would evacuate.

Practical jokes in our own barracks were often just as entertaining. Most everyone had at that time KP or Kitchen Patrol. To perform this duty meant the lucky person would have to get up at 3 am, report to the chow hall, start his day by peeling a ton of potatoes, and then enjoy the pleasures of washing dishes, pots, and pans throughout the day. Only after sixteen hours would the exhausted airman return to his bed. A practical joke we pulled periodically would be to set the clock of the person scheduled for KP ahead an hour or so. That meant they arrived at the chow hall an hour or more early to our childish delight.

Now that I am an adult, and presumably mature, that doesn't look as funny today.

I blended in with my fellow airmen. Drinking was high on our agenda. I purchased a Honda Dream, a 300cc motorcycle, and I know my guardian angel worked full time to keep me alive. Although at the time speeding and running lights and stop signs felt like fun, today I would be inclined to chastise youth who I see doing the same thing.

At the age of 22 my inability to form relationships should have been obvious, but it was not to me. I had very few friends, and no close friends. I rarely had dates that I initiated myself, although I did double-date a few times because someone else fixed me up. I did not think myself abnormal. I did not think about myself. Without giving it much thought I assumed I was normal. I had a very low self-image but was not aware of that either.

But I was aware that I did strange things, irresponsible things, and even bold or stupid things. For example, Lane Missamore got busted by the Shore Patrol (Navy cops) in San Francisco, and his mom called me to see if I could advise her on how to help him. I called the Shore Patrol and represented myself as Lieutenant Morgan from Beale AFB. I showed up in San Francisco in civilian clothes and found Lane in a cage in the middle of the floor where he was being held by the Shore Patrol. I signed a few pieces of paper and he was released to my custody for transport back to Beale. The seamen on duty never bothered to ask me for ID. If they had, I would have joined Lane in the cage.

We both had a good laugh at this, and I actually did not realize I was committing a crime. Guess I was just lucky. The fact that I was able to help a friend clouded my judgment.

It was clear to me early that I would not have a career in the military. I continued to look at the military service as me being on a vacation. So I used this time to enjoy myself. My relationship with Lane seemed to vanish. I can't recall how or why, but I suppose I was once again looking for greener pastures.

My job in the Air Force as a Channel and Tech Controller was a little like the internet is today. With the use of radio, telex machines, radio signals and landlines, I could find people in faraway places and have mini-adventures. One was with Jack Zicker who was stationed on the Island of Guam. He was from Milwaukee, Wisconsin. He and I would have nightly chats over the telex or radio lines. He was always calling home to his parents - free - through our switchboard. One evening he gave me the good news. He was being assigned to McClellan AFB.

So we became close friends. He liked to drink. And that was one way I now socialized. He was a womanizer and I tagged along. So now I was getting lots of double-dates. And, I was even getting laid, something that was not a part of my life for half a dozen years.

But after a short time together he was discharged before I was and went back to Milwaukee, Wisconsin to become a firefighter. That left me friendless once again. I had associations with people I worked with, but not any close friends. But again, my relationship with Jack seemed to evaporate, and I never examined the reason. I had not kept in touch with any other runaways from the orphanage like Bill Pegliaro, or with my first "mentor" Ben Alexander, or with my "quasi first love" Estelle Zinger. Had I been asked why, I could not have provided an answer. I had the makings of a loner/loser and did not recognize it.

Many years later Jack found me via my website and sent me a short story he had written in 2005:

San Francisco, a very sophisticated city, has long held a special place in my heart. (There's a song title in there somewhere.) The city is memorable as much for my Air Force buddy, Steve Mizera, as our experiences visiting Nob Hill, Chinatown and North Beach. All worthwhile destinations, to be sure, however, it's not where you go but who you are with that lingers.

Steve and I would sometimes drive (where shall we go today?) from McClellan AFB, Sacramento, 100 miles to San Francisco in his beat up, yellow '54 Merc. October 29, 1963, I had attained the age of 21, a time in a young man's life when adulthood ostensibly begins. (Growing up and growing wiser are two different steps.)

What did two off-duty airmen with very little funds think they were going to do in the City? Having been there, Steve had a plan. We parked the heap and walked up Nob Hill to the Mark Hopkins Hotel. At the Top O' The Mark cocktail lounge, 19th floor, the maitre d' looked askance as two out of place G.I.s were adding up their quarters!

Quarters, hell! We forked over our last singles for two scotch and sodas and felt very grown up. The view of San Francisco bay from the Top O' The Mark is indescribable.

From the Mark Hopkins we walked over to the Fairmont Hotel where well dressed guests were arriving for a concert. The occasion: An Errol Garner Sunday matinee in the main ballroom.. With no tickets, we managed to sneak a peek at Errol Garner as he performed "Misty" to a hushed crowd. And then we beat it.

Later Steve and I found ourselves driving through Chinatown badly in need of a wiz. Mid-afternoon we double-parked on Grant Street, leaped from the car and into a Chinese restaurant. *The manager denied us entry because we were not customers and hadn't time to become his customers! Calmly Steve said, "Don't worry about it. Get back in the car and piss in the back seat!"*

At a busy intersection, the red light holding us, I couldn't. People on the street were probably wondering what that fluid was leaking out of the back seat! Ashamed? Not Steve.

He then drove up to North Beach and the Filmore District. Relieved and broke, we parked and walked down Broadway, funky down Broadway. Observing some queer kind of guys, I turned to Steve and plaintively asked, "Can we get back to base soon?" (For a young serviceman, back to base means back to normalcy.)

From the Top 'O The Mark to the streets of San Francisco...it was quite a day!

Jack has had a career as a firefighter in Milwaukee. I once borrowed a $1,000 from him. One of the reasons I played the lottery twice a week is to be in a position to pay him back with interest. I never answered his letter but hope to send him a copy of my autobiography,

Besides a few good friends, the military did teach me to type, to socialize, and it modified my concept of discipline. The puke-green stick was replaced with a barking voice during basic training and written regulations later. The Air Force also gave me an opportunity to enter the world of politics.

On a base bulletin board there was an invitation for airmen to enter a writing contest. It was sponsored by *Let Freedom Ring* and asked applicants to submit 500 words to explain what voting meant to the writer.

Well, I had no idea what an election was. Voting was a foreign concept. But I entered the contest anyway. I have no idea what I wrote, or why, and after depositing the entry in the base mail, I forgot all about it.

Months later I was shocked to learn that I won second place. Max Rafferty, the Superintendent of Public Education for the state of California won first place. I was contacted by Josephine Spaulding from Auburn, California, a small town north of Sacramento. She was a political activist and extended an invitation to me to have lunch to talk about my medal and award.

At lunch I met her husband Ray who was in the lumber business. He owned sawmills in Truckee and Eureka, California. They lived on five acres outside of Auburn and invited me to spend time at their home. I had leave coming and was able to take 30 days without a problem. I now had new friends, and they were rich. They owned an airplane - a Cessna 180 - and I went on a few trips with them to both Truckee and Eureka.

They were very active in Republican politics. During my initial stay at the Spaulding's ranch, Ronald Reagan was campaigning for Barry Goldwater who was running for president. Because I had free time I sold tickets in the Auburn area to people who wanted to hear what Reagan had to say in support of Goldwater. The actor stayed at the Spaulding's home overnight and my career in politics was off and running. Josephine had the local radio station record me narrate my award-winning essay. They played it dozens of times each day to the accompaniment of big band, patriotic music.

A week later, Robert Welch was an overnight guest at the Spaulding home. I had no idea who he was or who the John Birch Society was, but quickly learned he founded the right-wing organization and dictated what they stood for. I did not hesitate to put a GET US OUT bumper sticker on the back of my car, although I had no idea what the United Nations was or why the US should get out. My education or indoctrination came fast and furious. I bought it without a question. I would do anything to please my new-found friends.

I went back to the base but now as a proud American. The Republicans held their Presidential Nominating Convention at the Cow Palace in South San Francisco. Ray and Josephine Spaulding were personal friends of Barry Goldwater and big contributors to his presidential bid. They invited me to join them at the convention.

I did not own a suit so I wore my Air Force uniform to the convention. I did not know what the *Hatch Act* was or that it prohibited anyone in the military from being active in politics or to wear a military uniform at a political convention. I showed up on TV waving my *Goldwater for President* sign. The TV cameramen had a field day at my expense. Goldwater was a General in the Air Force and I was an Airman 1st Class. Clearly violating the *Hatch Act* was what interested the TV folks.

After the convention I was back at work at McClellan AFB. Early one morning I made a telephone connection between our base commander and the base commander of Hamilton Air Force Base, located just north of San Francisco. We seldom listened in on most conversations except to make sure there was a good connection. But this call was an exception to that rule because I heard my name being mentioned within the first minute of their conversation. Yes, it was about the TV coverage. I listened to them discussing what should be done about me! I soon heard and understood that if Goldwater lost the election,

I would be busted. It is nice to know your fate in advance. It is easier to take. Barry lost and so did I.

I was demoted back to Airman 2nd Class. I always felt more comfortable as second class anyway. Besides, I was getting discharged in a few months as my four year enlistment would be completed in April, 1965.

Within a few months McClellan had a new base commander. I worked the midnight to eight shift. An older person in civilian clothing showed up at my job. I recognized that he did not have an ID badge and challenged him. He turned out to be the new base commander. He had been in our top secret building for an hour and I was the only one who questioned his right to be there. For this I was given a field promotion by him back to Airman 1st Class.

In retrospect, the positives of my Air Force career were an honorable discharge, veteran benefits, a skill of typing, and a few socializing skills. The negatives: still not able to develop relationships, (specifically, no girlfriend,) and no idea what lie ahead in my future. Regrettably, my relationships with Jack Zicker and the Spauldings had evaporated just as quickly as they materialized. I never questioned why?

I really hadn't given a second thought about a job upon leaving the military, but because of my relationship with the Spauldings I was introduced to Harriet Ross. She ran the Heritage Bookshop in Sacramento. It was filled to the rafters with right-wing propaganda, especially John Birch Society books, pamphlets, and bumper stickers. Her husband Loren Ross was the General Manager of the California Fruit Exchange, a farmer's co-operative; whose members grew a wide range of fruit. So I was offered a job as assistant to Ron Worden, the Export Sales Manager.

There was no resume, no interview, just an appointment based on my political connection.

Ron was very talented and a dedicated employee. He taught me a few people skills but was a strict boss. He was a disciplinarian but did not use a hickory stick. He was a true professional. We got along fine for a few years before he left to work with a competitor Levi Zentner in San Francisco. His replacement was an alcoholic who really had no idea what was going on, except he had a "Ben Alexander" method of communicating: a con artist.

Fortunately for him, I was well trained by Ron Worden and I was able to carry out the duties that he, Jack Muelenkamp, was being paid to perform. He took long lunches and would come back to the office intoxicated, and would leave early. No one ever called him on it because the job was being done satisfactorily. It was being done satisfactorily by *me*. No one ever acknowledged my contribution to his position as Export Sales Manager. When he departed after two years I fully expected to assume his position.

During my short, four year career with the California Fruit Exchange, I became active in politics. I joined the Young Republicans and lived at the Fairlake Apartments in Sacramento. The main character in both the YRs and Fairlake was Mike Abernathy. He and his younger brother Mark came to California from the farm country of Indiana.

Mike was a real people-person. He was good-looking, had a great, friendly personality, and always had half-a-dozen girls chasing him at any given time. One in particular was the proverbial sex maniac. Mike was also the farm reporter on KFBK radio and would have to be at work at 5 in the morning. His sexophile would jump in my bed after

Mike left for work. No conversation, no foreplay, just raw sex. She satisfied me long before she satisfied herself.

Being a member of the Young Republicans gave me the opportunity to have a lot of "friends" or at least associates. Due to Mike's leadership there were always lots of parties. We shared a three-bedroom apartment and it was always cluttered with guys and girls, night and day. One of my fondest memories with the YRs is something I organized called the *Joy of Giving* party.

I encouraged our group to actually do something beneficial in the community instead of just partying. As Christmas was not too far off, I suggested we throw a Christmas party for under-privileged kids.

Our goals were set. We would host 100 kids. We would pick them up from all over Sacramento from a list provided by the county welfare department. Early on the Saturday morning of the party, we would bring them to the Fairlake Apartment clubhouse, feed them hotdogs and other junk food, and have Santa give each of them three gifts. Then we would return them to their homes.

Most members got behind this idea enthusiastically. My contributions to the project were raising money and playing Santa Claus. As I was the California Fruit Exchange's defacto export sales manager, I suggested to our export trade that the winter grapes were in short supply. I bargained that if they would make a contribution to our *Joy of Giving* party, I would give them enhanced consideration when filling their orders.

I was able to raise $6500 in just a few days, and none of the contributors brought my noble endeavor to the attention of General Manager Loren Ross, who probably would have fired me. I also talked local companies into contributing food and gift wrapping materials.

Because I played the role of Santa on the day of the party, I was able to view the souls of children through their eyes. It was immensely rewarding. It took a lot of self-control for me not to cry. The occasion produced a flash-back to my being the recipient of brown bags at *St. Francis Orphan Asylum* three decades earlier during the Christmas season.

The *Joy of Giving Party* was a genuine joy and pleasure for me. I had always considered myself as a giver so this made me happy. I seldom examined my motives in anything I did. In retrospect, perhaps, this was my way of purchasing friendship. The inaugural party was a huge success. The YR *Joy of Giving Party* became an annual event.

My interest in photography was born during this period. I would take slides at the various parties and activities sponsored by the YRs. Later, at yet another party, I would enjoy showing the slides but was very interested in watching the reaction of those who were viewing the slides.

Hiding behind a camera was probably my way of socializing. I felt safe there. So it was normal that I took a number of photographs at the *Joy of Giving* event, starting with the purchase and wrapping of presents. Another YR took a few of me making the presentation of the gifts. I later assembled these slides together to tell a story. It included narration and Christmas music. Our club submitted this slide presentation to the National Young Republican organization at its annual convention and we received well-deserved first place and peer recognition.

The years 1965, when I left the Air Force, to 1968 were consumed by working at the California Fruit Exchange, and socializing or playing in the Young Republicans. Although I did not have a "girlfriend" while I was in the Air Force, I did get laid a few times in addition to being bedded by Lane's mom. These exploits were nothing to write home to Mother about, even if I had a mother to write home to. But being a member of the Young Republicans was to change my standing.

Judy Schaffer, a member of the YRs, caught my eye very early on. She was pretty and very soft-spoken. I learned from her that she was raised in Salt Lake City and was a Catholic. She mentioned that she suffered discrimination at the hands of Mormons, who apparently dominate Utah, especially Salt Lake City. What I did not learn from her was that she was in search of a husband. Initially, she focused on me.

We did a lot of things together, mostly partying with other Young Republicans, but we never had sex. I actually did not know how to initiate a sexual encounter, especially with someone I viewed as a sweet girl - wife material, even though I was not looking for a wife. I did not know where to begin. I had generally been a reactionary, like when responding to Mike's sexophile.

One evening I stopped by Judy's apartment. She had to go to the store for something. When she returned she related to me that while crossing the street she was almost hit by a car. I did not pay much attention, nor did I react to what she said and that was a big mistake. She became enraged and the message I took home with my tail between my legs was that I did not empathize with her and showed no concern. She was right. I was stupid and inattentive.

It was our first and last argument and resulted in our breakup. This breakup was a little hard to take for me, as I did not make relationships easy. I tried on a number of occasions to get back together with her, but she was determined to call it quits. It was difficult being in the YRs with her but she solved that problem for me. She was married three weeks after our breakup to someone she worked with. She never returned to the YRs. It became a little easier to forget about her. Janice Kling made it easy.

Janice was slim, very attractive, and had a sister Sherry who was absolutely gorgeous. The YRs have conventions where clubs from all over the state get together once a year. They elect officers and party hardy. They also invite candidates running for public office to speak for the purpose of endorsing the most conservative. YRs promise thereafter to work for the election of the endorsed candidates by stuffing envelopes, going door-to-door soliciting votes, raising money etc. At their state convention members also elect a "Miss YR" who goes on to compete for the national Miss YR title at a national convention held every four years.

The Fairlake YRs, who choose this name because most members lived in the Fairlake Apartments in Sacramento, were headed by Mike Abernathy, whose dominate characteristic was that he always had a dozen single girls trying to nail him. He was always polite to everyone and spent much of his time dishing out compliments to every female, not tipping his hand as to whom he favored. He therefore got laid quite frequently. He decided to enter Sherry Kling in the Miss YR contest. And he asked that I be her "handler." This required that I escort her to many caucuses and introduce her to as many YRs as possible. She was easy to handle.

And that is how I ended up with Janice. Sherry won the title Miss California YR. And I won the right to woo Janice. We were constant companions. There was a big difference between the Kling sisters. Sherry was naturally beautiful and did not wear makeup. Janice wore makeup but did not know how to apply it. This was actually the first time I became aware of makeup. Janice, who was two years older, looked a little like she had glued thin sheets of transparent leather to parts of her face, but I knew that beauty is only skin-deep so I ignored this. It was more important to me and my ego that I publicly replace the absence of Judy Schaffer.

We attended most YR activities together. One event was a local endorsing convention. There was a Black running for a county office, quite a rare event in Republican circles in the sixties. When it came time to vote to endorse someone in the upcoming election where a Black was one of the candidates, I was the only one who voted for him. I got a few boos and a few dirty looks from my fellow conservative Republicans. The right wing was in control of most of the YRs and I had observed for the first time that many of them were racist. "Why did you vote for that nigger?" I was asked by more than one member after the nomination process ended. My answer - that he was the best qualified candidate -fell on deaf, white ears. But as he did not get the club's endorsement, my sin was apparently forgiven.

Janice and I made out like teenagers, but never had sex. I assumed she was a virgin, and was saving herself for her future husband. And I assumed that would be me. Initiating sex was not my field of expertise. It was not even close. Republicans had a lock on family values, even though it seemed that Mike Abernathy and many others lost their key.

After knowing Janice for about a year, I decided to pop the question and took her to dinner one Sunday night. I had secreted a wedding ring in her drink with the help of a waitress. Janice almost swallowed the ring. When she recovered, she announced she would love to marry me.

About midnight we drove to her home to give Mrs. Kling, my future mother-in-law, the good news and to get her blessing.

There was a Mr. Kling but he was like a vegetable. He never said much of anything to anyone. Mrs. Kling did all the talking. She was such a dominating force in the family that Mr. Kling long ago had the winds removed from his sails by her, and he was content to remain silent. She apparently was raised in England and had been in this country for twenty-five years. Both of her daughters were born in the U.S., yet Mrs. Kling, who had a job with the state, was constantly running down America and praising Great Britain. We were not close and I assumed we would never be.

When Janice proudly displayed the ring and blurted out her plan to become **Mrs. Mizera**, Mrs. Kling went berserk. She started screaming at me, berating her daughter, and moving toward us in an intimidating manner. I backed Janice and myself out the front door and whispered to my frightened fiancée that we would discuss this later. Mrs. Kling followed us through the front door onto the porch. I couldn't get Janice and myself into my car fast enough. The last words bellowing out of Mrs. Kling's mouth was that I was a **"nigger-lover"**. So, my anti-bigot sin was not forgiven after all. All of the warnings I ever heard about mothers-in-law started echoing aloud in my mind. What did I get myself into?

I should have been more observant. What should have been the obvious reason Mr. Kling was vegetated was due to the domineering character of Mrs. Kling. I don't recall him ever saying anything to me. That should have raised a red flag. Initially I thought the reason was *me* but later concluded that he was mentally challenged or handicapped. I did not know that Mrs. Kling was the reason for his mental state. How on earth did he father two beautiful girls?

Janice was adamant. She was not going to let her mother screw up our engagement. She stayed at my apartment that night. I slept on the couch. The next day, Monday, I took the day off from my job at the California Fruit Exchange and found a nice apartment at 25th and H Streets in downtown Sacramento. Janice worked for the Sacramento Savings and Loan Association a few blocks away so she could walk to work. I plunked down almost $1000 for the first and last month's rent, and for a cleaning deposit. I was now broke. Not saving money reflected one aspect of my lack of a value system. "Easy come, easy go" had been my attitude. I now recognized that this would have to change. The prospect of being responsible for someone else weighed heavily on me. Marriage and starting a family were foreign to me but I was determined to forge ahead and succeed. The first hurdle and obstacle was Mrs. Kling.

Although we slept under the same roof in our new apartment, I was respecting Janice's virginity and slept on the sofa. I had explained to her gently that if we were to be married her relationship with her mother would be altered significantly and that we would be building a life together. Although she initially agreed with me, her mother got the last and final word. Within twenty-four hours, Janice changed her mind and moved back home with her mother.

Janice would not even talk to me when I tried to visit her at the bank. I was hurt and even angry, but I walked away in favor of her mother. What had her mother told her that would cause such a reversal in my relationship with Janice? Or, was Janice so overwhelmingly dominated she lost her ability to reason? My inability to maintain a relationship further confused and confounded me. How did other couples keep it together?

About a year later, I learned that Janice was pregnant out of wedlock and in a hospital in San Francisco. Because I still had dormant feelings for her I drove down to visit her. She had a miscarriage, and tried to convince me that she was still in love with the father of her aborted child. He, on the other hand, did not want anything to do with her once he found out she was pregnant. She finally lost her virginity. I lost the last vestiges of respect for her. How could she still carry a torch for someone who would abandon her when he learned she was pregnant?

I could only dream of the reaction Mrs. Kling had during this course of events. She might have been better off with a "nigger-lover" for a son-in-law. But she went on to die of cancer, Janice went on to follow in her mother's footsteps and become a state-worker. Sherry got married, had a beautiful son, and as far as I know, is living happily ever after in El Dorado Hills, a nice bedroom community to the east of Sacramento.

The Young Republicans did two things for me that I was not expecting. Previously, at a party at my apartment I engaged in conversation with a young black person. He was not a YR, and it was rare to see any Blacks in our circle or at our parties. He mentioned he was going to college. I mentioned I was a high school drop out. Then he suggested I take the SAT (Scholastic Aptitude Test). He told me I did not have to be a high school graduate to go to American River Junior College.

Have I mentioned that I was naïve?

There was so much I did not know. Going to college might help me overcome my naïveté. Overcoming my lack of a formal education might do me some good.

Perhaps I could learn to develop and maintain a successful relationship.

I signed up for the test and passed with grades high enough that I did not have to take any remedial courses.

Two other pieces to my puzzling life found their way onto the table. Although I was honorably discharged from the Air Force, I was not aware of GI benefits. Although I served *during* the Vietnam War, I did not serve *on the front lines* in the Vietnam War. I spent all my time in Lackland, Texas, Biloxi, Mississippi, and North Highlands, California.

That same black stranger at the party clued me in to the GI Bill, and he was never even in the military! This was very timely information because my relationship with the California Fruit Exchange was about to end.

Mike's other roommate moved out (because he got married) and Ray Robinson moved in temporarily until escrow closed on the house he was buying. He was not a YR but did attend a few of the parties. While his purchase was in escrow, he talked me into moving in with him by arguing that rent would be less expensive and that it was very close to American River College. I agreed. Little did I know but I was being manipulated. His escrow would close in about a month.

Jack Meulenkamp left the California Fruit Exchange in February for greener pastures. The position of Export Sales Manager was opened and I assumed I would be asked to fill it. I was not. Pat Sanguinetti, an eighteen year old son of a Lodi cherry grower who was a member of the Board of Directors, was given the job. He had no sales experience. This would be his first job. Somewhere I had heard that it is not *what* you know but *who* you know that counts. I should have been aware of this truism because this was how I got the job with the California Fruit Exchange in the first place. I knew Harriet Ross and I knew nothing about sales or fruit. I was expected to be his assistant and I was also expected to run the export desk until he learned the ropes.

The California fruit season starts in late April with Thompson Seedless grapes becoming available from the Coachella Valley in Southern California. I was more than a little pissed off because I did not get the Export Sales Manager position. I did not intend to stick around and wallow in a sea of rejection. I intended to quit. I had no idea what I would do for a living. I knew I would be attending American River College. I really was not qualified for much. Except for typing, my Air Force skills including the Morse code were not marketable. I did not even know what a resume was or how to go looking for a job.

Johnsey Raymond Robinson, my roommate and landlord, worked on the railroad as a brakeman. He ignored rules like I did, but I did not know it was against the rules for a non-employee to ride a freight train. He took me for a 400 mile round trip ride to Dunsmuir. He convinced me to apply for a job. The Southern Pacific railroad hauled much of California's fruit to eastern markets. SP was very busy in June and July. SP also did its hiring in May. I applied for a job. I was hired.

So now I was in a position to quit work at the California Fruit Exchange, get a formal education and have it paid for by the government, and start my railroad career. I was about to turn twenty-eight years of age. It was 1968. What was missing from my life was a decent woman. Maybe the college campus would provide one.

I gave my two minutes notice to Loren Ross.

The job on the railroad proved to be rather interesting. For generations, the only persons who were hired as crew members were sons of railroaders. Crews worked hours that ignored the natural clock. Just about the time one was ready to go to bed, the crew dispatcher would call two hours before you had to show up at the yard office in Roseville. Then you usually waited for about two hours for the train to be made up by a yard crew before you took it on an eight hour trip over the Sierra Mountains to Sparks, Nevada. There was something called the Twelve Hour Law that prohibited trainmen from working more than twelve consecutive hours. If luck was on your side you made it to Sparks before twelve hours. If you did not have that luck, you had to stop your train, wait for a relief crew and take a company taxi to Sparks.

After eight hours of sleep you were ready for the return trip, but it may be another twelve to twenty hours before a train would arrive needing a crew for the west bound return trip to Roseville. On the other hand, you could be called to return upon wakening. On those occasions, sleeping on the train home was commonplace. The engine crew consisted of a brakeman and an engineer, and sometimes a fireman. Often, all three crew members would be asleep on the engine as the train headed home downhill. This added a little excitement to the otherwise boring trip.

Brakemen and conductors seemed to always be away from home. Their kids picked up the language of the railroad after hearing it for more than a decade so they could hop on an engine and were comfortable hearing words like "dynamite the train," "big hole," "highball," "throw that switch," "dutch drop," "lay down a torpedo," etc.

To "dynamite the train" simply meant to put the train into emergency by pulling a lever. All the air in the braking system is released and it sounded like dynamite exploding. This procedure would only be used if there were a gas tanker or logging truck stalled on the track, and it was necessary to stop the train in a hurry. "Big hole" was a two-mile long tunnel drilled a hundred years ago at the summit of the Sierra Mountain. This was a little confusing because the same words could mean put the train into an emergency stop. Pulling that lever would put a big hole in the train's air line. "Laying down a torpedo" meant strapping a two-inch square packet of black powder to the rail. When the engine of a train ran over it, there would be a detonation and the explosion would warn the engineer that a train was stopped ahead of his. Learning the language made the job interesting. There was also a type of sign language between crew members. Moving arms signaled the engineer to stop or start a train, and conveyed distances. Lanterns were used when it was dark.

Going to work for the Southern Pacific Railroad was a blessing. Because the crews operated on a seniority system, I would only get to work during the summer and on holidays when regular crews did not want to work. And because I could work again after only eight hours rest, I could earn a lot of money in a short time. This would allow me time to pursue a college education.

There was no formal training for working on the railroad. The Railroad personnel simply showed you a faded ball of yarn that formerly was either red, yellow, or green. They wanted to make sure you were not color-blind. And they also wanted to make sure you had a strong back so you could throw 100-year old, iron switches. Thus a quick x-ray was the only other qualifier.

Railroading was a dangerous job. I learned this by listening to crews tell stories of brakemen or conductors who were crushed between two knuckles of a car when making up a train. Knuckles are sixty pounds of u-shaped steel on the end of each rail car that connected one car to another. Other stories told described vividly how a worker had one or more legs cut off trying to get on or off a fast moving train. This was sufficient education for me to be super cautious.

I was able to work all summer while looking forward to starting in September of 1969 as a 29 year-old freshman at American River Junior College.

Chapter Six
Conductor and Law Student - 1970

In early June, 1969, I acquired a seniority date and made my first trip. I worked on freight trains all summer. The through-freights were easy jobs. A brakeman would just walk from the rear of the train and past as many as 120 cars to the engine and get on, and then ride 110 miles to either Sparks, Nevada, or 155 miles to Dunsmuir, California. Although no one told you why you were to "walk the train," the purpose was to inspect it for any dangerous condition such as brakes still applied or freight hanging out of open doors. On a rare occasion, I would get to ride almost 200 miles to Fresno.

But it was the locals that made railroading interesting and difficult. The work was difficult simply because no one told you what to do, and that made it dangerous. You were expected to know. Picking up cars, either empty or loaded with freight, and dropping off cars either to be loaded or unloaded would seem to be simple enough. But the conductor or the other brakeman didn't give much guidance, mostly because they were unable to articulate what had to be done. Instructions were given in short bursts or barks, with no accompanying explanation. By the end of the summer, the job became much easier. Repetition surely is the mother of learning.

Perhaps the most profound thing I learned, though, was how to fake an injury and get the railroad to pay an out-of-court settlement to supplement my income. Yes, this was dishonest, but there was no green hickory stick to keep me in line. Very early in my career I observed quite a few brakeman who had enough seniority to work, but were not working. They were staying home "nursing" their make-believe injuries while waiting for their corrupt attorneys to negotiate their out-of-court settlement. Eventually, and then periodically, I found it profitable to fake an injury myself. I usually timed these make-believe injuries to coincide with the end of summer when I did not have enough seniority to work.

As with the railroad, in September of 1969 I found American River College to be the beginning of both a learning and an interesting social experience. I had not been in a formal education environment in fifteen years. The first notable difference was that I was older than most students. I think I was mistaken for a professor on one or more occasions. Older students generally went to college at night, but I was receiving veterans' benefits and that allowed me to attend day classes.

I was also receiving unemployment checks because my lack of seniority kept me off the railroad's extra board, except for holidays and a rare weekend. The extra board supported regular crews. It consisted of just enough workers who did not have seniority to hold a regular job who would only work when regular crew members took time off. There were not a lot of persons on the extra board in the winter, but everyone was on the list in the summer.

In college, I had no idea what a major was, so I did not declare one. Perhaps my background prepared me to be the epitome of a naive person. But I finally selected journalism as my major. I became used to reading newspapers on the trains. Now I would learn how they were published.

ARC published a weekly newspaper called *The Beaver*. I learned in an early class that I would be writing and using the "who-what-where-when-why and how" format. That sounded easy. And, I thought it would be fun. Prior to enrolling in this class I got my news from the TV. Reading newspapers were something one did while riding the train to avoid boredom.

Although I was recently introduced to marijuana by Ray Robinson, the weed was now readily available and often used by my fellow students. It was illegal to possess or smoke it. In Nevada, persons caught with as little as one joint were readily incarcerated for more than a dozen years. Although it was a felony, I did not notice any enforcement of this law on campus. I was not in the habit of looking at consequences of my behavior. Perhaps I should have started to look.

During my first year I took required classes to get them out of the way: English 1-A, an Introductory Geology class, as well as an introductory Psychology class, along with my journalism classes. All were interesting and relatively easy. I had plenty of time to study and curiosity was what motivated me.

Taking fifteen units was not a burden as I did not have financial worries and did not have to put in a forty-hour work week. Most of my expenses were covered by the Veterans Administration - the GI Bill. And that was supplemented by the very few trips I took on the railroad. A twenty-four hour round-trip from Roseville, California to Sparks, Nevada on the weekend was equivalent to the pay for someone with a full-time job flipping hamburgers.

But unlike a McDonald's job, the railroad did have its own doctor and hospital.

My grades were all A's or B's, even though I did very little studying or preparation for exams. For the first semester I did not socialize with other students. I think I was self-conscious and concerned about the age difference.

I still participated and partied with the Young Republicans, but that was getting old. The experience with the husband-hunting Judy Schaffer - the Catholic whose claim to fame was the discrimination she suffered at the hands of the Mormans - was still an active memory. And the dependent Janice Kling who saved me from a vicious mother-in-law also acted as a barrier to relationships with girls. But college was different. The girls were younger and not uptight. I would have to pay attention and wait for an opportunity.

I did pay attention in journalism classes. I worked my way up to Associate Editor by the second semester and really enjoyed the writing assignments. I even produced a featured story or two, and once, on my own initiative, I wrote an exposé. My fine investigative reporting was not printed because it dealt with corruption in the college's financial aid office. I was eager to let our readership know that the girlfriend of the Beaver's editor received money from the college financial aid office - a grant to help with her education. But instead of using it for education, she purchased a car. She was not qualified to receive any aid.

The financial aid office was run by the father of "The Beaver's" editor. The journalism professor was very conservative and did not like to rock the boat, so he prevented my expose from being published. His preventing the publishing of my writing somehow did not seem like real or legitimate journalism.

American River College received a lot of national publicity in 1969 for one of its unique programs. A professor in an advanced psychology class used rats to teach the principals of negative and positive reinforcement. Psychology giant B. F. Skinner's claimed that successful child-rearing required rewarding only positive or good behavior and ignoring bad behavior. It was tested in a class taught by Professor Jack Badaracco. The students trained rats that were fed cheese or peanut butter treats if they found their way through a maze, performed successfully in a high or long jump, or were able to navigate a high-wire act without falling. But some students used negative reinforcement when their rodents failed to perform and administered an electric shock to their rats.

Those students who did not punish their rathletes were rewarded by producing star performers. Those students who used punishment almost cooked their rats that would refuse to perform even when the rodent's feet were smoking. Some of the students appeared to relish frying or almost electrocuting their "pets." Observing those training sessions brought back memories of my butt welts and the nuns who enjoyed my pain.

Professor Badaracco used his rat class to raise scholarship funds. Jack was very thin, very hyper, and had a huge nose, but he was a brilliant teacher. It fell on me to write the news stories for *The Beaver* in order to promote his scholarship program. On a Saturday near the end of the semester, students mimicked the Olympics by putting on their Rat Decathalon. (The rats competed in five activities - twice!)

A pictorial magazine crammed with advertisements sold to the local business community, was also sold to those who attended the competition. The event raised a few thousand dollars each year by producing the decathlon and the magazine.

The editor of *The Beaver* was in Southern California for a journalist conference so the task of publishing the newspaper was delegated to me.

The journalism professor watched closely as I supervised the layout of the weekly paper. He left early satisfied that I was conforming to his dictates.

But readers were surprised to see that the name of their newspaper was changed from *The Beaver* to *The Rat*. So was the journalism advisor. He promptly fired me and angrily announced that my grade would be an F.

But for every door that closes, one opens. Jack Badaracco sought me out to thank me for the name-change. When he learned I was fired, he went to bat for me. He liked confrontation and rocking the boat.

I don't know what Jack did exactly, but soon the journalism instructor sought me out to ask that I re-join the staff. I agreed on the condition that the F grade be converted to an A. He reluctantly consented even after I demanded his written promise. I did not bother to attend any additional journalism classes that semester.

The following semester I enrolled in Jack Badaracco's rat class. I did not need nor did I desire any more journalism classes.

As my first semester was ending, I was living with Ray Robinson, helping him pay the mortgage. He was tough to live with. Once when my car would not start, I asked if I could borrow an extra car battery until I could replace mine. He turned me down with some lame excuse.

As I rode my bike the seven miles to ARC, I committed to memory my observation and warning that Ray would give anyone the shirt off his back, unless that person needed a shirt.

On a later occasion I would have been late for class if I stopped to do the breakfast dishes, so I left a plate, glass and silverware in the sink. When I returned from class Ray was not there but he left a note. It was a long *Rules of the House* list. Rule number one dealt with leaving dirty dishes. I did not bother to read further. I was packed and looking for new housing within a few hours. I found an apartment across the street from American River.

We resumed our friendship much later although I did not initiate the move. I had difficulty making friends, and I usually accepted blindly people who befriended me. But I was good at terminating relationships on the drop of a hat and generally did not need a very good reason. I was an expert in burning my bridges behind me, but never asked myself: Why?

After my second semester, it was time to go to work. Summer was the time when new brakemen with little seniority could earn a small fortune. Fruits and vegetables where shipped by train to the east coast so there were a lot of trains and a lot of work. A brakeman could earn more in a summer than many people earned all year. But it meant giving up any social life and adopting instead the attitude of a slave to a job and to money. By definition, this also meant, for me, no steady girlfriend. No summer school for me. I was able to accumulate enough money to have a social life but still did not have the skill. It was a railroad summer.

In the fall I enrolled in the Rat class. Professor Badaracco was a chain-smoking, likeable and funny person. He liked me and I liked him. He invited me over to his home and soon I became a fixture there. He had a few kids from an earlier marriage and was married to Adrianne, a sweet, nice looking and much younger person. She was also secretary to one of the ARC departments. She had a few kids too. They were a happy family and I felt very comfortable with them.

On one visit, we were all working on a project at the dining room table. The lights went out and in came Adrianne carrying a birthday cake she had made. There was a paper cutout of a beautiful blonde's face and the rest of the layer cake had two distinguishing features. First there were two pink mounds, representing breasts, and chocolate decoration representing pubic hair. This was the one and only surprise birthday party I ever had. Yes, I ate the pubic hair portion. It did not have an odor of fish, It did taste good!

I did not bother to train a rat in Jack's psychology class. I think I already knew the concept that the use of punishment to regulate behavior was a guarantee of failure. I was living proof. All I had to do was touch my butt and I would get a quick flashback of the asylum's negative reinforcement.

Jack's class was very interesting. Even though the rest of the class was fifteen or more years younger than me, it kept me young and tuned into the generation. Smoking marijuana, for instance, was a regular activity. One of the students in Jack's class was Jim Sanderson: a good-looking kid, who drove a nice new car purchased by his parents. He did not work. Many of the students in Jack's Rat Decathlon class met a few times a week at Jim Sanderson's home which was located within a few miles from American River College. His father was a doctor and they had a beautiful home in a secluded neighborhood on Park Road, between highway 80 and Auburn Boulevard. We got high after class and listened to music. Both of his parents knew we were all smoking dope but neither did anything to stop us.

Jim was a bit shy when it came to women. I could afford to be outspoken because of my age. He was too shy to ask one particular girl for a date, so I did it for him. I asked her if she wanted to go to the Rose Bowl, an annual football classic held on New Year's Day in Southern California. She immediately said yes which kind of shocked me. I then asked her if I was unable to go would she go with Jim. She sheepishly replied in the affirmative.

That happened. She was sweet and beautiful. I never got to really know Jim. He was friendly but not open. When they married, very soon after that date, and then divorced very soon after getting married, I suspected the problem was with Jim. But I was still his friend.

It seems Jim's father was too busy in medical school to pay much attention to Jim as he was growing up and there was a very distant relationship between them. Even after his father started his medical practice, money was a substitute for love. Jim got whatever material wants he had satisfied. So maybe it was his father's fault that Jim did not know how to make and keep a relationship with his bride. Jim had an older brother who had a similar relationship with his parents. And not being able to form relationships was probably what initially bonded Jim and me together.

Nevertheless, he and I did develop an interesting, symbiotic relationship.

A friend of Jim's father was a con artist who claimed to be an investment counselor. (I saw the Ben Alexander in him immediately) Jay Shack had "created" something called *The Student Guild*. He was selling directorships for $25,000 to ten persons, including Doc Sanderson and Jim.

Jay lived in Tacoma, Washington and had a connection with a printer there who produced a few plastic cards for the scam and colorful brochures that explained that students would get a significant discount on virtually anything they could purchase as a member of *The Student Guild*.

On one visit to Sacramento, Jay signed a lease for a very small office at 555 Capital Mall, one of the few local skyscrapers in 1970. The photo of the building implied that this was the Student Guild building. Jay tried to convince me that I had a future with the Student Guild. Being a director, Jim's ego was over-inflated and blinded him to the reality: *The Student Guild* was a scam.

Once I picked up Jay at the Sacramento airport. He made a telephone call to someone in the California Governor's office. Before the connection was made, he handed me the phone and instructed me to ask to speak to someone and to state that I was Mr. Shack's personal secretary.

Because of that lie, over the next few months I viewed *The Student Guild* with a lot of suspicion. One obvious flaw with the proposed organization was the definition of a student. Anyone wanting the proposed discount could claim to be a student. Thus the **entire population** could conceivably deserve and **demand the discount for virtually everything**. This is what made it a scam! What an illusion! The king was naked! But when it appears you can make a fortune by selling memberships, why would you want to look for negatives, especially if you spent $50,000 for a couple of directorships?

Ultimately I shared with Jim my suspicion that Jay was a con-artist who was bilking his father. But Jim did not want to hear it. He stayed in denial. I chose to avoid *The Student*

Guild. This was the beginning of the end of my relationship with Jim. I had burst his bubble. The truth did not set him free. It would only be a matter of time before we parted ways.

I poured my time and talent into making the Rat Decathlon a success. Our class made it an international event in that we had three colleges from out of state entering the competition, and someone managed to have a student from the island of Guam attend. We reasoned that ours was an international competition because Guam, although a US Territory 3,500 miles west of Hawaii, was west of the International Date Line. I am not sure how he got the rat through customs, unless he declared it was his pet.

My participation was to publish the magazine that accounted for most of the profit to be used as scholarship money. My hobby as a photographer, my journalism education and my experience as a salesman seemed to work together to produce a 56 page, color magazine. Because the cost of printing was donated, the sale of advertising and the magazine was profit. We had raised almost $4,000 for scholarships. That was a lot of money in 1970 when college units were only $3.

Between my job with Southern Pacific and obtaining veterans benefits, I was always flush with money. Easy come, easy go. So one way my popularity increased was by purchasing marijuana and distributing it gratuitously.

I was not related to anyone on the railroad. And I was an exception to the rule of hand-me-down father-to-son job. There were no daughters involved, so there were no female crew members. Of the more than four hundred crew members working out of Roseville, only two were black. One was Leslie Gentry Stafford. He was big and humble.

He was born and raised in Montgomery, Alabama. When I met him his eyes were cast down. He was a poster boy for racial discrimination. I formed a friendship with Leslie immediately. I genuinely liked him, perhaps because we shared a common background of suffering. Mine was at the hands of nuns and Catholic laymen. His was at the hands of white racists in Alabama.

Railroading was divided into two types: working a local or through freight, or working the passenger train. In the pre-Amtrak days, Southern Pacific ran a passenger train. There were only two trips a day. One was a six hour trip that went from Roseville to Sparks and returned the following morning. That train originated in Oakland, California and turned in Chicago, Illinois, but crews out of Roseville turned at Sparks, Nevada.

Another passenger train was called the *Coast Starlight*. It originated in Los Angeles and turned in Seattle. Roseville crews operated this scheduled train as it moved from Davis to Dunsmuir, California. It was always in the night hours so crews got to do a lot of sleeping on this passenger train.

Trains known as locals usually had a lot of work to do. Railroad customers either had a box car to be picked up, or wanted an empty one to be set out so they could load it with their freight. So there would be a lot of switching loads and empty boxcars. Switchmen in the yard would have the train ready. The trip might be as few as 20 miles, or up to 150 miles round-trip. And, it could take as few as 2 hours or as many as 12 hours. The federal law prevented railroad crews from working more than 12 consecutive hours. If a job took 12 hours and your crew did not make it back to Roseville, a taxi would be sent to pick up the crew and deliver another crew to finish the job. This was actually an incentive to drag your feet because you were paid a lot more if you did not complete your run within 12 hours. This is a prime example of inefficiency.

The weather factored into the job. Some jobs in the winter included taking snow removal equipment and clearing the track before regular train traffic could go to work.

During the summer the heat in places like Red Bluff could be torture - no shade, 110 degrees, walking along side steel cars on baked gravel.

There was absolutely no training when I hired out in June of 1969. Railroading had always been one of the most dangerous occupations. Because working on the railroad killed or maimed so many of its workers, Congress passed special legislation at the turn of the twentieth century designed to protect the workers by making railroads liable for any injury suffered by its crews. In 1908 Congress passed the *Federal Employees Liability Act* (FELA) in response to the high number of railroad deaths in the late 19th century and early 20th century. Under FELA, railroad workers who are not covered by regular workers' compensation laws are able to sue companies over their injury claims. FELA allows monetary payouts for pain and suffering, decided by juries based on comparative negligence rather than pursuant to a pre-determined benefits schedule under workers' compensation.

FELA was not intended to be awarded automatically. Unlike State Workers' Compensation Law, FELA requires the injured railroader to prove that the railroad was "legally negligent" at least in part, in causing the injury. After proving negligence, the injured railroader is entitled to full compensation. Such compensation is usually many times greater than that provided by State Worker's Compensation for non-railroaders.

It was this law that many of the railroad workers took advantage of when they faked injuries. Learning this aspect of railroading right away was profitable for me. When it appeared that my ability to work was disappearing because summer traffic slowed down, I would learn to "get injured" and go to the local law firm that was in bed with the United Transportation Union bosses. I suppose you could call this train chasing. It predated the liberalization of the law when it allowed ambulance chasing. They fixed me up with a corrupt doctor and fronted me money to handle my expenses until they settled my case.

Through-freight trips were very easy because they did very little work. Some through-freight jobs such as "the pigs" were very desirable. The *pigs* were flat cars each loaded with two truck trailers of freight. There were sometimes as few as 20 of these flatcars which, together with four engines, consisted of the entire train. These trains were very short, very light and very fast. Regular freight trains might have as many as 125 cars and less than four engines. Needless to say, they took a lot longer to travel from Roseville to Sparks than did "the pigs".

The pigs were a very high priority train, second only to the passenger train. They always had more than enough locomotive power to get over the Sierra Mountains at the maximum speed allowed. They never broke down and the trip took about four hours instead of eleven or twelve, but the crews were paid the same.

Regular freight trains, on the other hand, were so boring as they seldom exceeded 20 miles an hour going over the mountain and took about ten hours to go from Roseville to Sparks. Because they were so heavy and had insufficient locomotive power, they were subject to breaking down. A regular train usually had three engines on the front and one behind the caboose - a helper engine. If the train was very long, it had two engines cut-in about two-thirds the distance between the front of the train and the caboose.

Because there was a lot of terrain that ascended and descended it was necessary for the engineers to coordinate their use of power or braking. If they were not successful, the train would break a knuckle, the sixty-five pound hunk of steel that is used to couple the cars together. In rare cases, a drawbar, a much heavier part of the train, would break and brakemen used chains to pull the disabled car to the closest siding. A siding is any track not used for main line traffic. It is often used to allow one train to pass another in either direction. When there are more than one sidings parallel to the main line, these sidings are used to store rail cars, such as cars that have broken down.

When a knuckle broke, the brakeman had to carry a spare back to the break and replace it. Carrying a sixty-five pound piece of steel a quarter or half mile was not a lot of fun, especially when walking on unstable ballast or gravel.

Both kinds of trips paid about the same. A brakeman was paid about $110 and a Conductor was paid about ten percent more. A round-trip could take from six hours to thirty-six hours. If too many crews were waiting for return trains to Roseville, the company sent a company van to bring the crews back to Roseville. This was called deadheading.

To become a conductor required five years service as a brakeman and passing a written Conductor's test. The test required a brakeman to know the railroad rule book. This book was 176 pages and contained a lot of strange terms. Even the so-called definitions were way beyond the comprehension of most trainmen, many of whom did not have a high-school education. They would not take the exam knowing they could not pass it so there was a lot of old brakeman in their fifties and early sixties.

Today, most employees must have a college education and they are given thorough training before going to work. But in the old days, it was the repetition of doing something over and over that substituted for the requirement of knowing something that enabled some brakemen to become conductors. But so many knew they could not pass the test and remained brakemen for their entire career. They did not like taking orders from younger conductors.

Because there was a shortage of conductors, I was asked to take the conductor's exam before my third year as a brakeman. I was ill-prepared to take the test. As a brakeman, you followed the instructions of the conductor and let him worry about following the rules. But because being a conductor paid more than a brakemen received, I stole the answers to the exam from the yardmaster's office, took the test, and passed the written exam with flying colors.

Yes, yes, it was unethical but remember that I was super-disciplined for my "wrong-doings." Obviously at this stage of my life that discipline did not have the desired effect. My troubled upbringing did not really teach me how to recognize morality. Not following the rules is just one example. Perhaps I was getting even for the past abuse I suffered.

During the weeks leading up to the Super Bowl I suffered an injury playing football at ARC. I jumped into the air to catch a pass and three other players came down with me and on top of me and my left knee. When I tried to get up, I couldn't. I hobbled over to the college's nursing facility and was told to go to a doctor. I was given a crutch and excused.

Fortunately, Jim Sanderson and I were still friends. When I called Jim for a ride, he called his father who was an orthopedic surgeon. His father happened to be home. He put me on the kitchen table, bent my knee as he listened to it and informed me I had torn a lateral meniscus and would have to have surgery. Southern Pacific owned and operated a hospital in San Francisco. I spent a month there having the surgery and recuperating.

Two good things came of this experience, one right away. One of the nurses took a fancy to me and gave me a good lesson in sexual intercourse in her apartment after I left the hospital and before I returned to Sacramento. I had gotten a painful spinal tap prior to leaving the hospital so having intercourse was simultaneously pleasurable and painful.

The second benefit was now I was partially crippled. When a passenger works or rides on a bus or train the transportation company has a duty to protect the worker or passenger. If that person is using crutches or has an obvious handicap, the company has a much higher duty of care that must be exercised on his behalf. Southern Pacific had a legal duty to exercise an even higher duty of care so I wouldn't get injured. I would be testing their duty of care in a future injury.

On April 28, 1973, I had enough seniority to work as a conductor on the Red Bluff local. I showed up at the yard office at 10 am and heard on the radio that 18 boxcars loaded with bombs destined for the war in Viet Nam exploded for unknown reasons at Southern Pacific's Roseville railroad yard.

Ultimately, the disaster injured about 350 people with flying glass and caused more than $24 million dollars in damage, but no one was killed. More than 6,000 bombs detonated on the trains, destroying 169 freight cars and causing heavy damage to 5,500 buildings as much as 6,800 feet away. The trains were headed to the Naval Weapons Station in Concord to be shipped to Southeast Asia. Most of the evidence was destroyed, so the exact cause of the explosion remains a mystery.

Red Bluff is about 200 miles north of Roseville and I too was "injured" but not from the explosions. Actually, I feared that somehow I would get "bumped" from my job as the conductor on the Red Bluff local by one of any number of conductors who had more seniority and who would have been displaced from their jobs by the bomb explosions. So, I set up a situation where I could fake an injury. After coupling into a loaded freight car, I positioned my brakemen so they could not see me as the train pulled away.

Only the engineer who was almost a hundred yards from me watched me give a signal and saw me "slip" on a metal gallon can as I attempted to climb onto a boxcar. (I had previously buried the can myself in sand and gravel) I rolled on the ground and laid there until the crew came back and determined the hazardous condition that "caused my injury." I enjoyed the ambulance ride to the hospital knowing that my finances were assured for the summer regardless of who bumped me off the job. I took the initiative and bumped myself.

I did not bother to attend my graduation from ARC. I was heading to Sacramento State College as a prerequisite to law school. When I was a member of the Young Republicans I noted a number of them were young lawyers. I thought if they could be a lawyer so could I.

My finances were in order and I happened to get lucky and bought my first house at 50th and J Streets in east Sacramento. It was a small, two-bedroom, one bath house. It could not have been more than 800 square feet. I assumed an existing loan with a balance of $11,000 and monthly payments of $112. It was less than a mile to Sacramento State College.

I took the LSAT or Law School Aptitude Test during my second semester at Sac State. I passed but not with a high enough grade to get into McGeorge Law School. I had to settle for Lincoln Law School. Lincoln was an unaccredited school which meant a student would have to pass the Baby Bar exam to proceed to the second year.

Lincoln was created by Dean Victor Bertolloni, a disgruntled lawyer and former professor from McGeorge who had a falling out with the Dean there. He started his own law school to get even. I was accepted because of my grade on the LSAT. In an interview with Bertolloni he made it clear that he wanted some of that "fake injury" business. I dropped out of Sac State and attended Lincoln at their first "building" which occupied two rooms on a second floor in mid-town Sacramento.

I took a 2 unit class on Agency that summer. This course addresses basic principles of agency law, particularly the doctrines associated with authority, vicarious responsibility, and fiduciary duty. It also addresses how agency principles and doctrines are applied in such areas as legal ethics, corporation law, contract law, civil procedure, criminal law, torts, and constitutional law. I thought how things were looking up for the runaway from *St. Joseph's House for Homeless and Industrious Boys*. In September, Lincoln moved to a new facility: a basement and two floors of classes and offices. Things were also looking up for the Dean.

Part of my treatment for my Red Bluff "injury" was to wear a cast from hip to ankle. The cast was a nuisance but if I was to profit from my injury I would have to wear it for a while. I had been riding motorcycles since I was in the Air Force. I always bought a bigger and better one as the years went by. So now I bought another Honda motorcycle. It was a big 750cc and it was an automatic. Now I could ride with the cast. The cast come into good use as it enabled me to trip on the stairway carpeting at Lincoln Law School. Victor Bertolloni was quick to offer me tuition-free classes. As I had not yet taken the first-year class in Torts - which is about liability to injured persons - I relied on my experience faking injuries with the railroad to see me through. Why would people have to burglarize or rob when getting injured was safer and much more profitable? Although things were looking up for me, they would be much better if only I had a woman with whom I could share my adventures.

The issue of finding a woman was resolved when ARC's Professor Jack Badaracco's wife Adrienne phoned me. She set me up with two different women to see which one I would like. Being a law school student apparently had benefits I had not contemplated. Women want to marry a doctor or lawyer and I was en route to becoming a lawyer. It seems that the egos of many first-year law students get inflated. Most see visions of money in their future, but some see the challenge of public service. A lawyer is supposed to help the downtrodden. So many first-year law students look at filthy rich, corrupt corporations as the down-trodden. It must be that vision of lots of money that clouds their judgment.

I settled my "injury" claim with Southern Pacific and went back to work. I now had enough seniority to work the passenger train. I was its Baggage Master. An easier job is not to be found anywhere. At Oakland, the baggage master received from a wagon about eight suitcases. The train departed for Sacramento where maybe another bag or two was handed up to him. On a rare occasion a person detrained at Reno and his or her bag was handed down. That was it! Another baggage master got on in Utah and the train proceeded to Chicago.

I found this job to my liking. I could actually do a little studying on the train as there was about six hours of free time. So occasionally I used the time for my reading assignments. The first year of law in an unaccredited school included the study of Torts (or negligence), Criminal Law, and Contracts. The Baby Bar exam would test what one learned a year later in an all-day exam. The actual bar exam is a three day test of your knowledge in twelve areas of the law.

One of the first admonitions Bertolloni offered was that the person on both sides of you would not be going into the second year. On my right was Dorian Wright. On my left was David Dratman. I looked at both and felt sorry that they would not be joining me in the second year.

I had brought my marijuana smoking with me to Lincoln and spent a lot of time in class high, and in awe of the law. And accumulating knowledge of the law further inflated my ego. Marijuana has a way of distorting reality but I enjoyed looking at my world through rose-colored glasses. How could a person of such humble beginnings find himself in such a lofty position?

I was able to play the field with both women Adrienne set up with me. But soon one vanished because I would not play dad to her two kids. The other was not anything to get excited about so I didn't. But another lady came into my life on her own. She was a voluptuous blonde with two Japanese kids. She was from Missouri.

I took the Baby Bar in San Francisco in mid-June and my ego required that I take a position as Conductor on the passenger train. My ego also required that I delegate any work to the brakemen as I spent my time socializing, or trying to. On one occasion I brought a lady passenger who was wearing a Navy uniform home. She accompanied me assuming we would start a relationship. I was rather impatient. We had sex, although it was not quite consensual. I had never learned that when a woman says NO, she means no. Although I did not quite force myself on her, I was treating her like a sex object and not like a person. I believed erroneously that my status as a budding attorney entitled me to take what I wanted. I never looked at the consequences of my action. How close to raping her did I come? She did not have me arrested. I was lucky. Or was God looking out for me?

In early August I dropped by Lincoln to register for the second year, and the Dean looked at me quite somberly. "You didn't make it," he said softly. I couldn't believe what I was hearing. I was embarrassed, annoyed, angry, bitter, and depressed all at once. Earlier in the summer my ego required that I purchase a Porsche. It was actually a Porsche wannabe: the 914. This model was a lot less expensive then the normal Porsches. It had its motor in the middle and had a hard roof that could be stored in the trunk. It was bright puke green, almost the color of the hickory stick. The Porsche and I picked up the mother of the two Japanese kids – a 9 year-old boy and an 8 year-old girl. I asked if she would like to visit her parents in Missouri. She was surprised, overjoyed and dumbfounded simultaneously. We left for the southwest corner of Missouri the next day, the four of us in a two-seater sports car.

The trip helped me overcome my depression, but just a little. I found myself burying my sorrows in pussy. My ego was slowly deflating. Her parents thought I was a little crazy as they observed me taking a photograph of the six pair of socks worn by her grandfather which were drying on a clothesline on Sunday as he walked around barefoot. I also found myself appreciating a drive in the countryside, stopping to photograph a pair of men's and women's outhouses. On the return trip I wondered if I should spend my time making photographs instead of pursuing the law. That distraction did not last long. I busied myself in a course of study in preparation for passing the Baby Bar and a year later I did. I was now a second-year law student. David Dratman and Dorian Wright, the guys on my right and left during my first year, were now third year students.

I concluded that the Missouri girl with two kids was not to be in my future so I stopped seeing her. The new unresolved issue of a woman for me was about to be resolved once again. I received a phone call from Jack Badaracco. Apparently a student in his rat class lied to him when he claimed he had experience and the education to publish the scholarship program's magazine. Jack asked if I would publish it. I attended one of his classes and announced I would need an assistant. A buxom blonde, not yet twenty-one, volunteered. Her eyes were very glassy. Judy Nelson had big tits and wore cowboy boots. I did not like either. I was of the opinion that what you could not fit in your mouth was wasteful. I don't know why I did not like cowboy boots. I still don't. Maybe I should buy a pair.

Judy Nelson and I worked closely together and made great progress toward publishing the program. She smoked grass and was stoned much of the time. Judy told me that she had been smoking dope since she started high school.

I returned to the rat lab at ARC's campus to make lots of photographs of the rats in action. One of my bedrooms was converted into a darkroom and I processed the film and made prints. One day coming out of the darkroom I was a little shocked to see her standing naked, stoned, and asking if I would take photographs of her. I complied. After a session of photography we had a session of sex. She was good. She was especially good at oral sex. I learned to ignore her cowboy boots and accept her big boobs. She would accompany me in my car and after spending time on the program or in bed, I would return her to her home.

Judy's mother was a principal at Mira Loma High School. She told me that her mom provided her with the final exam answers in most classes and that was how she graduated.

When I dropped Judy off at her home one day I viewed her mother with more attention. I quickly noticed that she too had a vegetated husband, most likely a product of her abuse. We were alone when she gave me a warning. "I hope you have no intention of dating my daughter," she threatened. Her last words were "She is much too young for you." That pissed me off as I had no idea of doing anything but having sex with Judy. I thought it sounded a little like: you are a dime a dozen because you are old.

I took a closer look at Judy. I suppose when a parent tells a child not to do something, there is a desire to do what is not wanted, so I sent Judy a dozen roses. Why did her mother challenge me? Why did I retaliate?

A week later Judy moved in with me. In a few weeks, I put the house up for sale and we moved to Pollock Pines, about fifty miles east of Sacramento at the 4,000 foot elevation on the west slopes of the Sierra Mountains,

I noticed the town did not have a newspaper. So she and I created the **Pollock Pines Press.** Judy was listed as the Editor, and I assumed the position of journalist and photographer.

Chapter Seven
Publisher and Failure - 1980

I dedicated the first issue, **Volume 1, No. 1 Wednesday, May 4, 1977,** of *The Pollock Pines Press* to Judy's parents and to Jack and Adrienne Badaracco, the closest persons I had to parents. The first issue was filled with only good news. The twelve page "newspaper" was printed in three colors: green, brown and gold, in addition to black ink.

Publicity preceded the first publication with color posters that read "Coming Soon – News You Can Use - *Pollock Pines Press.* It had a rider on horseback representing the Pony Express Trail because Pollock Pines was a stop on this historic letter-carrying service.

One photo on the first page was taken at the Ghost Mountain Resort of a horse rearing with the rider ready to fall off the back as he was performing in a skit at the new campground. I had just bought a motorized Olympus 35mm camera and it could take five frames a second.

There was also a photo of Al Benson and other local civic leaders and members of the Lions Club who were holding an auction to benefit firefighters. And there was a photograph of Lulu who was celebrating her 80th birthday with 300 of her friends and family. Lulu owned an apple stand and operated it on the honor system. Buyers would take a case of apples and just leave the money in a box on a table while Lulu took her nap.

The news included stories of the historic Pony Express Ride going national, the Roy Bean Club installing officers, the grand opening of the Ghost Mountain resort, and the Chamber of Commerce seeking "Miss Pollock Pines" candidates.

Inside were two editorials, one chiding the phone company for maintaining a busy signal instead of answering calls from its customers. Another asked the California Department of Transportation to post a few signs on Highway 50 announcing the availability of gas and food for travelers to the benefit of the business community. The editorial claimed the general public using the highway on their way to or from South Lake Tahoe only knew that Pollock Pines had two exits as they were the only signs posted.

An **Inquiring Photographer** column asked a half-dozen five and six year olds if they believed in flying saucers. Billie Jean Haskill answered: "Ain't such a thing...wouldn't go with them if they landed. Mommy wouldn't want me to go." Sean Bass replied "Hardy Boys saw one. I would go for a short ride... if they got me back by morning... would like to go to Mars." Troy Keifer offered: "Have heard of them. Saw one at Disneyland. It was a round one with spacemen inside. Went inside and wasn't scared."

There were twenty-seven paid display advertisements. Businesses that advertised included Anderson Backhoe and Trucking, Faye's Coffee shop in Camino, Bob's Auto Repair, The Bean Hut's Mexican Food, City Answering Service, The Placerville Press, Wayside Village Shops, Passetti's Quality Meats, Pollock Pines Log Splitting, 49er General Store, Avery Furniture Store, The Donut Corral, Rich's Arco station, Gary Tanko Well Drilling, Kyburz Lodge, Pollock Pines Florist and all four Pollock Pine's Realtors. A classified ad section featured a dozen ads for 5 cents a word. The newspaper was profitable on day one.

I had taken all the photographs, sold all the advertising, wrote all the stories and layed the paper out. Judy accompanied and motivated me by providing me with both sex and marijuana.

There was a made-up or invented staff announced in print, but in fact only Judy Nelson and I were involved. I named her Editor, and hid behind her skirt as photojournalist.

There was no printing press. We contracted with *The Auburn Journal* fifty miles to the north in Placer County to print our budding journal. We printed 4,000 copies and distributed them from El Dorado Hills to the west, to Mount Aukum to the south, to Strawberry to the north. Distribution started at Cool as we drove back from Auburn. We had news stands or boxes set up in four businesses in Camino and eight in Pollock Pines. The first issue was well read and based on the number of phone calls we received, it was also enjoyed. But controversy was about to erupt.

Volume 1, No. 2   Wednesday, May 18, 1977

Sacramento, a budding metropolitan city in 1977, had been running stories almost daily in its **Sacramento Bee** about what they dubbed **The East Area Rapist**. He was committing his crimes in the east area of Sacramento. The rapist struck again on Tuesday night, May 17. In the morning of May 18, The Bee headlined his attack to warn Sacramento residents. May 18 was also the date of the second issue of **The Pollock Pines Press**.

Our headline in one-inch high letters read "RAPISTS IN AREA". But it had nothing to do with Sacramento's east area rapist. Our news story began: "Logging companies, many from out of town, are approaching residents in this area and are offering large sums of money for permission to cut trees on local property. According to a number of callers to **The Press** this week, what results instead is "a rape of the land and an under-compensated landowner." The story continued, "Reliable sources in both Pollock Pines and Camino confirmed that this activity has started and they gave **The Press** an example where $12,000 offers were being settled for less than $5,000 after the trees were cut and removed.

I vividly recall hand-delivering stacks of papers that morning. In one delivery I dropped off 50 copies at The Sportsman's Hall, an historic Pony Express station and a favorite eatery in Pollock Pines. Eighty-year old Lulu was there having breakfast with half a dozen friends. When she read the headline- RAPISTS IN AREA - she exclaimed to the laughter of her companions: "Great, I still have a chance." Regrettably, people in her generation viewed rape as sex instead of the violence it really is.

Much of the rest of the community reacted differently and some with anger. Of course I had given them an additional reason. The editorial cartoon depicted the Pollock Pines billboard on Highway 50 that proclaimed the area as **Nature's Wonderland.** In addition, there was a drawing of a lumber truck with a sign *Gypo - Out of Town Lumber Co*, painted on the side. And it was departing town leaving nothing but tree stumps behind. The billboard was altered to read: "Pollock Pines FORMERLY Nature's Wonderland." The lumber industry took it personally.

Camino had two major industries. The lumber industry was its largest employer. The apple growers were its second largest. Many of the larger apple growers were landowners who fed the lumber mill harvested trees. Another significant organization was the El Dorado Irrigation District, EID for short. Of course, the apple growers managed that public organization in order to have plenty of water for their orchards. The area's biggest drought started in 1977. Nevertheless, because the growers were on EID's board of directors, the growers would not suffer due to the drought.

A second news story in our second edition concerned the El Dorado Irrigation District and its effort to replace a 117 year old canal with a pipeline. EID claimed leakage from the "ditch" amounted to 820 acre feet of water lost annually. It was clear to me that EID wanted to regulate the flow of water for the benefit of its board of directors, the apple growers, and not the public. So the main photograph on the front page was of the pipes, ready to be installed. EID had previously published a press release in the **Mountain Democrat,** El Dorado County's other newspaper, proclaiming that the water would remain in the ditch. They deceived the public by failing to inform them of the pipeline project. The pipes would be laid and covered and the canal would disappear.

I believed I was performing a public service with my news story. Many readers agreed. But the apple growers, EID Board of Directors - the same people - and the lumber industry did not.

It is amazing what corporations and big business can get away with when there is not a free press to hold them accountable. With the advent of the internet and the corresponding loss of so many newspapers in 2010, will there be a revival of undetected corporate corruption?

A third story on the front page of the second issue of *The Pollock Pines Press* dealt with The Board of Trustees of a very small school in Silver Fork, about 30 miles north of Pollock Pines. They procured the resignation of teacher Sue Petersen by "offering to drop criminal charges against her." Perhaps they were not aware that only the county District Attorney had that power. Nevertheless, this story informed the public that the "crimes" the popular teacher allegedly committed concerned the use of the school telephone for long distance calls. Sue Petersen and others at the school admitted that use of the phone was a common practice among most personnel. She was also charged with claiming reimbursement for five trips to Placerville for a seminar on Early Child Education. She made all five trips but pointed out that one was cancelled and she was not notified. She further stated that the claim was inadvertently turned in by someone else. The teacher had paid for the calls upon notification that the two year practice was unlawful.

A former principal, Bill Scarborough, had also been forced to resign recently. According to a letter sent to him on May 10 by Rod Wright, the Superintendent of the school district, Scarborough failed to exercise good judgment when he allowed a child to stand up on a moving bus. Bill Scarborough told **The Press** that two children were scuffling in the back of the bus and he asked one child to sit across the aisle to restore order. The news story continued: "Scarborough has recently been evaluated by Graham Rankin, Associate Superintendent of El Dorado County Schools". In his report he stated: "Mr. William Scarborough is very highly structured, extremely organized and a disciplinarian of the first order." The evaluation, only three weeks ago, also found Scarborough "to be a caring teacher and one who spends a great deal of his time devoted to the learning of the students."

It seemed that a group of concerned parents representing more than 80% of the students in the school had raised charges earlier that Wright was waging a vendetta against all those who dared to vote against him. Earlier in the year Wright had cancelled a ski program because a number of parents of the children in the program had campaigned against him in his bid to be re-elected school superintendent. He was re-elected to a four year term in March, 1977. He apparently won because of the large number of absentee ballots from absentee landowners who were not aware of his true character. **The Press** had requested an opportunity to photograph some of the children for its Inquiring Photographer column. Instead of answering **The Press,** Wright, independent of the school board, sent each teacher a memo which stated "…no student shall have their picture taken by local newspapers." He sent this memo because he learned our newspaper would be attending the school board's next meeting.

So I put at the top of my agenda a visit to the next board meeting. Certainly this was an opportunity to right a wrong or two. And Rod Wright was that wrong.

Volume 1, No. 3   Wednesday, June 1, 1977

Two headlines graced the front page of this issue: **SILVER FORK TRUSTEE'S WIFE ATTACKS REPORTER,** and **Court Stops EID**. Another headline reported on the "massive PG&E leaks."

It is better to quote from the newspaper article than to rely on memory, so here goes. "KYBURZ -- The wife of Rod Wright, a trustee of the Silver Fork School District, stormed into the offices of *The Press*, handed a note to photojournalist Steve Mizera and, after being asked a question, threw a punch which missed him but broke an expensive camera. The note had demanded that the name Silver Fork Store be removed from the list of *Press* distributors. Mrs. Wright left the office before the arrival of the El Dorado County Sheriff. Mizera had asked the irate woman whether she had disrupted an Early Childhood Education meeting two weeks earlier by shouting obscenities, or if she made threats to Sue Peterson. The note also indicated Mrs. Wright was offended because *The Press* reported that her child, Bowdre Lemp, had been telling Miss Peterson that she would be fired. (Young Lemp had actually told this to Bill Scarborough who was also forced to resign because he was politicking against Rod Wright. The choleric woman has been despondent since *The Press* made public her husband's irrational behavior. According to Rod Wright, Bill Scarborough handed in his resignation on May 19, 1977. The popular and talented professional told *The Press*: I couldn't take them (the trustees) anymore. In response to his resignation, parents and property owners signed a petition directed to the El Dorado County Board of Health to investigate Rod Wright's mental competency."

In response to the photo and story of the pipe, The El Dorado Irrigation District was stopped by readers who filed a writ of mandate enjoining EID from proceeding with the project to destroy the beautiful canal by burying a pipeline in it. That triggered action by the Board of Supervisors to withhold money from the county general fund pending a judgment by the county council as to EID's responsibility.

It is true that no one should believe everything one reads or every photograph one sees in a newspaper. (Especially because of software today like Photoshop) Here is one example of how this was true at that time. The headline on the front page that read: **Massive PG&E Leaks** was true, but the story behind that story needs to be told. *The Press* honestly reported that "More than 15,000 acre feet of water -- almost twice the present capacity of Jenkinson Reservoir -- were leaking annually from a 55 year old wood stave pipe. The pipe supplied the El Dorado power plant on the American River north of the mountain community which is presently embroiled in a battle with the El Dorado Irrigation District over an alleged 820 acre feet of seepage. A knowledgeable source in PG&E's maintenance department, who wished to remain anonymous, told *The Press* "the leaks won't be repaired because PG&E is competing with $16 barrel oil." The photograph that accompanied the story needs clarification too. The pipe, as it existed, would not have made a good photograph. I needed to embarrass PG&E but the tiny leaks could not be seen. So I walked along the top of the pipe and enlarged a few of the tiny leaks until spouts could be visible and a stream of water flowing beside it could be seen in the photograph. Enlarging the leaks made this story more newsworthy. I printed the photo on the front page and it got PG&E's attention.

Readership was increasing with each issue. The size of the paper was now 16 pages, and advertisers were calling us. So it made sense that our imaginary staff be enlarged too.

Volume 1, No. 4   Wednesday, June 15, 1977

The Olympus 35 mm camera with the motor drive that enabled me to take five photographs a second was my weapon of choice when I attended the Silver Fork School Board of Trustees' meeting. I sat in the back of the room and went through three rolls of film, or 108 shots, in order to obtain the photograph I published in this issue. It showed Wright with his eyes closed and smoke from his cigarette billowing from his mouth. The caption read: "Silver Fork Trustee Wright displays arrogance while Trustee DePaepe listens intently to a parent's question."

The headline that accompanied this photo read: **Riles Writes: Remedy: Recall Wright.** (Wilson Riles was the State Superintendent of Education) The story read: "KYBURZ -- Two El Dorado County Sheriff Officers attended the Silver Fork School Board of Trustee's meeting on Tuesday, June 7. When asked why they were present, Rod Wright -- after several evasions of the question -- answered: 'I'm the one that asked for them because of threats.' He declined to discuss who made the threats with the concerned parents and residents who had filled the meeting room to capacity. Mrs. Wright, who threw a punch at a reporter for **The Press** two weeks ago, ran out of the meeting muttering obscenities after having been photographed. She was wearing a neck support, obviously for her fake injury and as a pre-requisite for a law suit."

It should be mentioned here that I *did* pick Mrs. Wright up by the head and remove her from my office. And that the Wrights were planning to sue me for damage to her neck. I was still going to law school. My friend and fellow student Mike Montbriand, who worked for the law firm of Sullivan and Turner in Sacramento, tipped me off. His bosses, who were hired by the Wrights, had asked Mike to check if I had any assets. Lawyers won't sue someone unless that someone has money.

The news story continued. "Parents had written to Wilson Riles, whose chief counsel, Thomas M. Griffin wrote back "If enough citizens in your community feel the same dissatisfaction as you with the actions of the board, the recall remedy is available to you." Parents had requested information on a recall election but Rod Wright refused it saying an election would be too expensive. One father left the meeting saying aloud, we have another Nixon here abusing his power.

I couldn't help but throw fuel on this fire. I asked, and my story reported: "Before the meeting adjourned Mizera a Press photojournalist asked Wright: 'Are you hiding boats from your brother's marina from a Southern California bankruptcy proceeding?' Wright screamed: 'get away from me'."

Yes it might have been both slanderous and libelous. I was not sure if he had a garage or a brother, but where there is smoke there is fire, and I was enjoying creating the smoke. Without checking the facts, I was helping to circulate a local rumor. It turned out he had a garage and there was a boat in it.

Weeks later Mike Montbriand reported to his boss at the law firm that I was heavily into debt and on the verge of filing bankruptcy. I had no assets. My only asset was my version of freedom of speech. Lawyers will generally take a case if there is something in it for them: money. They so notified the Wrights that filing a lawsuit against me would be a waste of their time and his money.

Nevertheless the paper was threatened with legal action by EID, PG&E, Silver Fork School District and the publicist for the lumber industry. As I was a law student and knew I could get tons of information from their files through the legal process of discovery, I invited all to proceed. None did. What could be in their files that they feared I would share with the public?

The publication of **The Pollock Pines Press** was now part public service and lots of fun. My favorite local resident, an artist named Chip Fyn, was already famous for creating life-sized wood carvings of store-front or cigar store Indians, dockside old salts holding lanterns, Charlie Chaplin, Superman, and so many others. One feature story in The Press explained how Chip put Pollock Pines on the map. Chip was scheduled to have a one-person exhibit at the prestigious Crocker Art Gallery in Sacramento. To promote it KCRA-TV came up to Pollock Pines and installed cameras to record him at work making a carving. The cameras took a few frames every few minutes. After thirty days, Chip finished the carving, and the film was ready for prime time. The intent was to show an entire carving completed in a few minutes. During the last week Chip removed a piece of clothing each day until he was stark naked. The news crew had to censor part of this.

I first met Chip on the K Street Mall in Sacramento where he was exhibiting and putting the finishing touches on his carving of Ronald McDonald. He had been threatened in a letter by McDonald's attorney demanding he not reproduce Ronald, but the letter was hung around the wood carving's neck. Chip told me this would increase the value of the carving. He was a genuine artist who lived in his own world. I liked him and he was a factor in my decision to move to Pollock Pines.

In addition to publishing the **Pollock Pines Press**, my time was spent keeping Judy satisfied sexually, and this kept my sexuality in check. I was commuting to Lincoln Law School in Sacramento, a 100 mile round trip three days a week. I was also commuting periodically to Oakland to fulfill my duties as conductor or baggage master. This was a 140 mile commute one day, a railroad trip to Sparks, a return trip the next day to Oakland followed by a return commute to Pollock Pines. To manage publishing, law school and working on the railroad, I would skip class one day a week and I would skip one or two round-trips to work. The newspaper was like a hobby. Sometimes Judy was a help, sometimes she was a hindrance, but I ignored those times because she always satisfied my sexual appetite and that was the glue that held us together.

I really enjoyed using a camera, and working in a darkroom processing film and making prints. I enjoyed writing. When I was preparing to write a news story, there was often no time to check or double- check the facts as journalists are supposed to do. At times calls would not be returned by public officials or they did not respond to my questions. I did not hesitate to invent the news by concocting what they might have said and putting it in quotes. Sometimes I would just use the "reliable source who wished to remain anonymous" method of lying.

I was selling ads, taking and making photos, laying out the paper, writing news stories, coordinating with cartoonist or graphic artists, delivering the paper layout to Auburn and then spending all day distributing it. And concurrently, much of my time was spent getting high with Judy and having more sex. I was also snorting cocaine with members of the train crew and popping prescription pain killers for my "injuries." Time flew by. There never seemed to be enough of it. When one paper was delivered, another had to be created. I was not really equipped to publish a newspaper single-handedly, although I appeared to be doing just that.

Weekly newspapers sell advertising by the quarter of a year, or in blocks of thirteen weeks, at a time. For the first year, I was selling ads individually - every week! This was really inefficient and a waste of time. Remember, you are dealing with Mr. Naive. I am sure now that my ability to think then was also seriously harmed by my use of drugs. But then, who among those that use drugs would believe it at the time.

In retrospect, another area that would have helped is knowledge of bookkeeping. I had no idea where the money came from or where it went. I was making enough from the railroad to subsidize publishing the paper. Knowledge in both of these areas would have guaranteed a successful and profitable venture. Instead of collecting money for many ads, I swapped. I swapped for gas, for dining out, and anything else that was able to be bartered. I guess I was more interested in feeding my ego than feeding my bank account.

Volume 2, No. 1   Wednesday, June 29, 1977

"Bill," I spoke in a measured tone, "take a look at the paper." He was the editor of the Auburn Journal and had been doing an outstanding job printing our newspaper. But with this issue there was a serious problem. I noticed it when the papers were delivered to my office. Judy held one up as she got out of her car. I knew she was high even though it was still morning. I could tell by her glossy eyes and her shit-eating smile.

It was our Fourth of July edition. A US Flag took up the top third of the front page along with our new motto and claim: **We Tell It Like It Is Because It's Made For You.** But this flag had six white strips and seven blue stripes and the 50 white stars were on a field of red. I heard Bill order a re-run of this issue. Had that issue been distributed before the error was discovered, no one would have ever believed that we were telling it like it is.

It was a good time to visit Chip and we had a good laugh over this mistake. He even had a good use for the newspapers. He had been illegally adding a room to his studio known as the Sawdust Gallery situated on Pony Express Trail in Pollock Pines. He used the 5,000 misprinted papers for insulation. One day someone will find those papers and they too will have a good laugh.

The headlines of this issue showed that battles were still raging. **EID Boycotting Press. $1,000,000 CLAIM FILED AGAINST SILVER FORK.** And inside: **Large EID Leak on Land of EID Director's Relative.** and realtor **EBER ASHER TRIED SELLING PG&E's LEAK.**

Each of these stories has a story behind it. And in the interest of honesty, I feel an obligation to reveal them to readers of my autobiography.

The publicist for EID was also the publicist for Camino's Michigan Cal-Lumber. I first got wind of her boycott plan when delivering this issue, as the businesses that normally distributed **The Press** in Camino refused to do so anymore. Then a few advertisers called to say they would not be advertising in future editions. Confidentially they mentioned that they liked the paper but were pressured by the publicist Halmar Moser who told them she vowed to "bury **The Press**. " I had found a way for youngsters to make a little spending money. If they came by the office I would give them one hundred copies of the paper that they could sell for $.20 each and keep all the money. Two ten-year old girls from Camino did this for the previous issue but their fathers worked in the lumber industry and their kids fell victim to Moser's boycott. He said they couldn't sell our paper in the future.

Placerville attorney Stephen Keller, submitted a claim to the Silver Fork School Board for $1,000,000 on behalf of teacher Susan Peterson. The claim stated that the resignation of the teacher was procured and accepted by means of fraud. Although the board was expected to deny the claim, filing a claim was a procedural prerequisite of a law suit against the school district and El Dorado County.

In order to have **The Press** interact with its readers, we started a *Letters to The Press* column in this issue. Although we did not receive letters to be published yet, I created one and signed it Mary Jane Wright, the wife of school superintendent Rod Wright. It read: "Dear Editor: The purpose of this letter is to apologize for throwing the punch at your reporter **and missing him.** No one in our community is interested in your biased news reports. It is none of your business what my husband is doing with his brother's boats. Furthermore, neither you nor your advertisers are welcomed at out grocery store and gas station."

The water leak cited in the story about the leak on EID Director's Relative land was important for a few reasons. EID had received a grant and loan of more than $5 million from the federal government on the condition it continue to conserve water and to develop additional ways to conserve water. The leak was on land owned by the widow Larsen, who was married to EID Director's Larsen's second cousin.

EID established new drought rates which penalized water consumers who used in excess of 70 cubic feet per day by shutting off their water and charging a $50 reconnection fee. The leak on the EID Director's property was measured at 5,760 cubic feet a day, or 82 times the amount considered excessive by EID. The drought rate exempted commercial, metered irrigation customers. If the penalty a homeowner had to pay for excessive use was applied by EID to its director's relative, it would cost her $4,100 a day. This story was intended to have readers attend the monthly EID Board meetings. And did they ever! The next EID board meeting was played to an overflow crowd.

Although his real estate business was an advertiser with **The Press**, Eber Asher was offended by our story that his firm was trying to sell a home on Forebay Road "with a year round stream." We pointed out in our news report that it was not a stream but runoff from the PG&E leaking, wood stave pipe. He not only stopped advertising but stated he would not pay his outstanding bill for his previous ad. I published his statement because we were simply being true to our slogan: We tell it like it is. This issue was twenty-pages, readership was up, we were being fed many tips dealing with corporate corruption. Things were looking up.

In this issue I ran a story announcing **Mizera Named Publisher**. I quoted Judy: "Steve is immensely qualified and he is a just person. You can count on him to locate the facts. All of them. He fears no one."

Volume 3, No. 3   Wednesday, July 13, 1977

Each issue seemed to have something a little different than the preceding one. Next to Safeway on the east end of Pollock Pines, there was a clothing store in the shopping center. It was named the Toggery. Our front page story read: TOGGERY GETS NEW WINDOW.

It was about Mildred Ayres, aged 58, who crashed through the Toggery's plate glass window with her big Cadillac. Mildred had a driver's permit and lots of health issues. After she had completed parking, her husband Clarence, 65, had patted her on the back and complimented her by saying, "You did a great job." At that moment the car leaped forward through the window. No one was in the store. Clarence asked, "What did you do that for?" and the car lurched forward a second time burning rubber on the linoleum floor. Clarence turned off the key.

Mildred told **The Press** she had just gotten out of the hospital two days earlier after having lung and gall bladder problems, and had taken a pill for her bad heart earlier in the morning. She said she would not be driving again because she was too nervous. The gas pedal on her vehicle had a four inch extension attached to enable

Mildred to reach it. Ayres had been involved in another accident earlier in the year. She had been receiving therapy for a neck whiplash. She told **The Press** "I think this accident must have unlashed my neck. It hasn't troubled me since driving through the window."

I never learned if her attorney or the insurance company read that admission.

Volume 2, No. 3   Wednesday, July 27, 1977

In this twenty-four page issue we started to look legitimate. The front page announced that the State was to investigate EID, and a Recall Wright Group was formed. That gave me an opportunity to re-run the photo of arrogant Rod Wright blowing smoke.

Our advertising base was broadening. We had a history column entitled El Dorado's Yesterdays, and California Senator S. I. Hayakawa contributed a column. We started a series on Laetrile, the controversial cancer treatment derived from apricot kernels. The 28th Annual Wagon Train took up a lot of space, especially with photos of the horses, mules and wagons and the participants in 1850s clothing. County supervisors lined up to submit columns in **The Press** for the free publicity.

Volume 2, No. 4   Wednesday, August 10, 1977

Pollock Pines had a population of just fewer than 3,000, but activity came to a crawl at the end of summer when the flow of tourists slowed. We announced **The Press** would be a monthly periodical until April, 1978.

This issue featured a column written by Sheriff Richard Pacileo who was calling for public support for various public safety bills hung up in the legislature. Our Letters to The Press featured a demand from Attorney George Maul, who was representing EID and took issue with our news report which quoted him as saying "EID was not responsible to anyone, not even God." His letter demanding a retraction cited the appropriate Civil Code sections and noted that the **Sacramento Bee** published a retraction.

In our Editor's note we informed him that we were present when he uttered those words, and were not just re-publishing what the **Sacramento Bee** printed. We also notified him that we would not retract the statement. We never heard from his law firm again.

Volume 2, No. 5   The September Pollock Pines Press 1977

Publishing monthly gave me a break. It allowed me to finally start to focus on law school. I continued my pursuit of photography by incorporating photos in advertising. People were actually providing much of the news. The California State Fair was underway and I had successfully applied for press passes. These were passed around to different people each day so more than fifty people got in the State Fair gates without having to pay. In 1977 the price of admission was $2.50 and there was a $1 parking charge.

The front page of **The Press** told of a mid-air collision which took four lives including that of Hugh Killebrew, owner of Heavenly Valley Ski Resort. A pilot of a twin-engine plane collided with Kellebrew's plane who apparently was circling, trying to gain altitude. The other pilot was uninjured and he was able to return to the South Tahoe airport.

The EID canal dispute was the subject of a public hearing. A letter to **The Press** was critical of our series on Laetrile. Our Inquiring Photographer asked half a dozen people if they enjoyed the State Fair. Jeff Banks, local dentist, did not go yet. Five did and stated they enjoyed it. Although the centerfold featured two pages of advertising for Safeway, I had given them the ads at no charge hoping they would become a regular advertiser. They never did advertise. Politics?

Volume 2, No. 6   The October Pollock Pines Press 1977

An interesting front page story told of a Sly Park Hills man who fired five shots from his 16-gauge shotgun and killed his neighbor's Doberman pinscher who had sniffed at his 11 year old daughter on her way to the school bus stop.

Another noted the Grand Jury was to call EID to probe the water district's violations of the Public Records Act and self-dealing by its directors.

The Recall Wright Committee initiated a petition. This was required prior to circulating a formal petition. It seems that Superintendent Rod Wright got caught using school district stationery for political purposes. Nothing new.

Because the town of Camino is famous for its apples, it was an opportunity to tell about 81-year old Lulu (Louis Lanigir) who raises and harvests the crop from 180 trees. She is the one who ran her apple stand on the honor system, a system that has long since vanished from society.

Volume 2, No. 7   The November Pollock Pines Press 1977

The main headline in this issue of twenty pages informed our readers that the State Water Resources Control Board was covering up an EID investigation. That is what happens when you put a fox in charge of the chicken coop.

Volume 3, No. 1   The December Pollock Pines Press 1977

Santa Claus and his pending visit to Pollock Pines was the main headline in the December issue. This issue was 32 pages. Merchants were being warned of fraudulent

Postal Money orders being passed. But the only photo was of **Happy the Hitchhiker,** Chip Fyn's latest carving.

Happy was a four foot, two-inch, 94 pound Ponderosa Pine statue, He sported a straw hat, and a red and white striped shirt. Chip carved this for "Mom and Dad Tramposch". A plastic envelope dangled from *Happy* and contained self-addressed envelopes along with a letter which asked drivers who picked up *Happy* to help get him to Connecticut. One of those envelopes was received by Chip and contained a note reporting *Happy* to be in Salt Lake City, Utah, eight hundred miles to the east.

Businesses being business, they know the value of advertising, so many were coming back to *The Press* despite our reports of corporate corruption. We even obtained large, paid ads from realtors. There was even a small ad for the realtor Eber Asher who we reported as trying to sell a home with a year-round stream, which was actually the leaking PG&E pipe. The check for his ad included payment for previous ads he said he would not pay because of our news story.

This issue contained an *Ask Al* advice column, a crossword puzzle, half a page of comic strips and a horoscope column by local astrologer Ruth Moscrop. Our classified ads were now free ads and were spread out over five pages. It was getting easier to publish. Perhaps a new adventure was on my horizon.

The phone call was from Alaska. It was from Juneau, Alaska. It was from Joe Orsini, Senator from Anchorage, Alaska." Would you like to come up and play politics?" he asked. Joe and I were in the YRs at the same time. In response to a cry of "Burn Baby Burn" by protesters during the Vietnam War, I had organized the building of a small community center in Rio Linda and we had a rallying cry of "Build Baby Build." Joe was very active on that project.

Volume 3, No. 2   **The January Pollock Pines Press**
1978

A photographer from Placerville's **Mountain Democrat** made the photograph of me that appeared on the front page of this issue. The headline - **Press publisher departs for Alaskan Senate Post** - was accompanied by a news story.

"Steve A. Mizera, publisher of the Pollock Pines Press, left for Alaska today. He has accepted a position as administrative assistant to the republican caucus for the Alaskan State Senate in Juneau. Mizera, 37, will be working with Alaska republican senator Joseph Orsini during the session which is expected to last until early June." It went on to give a short biography of me.

Another headline in this issue told of three persons charged with the sale of cocaine. It reported that a salesman for a local realtor and his wife were busted trying to sell an ounce of cocaine for $2900 to an undercover officer in Sam's restaurant in Cameron Park. The salesman's wife was a substitute teacher for El Dorado County. She was put on unpaid leave from the school district.

But the headline that I relished read: **"Stream" stops; Family Evicted**" The news story read: "A family of four was evicted from a rented house on Forebay Road in late December because a water supply dried up earlier in October. Daniel J. Farla, 27, his wife, and two young children were given a three-day eviction notice on December 28, 1977, because he was using the $150 rent to pay to have 50 gallons of water hauled in daily. Dogwood Springs, the name given to the house located one mile north of Pony Express Trail on Forebay Road, is a four bedroom structure. Its water supply was said to be a stream but was actually the runoff from a Pacific Gas and Electric pipe system that had been leaking for years."

"The house is presently being offered for sale by Mother Lode Realty of Placerville. Lee Woods, a salesperson with the real estate office said: 'the owners told me it was a year-round stream and that it never stopped flowing during the drought." But Faria said 'The stream stopped flowing completely when PG&E repaired its old wooden pipe'."

This issue also reported *Happy* in Denver, halfway home.

An exposé on **Amtrak the Bureaucrat's Railroad** started in this issue. It included a photograph of a $15,000 train window washer. The tone of the caption for this photograph is similar to the tone of the article. It read: "Pictured above is Amtrak's $15,000 train window washer. For the past 18 months it has been parked under a no parking sign in the Oakland railroad yard. The machine has not been moved because none of Amtrak's employees know how to operate it. Amtrak also has additional window washers in Ogden, Utah, Denver, Colorado and Chicago, Illinois. Congress is expected to appropriate $18,000,000 for Amtrak in January."

On my last trip as Conductor before departing for Alaska I distributed 100 copies of this issue to the porters on the passenger train that departed Oakland. They would make sure the article was circulated in each of the cities mentioned in the news story.

Senator Joe Orsini asked me to bring his automobile up to Alaska with me, so I drove it to Seattle and took the ferry to Juneau. He also asked me to find a secretary for him as the person who was to work for him was not able to. So I found one willing YR who was to fly to Juneau and arrive a few days after my arrival.

The voyage to Juneau was a three day trip in mid-January and one of the better times I enjoyed in the previous few years. No newspaper to publish, no train to conduct, and no law books to read. I had just dropped out of school without mentioning my plans to the Dean.

My ferry ride was even a bit entertaining. The crew was starting to practice what it would do if the ferry was about to sink. I was in the dining room having a late, expensive breakfast when over the loudspeaker an announcement asked crew members to report to one side of the ship for their scheduled rescue drill.

Immediately after a few crew members departed for the lifeboats on that side of the ship, the announcer corrected himself and directed the crew to the opposite side of the ferry. So I watched as only half a crew started to lower a large rescue boat toward the water. Life rafts stored in that boat poured out the back and splashed into the sea. Initially I thought this was funny but then the realization hit me that they were in charge of my safety. Small icebergs were visible so I knew the water would be very cold.

But the ferry is a wonderful way to get to Alaska. It stops at small fishing villages en route to Juneau and allows the passengers to disembark and spend a few hours in each town. The ferry system is called the Alaskan Highway. I left Seattle in the early evening on a Tuesday and arrived in Juneau at 6 am on Friday. I drove Joe's car to the state capitol building a few blocks from the dock. He helped me get settled. About eleven in the morning he took me up an elevator to a conference room on the sixth floor of the state office building. We sat and watched the sun rise over and between Mt. Juneau and Mt. Richards. The sun set again by 2 pm. Welcome to Alaska.

Working in the legislature was actually fun. I had plenty of time to make believe I was a reporter/photographer and got to rub shoulders with Associated Press journalists. It is always important to be careful what you say around journalists. I did not learn that lesson until it was too late.

I became the subject matter of the **Anchorage Daily News**, the state's major newspaper. It seems there was a controversy going on in Alaska about hiring out of state folks instead of local Alaskan residents. The news story was about Senator Joe Orsini hiring me. He and I laughed at this article and he then showed me how to use the press.

He introduced a bill the next day that called for a moratorium on commercial fishing, blah, blah, blah. Joe represented the people in Anchorage who fished for sport. It seems that the number of days for them to fish was being cut short by a regulatory agency. Joe's proposed legislation got everyone's attention and pushed me off the front-page. He told me with a smile: "if you want to get someone's attention, you need to hit them with a 2x4". In typical quid pro quo fashion the regulators backed off and increased the number of sport fishery days for the upcoming season. Joe dropped his bill.

My job was interesting and it gave me an opportunity to see how the legislature worked. I was answering Joe's mail. The state had state of the art typewriters at that time. It was an IBM selectric but it had a memory big enough to store a few template letters. So when someone sent the senator a letter calling for a response favoring that position, letter A was sent. If a letter was received in opposition, letter B was sent. All I had to do was add the name and address. The rest was automated.

One letter was from a self-employed person who had a small landscaping business. A regulatory agency had recently publicized a rule to raise revenue. But that would have been costly to entrepreneurs like Joe's constituent. So I called that department and told them we needed someone from their department to appear before the Senate Finance Committee, of which Joe was chairman. I informed them that the committee wanted to see how they spent their money last year, so detailed records would be necessary. Before I hung up I mentioned that one of Joe's constituents, the landscaper, was having what appeared to be an unnecessary expense as a result of rules recently passed by his department. I asked them to provide us with an executive summary of the problem along with a solution.

Sure enough I received a call the next day informing us that the landscaper need not worry as the rule was revoked. In turn, I informed him that it was not necessary for their department to appear at the hearing as it was cancelled.

I also spent a little time doing investigative work. The state did not have the equivalent of a state coroner nor did they have a dedicated facility in which to do autopsies and related lab work. I found some characters – masquerading as Forensic Sciences - who were trying to fill these voids by trying to get the state to pay for a lab that they would build. I suspected what they were doing was at the least unethical and possibly criminal. Eventually as they were executing their plan to purchase influence I gained their confidence. I started to compile a large file on them based on numerous phone calls I had with them.

A consequence of what they were planning might have been a disaster for another legislator, who headed the House Judiciary Committee, and who was a good friend of Joe's. My plan was simply to give Forensic Sciences enough rope. And they went for it.

Housing was the first difficult problem I had to overcome. Juneau in 1978 had a population of 25,000. It was Alaska's third largest city after Anchorage and Fairbanks, 800 and 1200 miles away, respectively. The legislature was known as a citizen-legislature. It met for four months every other year. The governor wielded most of the power. The legislature's primary responsibility was to pass a budget.

Most staff and employees lived somewhere other than Juneau but when the legislature was in session they all came to town and consumed all the available housing. When I arrived, the only place available was *The Baranoff Hotel*. And it was expensive. I got a rate for the first month of $1600. I called Joe's new secretary before she left Sacramento and got a commitment from her to split the month's rent with me. I assured her we would have a platonic relationship while looking for separate quarters. She agreed.

My pay would be $2000 a month. I already knew Alaska would be expensive. On the ferry I had to pay for three meals a day and that gave me a warning of what to expect. On my first night in Juneau I ate out at a pizza place. A small pizza cost more than $20. In California at that time it would have cost about $4. I must have looked like a tourist as I was observed photographing the menu on the wall.

Before leaving Pollock Pines I had offered to shut **The Press** down and bring Judy with me. She had just started law school and had gotten enough on-the-job training to put the newspaper out for a few months. She insisted she could handle the newspaper and urged me to go to Alaska. Our relationship was strange. First and foremost it was bound together with sex and based on revenge for her mother's threat. We both enjoyed intercourse and oral sex. Neither of us looked to a future where we would be married. There were no plans. I knew that our relationship had started off on the wrong foot because of my reaction to her mother. We seemed to be treading water. Neither of us cheated on the other. Once she claimed she loved me, but that was just moments after she dumped a bowl of cereal on my head in response to an insult I flung at her. No, I did not hit her. I clung to the value of respect for womanhood. I could not comprehend how having a bowl of cereal poured on one's head and hearing I love you were compatible. This incident just added confusion to my lack of understanding on what makes a woman tick. So I went to Alaska alone.

Fortunately, Barbara arrived at the hotel after the issue of hiring an out-of-state resident subsided. The press would have had a field day had they known that Joe hired not one, but TWO Californians. We shared a large bedroom. Judy kept me sexually satisfied and I looked forward to returning to her. I had no intention on having sex with Barbara.

Alaskans suffer from cabin fever during the long, dark winter nights so they find something to occupy their time. In the evenings the schools are packed with various types of informal adult education. Classes range from learning to belly-dance to airplane pilot classes. I bounced around amongst many of them plying my photography hobby. I also took flying lessons which included classroom sessions learning about radio frequencies, flight plans and weather.

I especially enjoyed photographing the belly-dancing students. The teacher of this class complained to me one day that the legislature was cutting funds and she would have to cancel her classes. I suggested she have some of her students show up in the legislature - in costume, but for them to wear long coats to initially hide their outfits, and they could lobby all the legislators at once. She agreed. I tipped off the Associated Press and we all got great photographs. AP got a good front page story to go with their photos as the girls disrobed and charmed the senators holding the hearing.

I attended a legislative party cluttered with lobbyists one evening and managed to get a photograph of the governor with his eyes closed. (Film camera's shutters open and close in 1/1000 of a second, but if a strobe light is used the speed is increased 50 times.) I later sent the print back to **The Pollock Pines Press** together with a story about how the governor was ignoring scandals, in particular the one dealing with the autopsy lab being funded by the state.

I met an entrepreneur who wanted to build a tram that would travel from the top of Mount Roberts to the docks. I was able to photograph his artist's rendition of his project and I sent that story to Pollock Pines.

I finally found new housing, cheaper and even smaller, and so did Barbara. But before we checked out of the Baranoff Hotel, Judy called me. I was not there and Barbara answered the phone. I should have but did not inform Judy of my platonic rooming arrangement. She assumed I was cheating on her and went a little crazy. It was not until after I returned to Pollock Pines that I learned she started having intercourse with anyone in the area who wanted a piece of her. That was her way of getting even, and that is what ended up terminating our relationship.

She actually flew up to Juneau to accompany me back to Pollock Pines. When I returned I heard about her promiscuity from way too many people. One night I called her parents and told her if they did not come up and get her and her belongings in an hour they would be responsible for the corpse I would leave them. They came. They took her to safety. I have never seen or spoken to her since.

I increased the publication from a monthly to a weekly with the May 2, 1978 issue. On my way out of Alaska, I provided my investigative file to both Joe and Bob Speed, administrative assistant to the chairman of the House Judiciary Committee. But I also used it to provide my readers with a little about Alaskan politics and some of the corrupt people with whom its legislature was dealing.

The photograph I made of Alaska's Governor Jay Hammond with his eyes closed came in handy and accompanied the story I entitled: SHOULD ALASKA MOVE ITS CAPITAL OR JUST WAKE UP ITS GOVERNOR?

While I was there Alaska was on the verge of spending 4.5 billion dollars to move its capital from Juneau to just north of Anchorage to a small town called Willow. Plans were ultimately cancelled due to the expense, but it was a hot issue.

Forensic Sciences Inc. had contracted with the Alaska Court System on February 23, 1977, to construct an autopsy facility. They had breached that contract by not having the facility built by May 1, 1978.

This breach occurred two months before a prepaid contract was awarded to Forensic Sciences by the Department of Public Safety's Director of Administration Trygve Hermann. He authorized pre-paying $135,000 to Forensic Sciences instead of paying them $141,000 in twelve monthly installments, which was permitted in the July 1, 1978 contract for laboratory testing of evidence to be used in Alaska's criminal prosecutions. He claimed he did it because it was a $6,000 discount.

He did not bother to check the credit or background of the principals of Forensic Sciences. Had he, he would have discovered that Forensic Sciences Inc. had a balance sheet of $1,000. Had he asked basic questions he might have learned what I did. Forensic Sciences Inc was run by the same people who ran Associate Laboratories of Alaska.

Before I left Alaska, the House Judiciary Committee was conducting hearings on HB392, an act relating to the establishment of a state medical examiner's office. That office would need both a lab and an autopsy facility. An opponent of the bill representing a major Anchorage mortuary testified that the authors of the bill were the same persons responsible for negotiating the ill-fated contracts for both a lab and an autopsy facility. Dan Hickey, Alaska's

Chief Prosecutor, who authored HB 392 and drafted the advance payment contract, told the committee no one connected with Forensic had anything to do with drafting the medical examiner bill. Dr. Patrick Mathews a former medical examiner for King County in the state of Washington told the committee he had conferred with Dan Hickey on HB 392 a number of times in 1976 and 1977 while HB 392 was being drafted. Dr. Mathews was on the payroll of Associated Laboratories of Alaska Inc., which was incorporated by the same incorporators of Forensic Science. Associate Laboratories of Alaska owned 100% of Forensic's stock.

During my investigation I had learned that two principals of Forensic had a falling out prior to the two contracts for the lab and the autopsy facility. Forensic's President Collins fired its vice-president Douglass. Eight weeks later Collins signed the contract with the Court System. Douglass signed the second contract which exchanged future services for the $135,000. A month later Collins was demanding $40,000 from Douglass or as he told me "he would bring it all down." When I asked him what power he possessed to "bring it all down" he said he would not answer any further questions unless his attorney was present. His attorney Jim Johnson of Anchorage was the incorporator of both Forensic and Associated Labs.

I ended my story with a question. If the House Judiciary Committee digs deep enough, it may discover others who received part of the $135,000. It may also discover the real reason state officials authorized the advance payment and didn't check the character and business reputation of Forensic. I concluded my story of Alaska's politics with a suggestion. Governor Hammond still has a belated opportunity to resolve Alaska's little issues. Only then can he claim the qualifications necessary to decide whether

Alaska needs to spend $4.5 billion to move its capital city from Juneau to Willow.

Juneau as we all learned in school was, and still is, the capital of Alaska.

Publishing a weekly newspaper was taking all of my time. I was still working as a conductor for Southern Pacific, so commuting took a bit of time too. I was driving a Porsche which made the commute easy and that was still feeding my ego battered from my failure of the baby bar exam. I reverted to having no social life. It was very lonely, and I was not even close to the top.

Volume 5, Number 1   The Pollock Pines Press   May 23, 1978

Judy was gone. But a professional journalist took her place. The front page story was headlined: **Dorothy Ingram Now Press Managing Editor**. A quote from her said it all: "No one has taken the **Pollock Pine Press** seriously but now it is time for the publication to get to work and take its place in the community as a viable and permanent newspaper." Timing is everything. Had she been around when I started publishing and was highly motivated, **The Pollock Pines Press** would certainly have been a success.

At our first year anniversary we were printing twenty pages a week. Our editorial was supporting the re-election of Sheriff Dick Pacileo. Our editorial cartoon was depicting the county's superintendent of education, Hazel Hoak, as a puppet of Halmar Moser. (She was the publicist who started a boycott of The Press a year earlier.) We had legitimate ads producing enough income to hire a graphic artist, an advertising executive, and a reporter in addition to Dorothy Ingram. We had resumed the Silver Fork affair, writing about the lawsuits brought by the teachers who had been forced to resign a year earlier. Because there were many seniors residing in our area, we instituted a policy of using large type to make it easier to read **The Press**.

But my heart was not into publishing a newspaper. I limited my involvement to photography, which was my only love. For me it was easy to love an activity but difficult to love a person.

**Volume 5, Number 3   The Pollock Pines Press
June 6, 1978**

This issue featured a two page spread of photographs of a 1,350 square foot geodesic dome being assembled in eight hours for and by owners Greg and Sharyl Laurel who were my neighbors to the north. I owned forty acres along Starkes Grade on which I had built a small cabin, without a permit. These domes enclosed the greatest amount of usable space with the least amount of volume compared to a standard rectangular home. They also eliminated dead air pockets and cold corners. El Dorado County had thirty domes. Its Building Department had been very cooperative with this new concept in building.

Another neighbor who lived close to us owned a breakfast cafe in town and Judy and I were regular customers during the past year. While having breakfast alone one morning, I suggested to the owner that he might like to buy an ad in **The Press** as our circulation had exceeded six thousand readers. He must have fallen out of the wrong side of his bed because he used sarcasm to tell me he did not need my little paper to get customers.

A week earlier he had been visiting with Greg and Sharyl, who built the dome, and was bragging that he was an SS Captain in the Nazi army. He actually proved it by showing them photographs of him in uniform. I now seized upon this to explain that he may want to at least read **The Press** because the next issue would feature a story about a former Nazi officer hiding in Pollock Pines. He produced fifty dollars and said he would be glad to advertise.

As I won that battle I did not need to prove anything by actually writing the news story that would certainly have produced national and international publicity. I was not motivated to be a publisher, but that did not mean that I forgot how to be a yellow journalist.

Advertising was paying the bills but I did not run **The Press** as a legitimate business. No taxes, no insurance, no record keeping, no interest. I still did a lot of bartering of gas or food for advertising. We finally did have a full page ad from Raley's in Placerville. I enjoyed publishing it as Safeway was not advertising. And in an effort to prove our newspaper produced customers, we ran a full page ad for Stancil's Toyota in Placerville that offered readers a dollar if they brought the ad in. Stancil shelled out $626 and became a permanent advertiser. Even all of the local realtors were advertising again.

And Dorothy was doing a super job. The headline in this issue cried out: BOS RECINDS PAY RAISE. Dorothy loved politics and now she had a vehicle in which to ride the politicians, including the Board of Supervisors. She was on a natural high as she reported **Women Charge EID with Sex-discrimination**. She had cultivated a lot of reliable sources over the years and was producing first class news. I had to chuckle when I read **The Press.** She was out-doing me and did not resort to "yellow" journalism to connect with readers. Our headlines were reporting on the Grand Jury, Illegal Parcel Splits, County Budget Manipulations, and so many of the dirty little secrets that lived below the surface for so many years in El Dorado County. The size and distribution of the paper was growing thick and wide. Why couldn't this have happened earlier?

Volume 8, Number 3   **The Press and Sierra Recorder**
August 22, 1978

We had changed the name of the paper to reflect a much larger readership which extended from Cool to the north, to Mount Aukum to the south, and El Dorado Hills in the west to South Lake Tahoe to the east. We had readers in South Lake Tahoe although we did not cover news on the eastern slope of the Sierra Mountain. This issue was quite meaningful to me because it depicted age discrimination in an unusual manner. The headline in this 28 page issue announced: STATE FAIR IGNORES EL DORADO ROSE. Telling the story as it appeared in my newspaper is appropriate.

"SACRAMENTO -- El Dorado County's entry in the Maid of California contest was excluded from participation because of her age and missed her chance to become Queen of the California Exposition and State Fair.

Betty Yohalem, 77, was crowned El Dorado Rose in early August at the county fair and accepted an invitation to compete for the Maid of California pageant.

She drove the fifty two miles to Sacramento on three consecutive days but was not included in any pageant activity. The former movie star was excluded from a banquet, an awards dinner, dress rehearsal and a photographic session.

Her name and sponsoring county did not appear in the official printed program.

Although she was well treated by the thirty-five contestants who ranged in age from 17 to 25, Yohalem was ignored by the pageant director, Del Barta, who runs a clothing store on Arden Way in Sacramento.

During the closing minutes of the contest on Saturday night, Barta attempted to defend her position. 'She's cute, she said, but you don't really expect her to compete with these girls, do you?'

Paul Costa, a fair official, offered to 'make things right later in the fair.' He promised 'a special certificate and maybe a trophy' when she appears for Senior Citizens

Day. Costa, apologizing for the poor planning, noted that Yohalem was on stage Friday night for about fifteen seconds while the 'girls changed from bathing suits to evening dresses.'

Terri Ann Doan, the contestant from San Benito County, said 'That's bad, really bad' when she learned that El Dorado Rose was locked out of the contest. 'I've never met a woman with more poise and natural beauty,' she exclaimed.

Los Angeles County's candidate, Joan Patta, 17, also sympathized with Yohalem. 'There ought to be a pageant for older women,' she said. 'Betty would have won hands down.'

After the pageant closed, Jack Wendell, sales manager for Hubacker Cadillac in Sacramento and one of the five judges for the pageant, scratched his head when asked about El Dorado Rose. 'El Dorado County? I didn't know they had an entry.'

Fellow Judge Rosemary Weaver, an official with Safeco Title Insurance in Roseville, reminded Wendell that 'she was the older lady.' Wendell then said: 'We were judging only the people we saw.' He commented that the pageant should be open to anyone and age should not be a factor. Weaver said she was told that 'the El Dorado Rose situation was just kind of pulling our leg.' 'But, she added, the idea is stupendous and more older women should have a contest of their own'.''

Yohalem, author of a pictorial history of El Dorado County titled "I Remember," was totally forgiving. She said all the contestants were given an opportunity to extol the virtues of their respective counties, and she would have appreciated an equal opportunity to tell more than one thousand members in the audience of the beauty of El Dorado County.

The master of ceremonies for the pageant, Stewart Rose, was asked if the result would have been different if El Dorado Rose would have been allowed to compete. "She was absolutely gorgeous, he said, but I did not see her in a bathing suit, and the bathing suit is part of the competition."

The pageant was won by Janette Guerrero, who represented Alameda County. Betty Yohalem was co-sponsored by the **Georgetown Gazette** and **The Press and Sierra Recorder**.

Summer was coming to a close and I had spent a lot of time working on the railroad. Although we were selling advertising, I wanted to be in a position to subsidize the paper. I really did not know where we stood financially. I was meeting the payroll by writing checks from my personal account. All employees were independent contractors so I was not paying the state worker's compensation or withholding taxes. I was still swapping advertising for fuel, food and whatever else I needed. And I did not resume a social life. It was at times like this when my natural sexual urge reared its ugly head.

With guilt and shame I recall a young couple hitch-hiking back to Colorado after enjoying their adventure in California. I had picked them up in Placerville as I returned from Sacramento after a long trip on the railroad. I invited them to stay with me for a few days. They were in their teens. The newspaper's office had an extra room that was converted to a bedroom where I spent time when I was working late.

I took the kids out for supper to one of the restaurants where I had a swap account. After supper when they went to bed, I barged in on them because I wanted to enjoy a sexual encounter with them. I did not ask. I just climbed into the bed and began to fondle both of them. There were mild objections. I was satisfying my lustful desires. It was a non-consensual three-some. I did not feel good about it. In the morning, I brought them to the freeway exit, gave them $100 and wished them luck on their return to Colorado. I apologized for ruining their California experience. Although they indicated it was no big thing, I knew better. I was in fact a monster. They were my victims. Although they were not intimidated by me or afraid, I knew my illicit behavior was something they would remember and it would affect them for the rest of their lives. I felt real guilt then and still do. Maybe I was on a power trip. Maybe I was sick. I did not stop to analyze my behavior. Perhaps I should have. My future may have taken a different path.

The winter approached rapidly. **The Press** published a 32-page edition in color every month through January, 1979. So many advertisers participated it seemed that the paper had finally become a part of the community and had a bright future. I knew better.

I made an appeal for investors to buy into the paper in early February, but none did. My intention was to raise sufficient funds and turn it over to Dorothy Ingram. I knew she could continue what I started: to tell it like it is.

Because no investors responded, I did not bother to publish another issue after February 2, 1979.

My Porsche was covered with unusually deep snow and was hit by a snowplow driven by a county employee who used booze to keep warm and distort his view of his work. I had traded advertising for a motorcycle so I left town when the snow cleared. I simply abandoned everything - newspaper, cabin, and everyone I had known. I went back to work at the railroad. I did not have any plans to resume my legal education. I was all alone. I was all alone again.

The rest of 1979, all of 1980 and half of 1981 found me suffering from depression. I always dealt with depression by myself. I would toy with the idea of suicide but was probably too much of a coward to carry it out

In the summer of 1979, I was fired from Southern Pacific for a rule violation. While waiting for my union to adjudicate my case I moved to Tacoma, Washington. I applied for a job as photographer with the City of Tacoma but ended up getting hired by a railroad they owned. The railroad owned a few switch engines and operated out of the port of Tacoma moving cars between four other railroads. The superintendent of that railroad was a tyrant. He had its thirty employees shaking in their boots. I became active in the union and started a letter writing campaign to regulatory agencies complaining that the safety laws were being violated. When the superintendent came down on me for writing the letters, I found wild blackberry bushes growing close to a rail switch and "got injured."

Fortunately my United Transportation Union griever in Roseville notified me that SP had to re-hire me and give me back pay. A lawyer in Placerville was supposed to take care of my claim against the county for the damaged Porsche. Unknown to me, he notified the business with which I traded advertising for the motorcycle where I was living in Tacoma. It came as a shock when I found that the motorcycle had been re-possessed. How unethical! How unethical it was for both the attorney and me. I contracted for a Rent-A-Wreck car and drove back to Sacramento. I bought a house in North Highlands, a three bedroom house and I would be the only one living in it. Being all alone for the past year kept me in a state of depression.

Before I left Tacoma to resume working for SP in Sacramento, I had an illicit sexual encounter with a young boy about fourteen years of age. He was a teen prostitute who I met by accident. We had a one night stand that seemed to satisfy my sexual urge and loneliness. When I went to work, he robbed me of money, sleeping bag, TV etc. I am sure I deserved it because I had robbed him of a little of his innocence. He was a runaway and was using sex to survive. I did not have the moral guts to recognize that he was where I was when I ran away from St. Joseph's House. I was in a position to really help him, but I did not. My sex drive overpowered my morality once again.

Living in the house in North Highlands on Thomas Drive I continued to live a lonely, depressing life. I had no goals and no plans for a future. How did I get to be forty years of age and not have a close friend?

The summers in Sacramento get very hot. Most summers find a dozen or more days where it is more than 100 degrees. I don't recall how it happened but I met an eleven year old boy. I ended up going to his home a few blocks from my house. I met his mother. After knowing her a very short time, I had it in mind to marry her. I was too old to be single and too alone to be happy. Being married must be better than what I had.

But his mom was not interested in me, except that she was glad her son found a "father figure/baby-sitter". She had been married four times. Danny was the youngest. He had three older sisters, each of whom had a different father than his. He was overjoyed to have had a relationship with me. I finally found a friend, a companion, someone who made me happy with his smile. I had known him for about three weeks when he invited me to a sleepover in his back yard. Although I did, I should not have. We shared a sleeping bag. And I committed a most horrible sin. Why did I take advantage of his youth and friendship, and let my sickness out of the bag.

Over the course of the next six weeks in July and August 1981, he came to my house, and stayed in my bed. He tolerated my molestation. I had previously observed that he was ignored by his mother and three older sisters. That was the primary reason he clung to our relationship. I really did not think I was hurting him, but that was because I was trying to justify my selfish, sexual satisfaction.

I even took him to work one day. I was called to be a flagman at a location where rails were being installed. I had an El Camino truck then with a camper. I loaded a couch in the back. We spent hours in a wooded area alone. Even there I molested him.

At times I did flash back to what Whalen did to me at St. Joseph's and halfheartedly compared what I was doing to what Whalen did. I was a Whalen clone regardless of how I tried to sugar-coat my behavior. I was selfish, stupid and sick. I was about to find out that I was also a criminal. In all of my studies at Lincoln Law School I had never read a case about child molestation. I wish I had.

PART THREE

Chapter Eight
Crime, Folsom State Prison and Punishment - 1982

It was on one of those hot Sacramento mornings where the temperature at nine in the morning was already in the nineties. I rode my new motorcycle from work in Roseville to my North Highland residence. The front door was open. No one was parked in the driveway so I entered with caution. The first view I had was of a note on the dining room table which informed me that the police had hired a locksmith and departed with a bag of marijuana, some photographs, and a utility bill.

I bolted out of the house and jumped on my Honda 750, trying to collect my thoughts. I started to drive toward Mike Montbriand's home. Within a block my whole body shuddered violently, like it was freezing outside. The bike was hard to control so I had to pull over and stop. I asked myself what happened while I was at work. Mike Montbriand was one of the few students in my first year at law school with whom I maintained a friendship. His wife Marcia worked as a nurse and both were the original yuppies. They had a son Phillip who was also twelve. No, I did not do anything inappropriate with him.

It was a Saturday and they were sleeping late but welcomed me into their home. Although Mike was an intern at Sullivan and Turner, a firm that specialized in civil litigation, he had made a lot of contacts in the legal field and quickly fixed me up with a criminal law attorney. I showed Mike the note that was on my dining room table. He looked up the penal code that was referenced in the note: Lewd and Lascivious Conduct with a child under twelve. That attorney called the sheriff to surrender me. I went through the booking process still in shock. I was being charged with five counts.

I was released on my own recognizance. Southern Pacific railroad was informed of my arrest and I was immediately fired. I have never been one to save money so I had serious financial problems. Most of the cash I had received from the back pay award went to buy the house and motorcycle.

Had I been a man, things would have turned out differently. That is to say, had I plead guilty I would have been shipped off to the Atascadero State Hospital where all sexual deviates were treated in 1981. But it was slated to close at the end of the year, and sexual deviates were to be treated entirely as criminals.

I put the house up for sale to try to recoup my down payment so I could afford an attorney. But that did not work out as quickly as I had hoped, so I had to seek the assistance of the public defender.

Once again I had an opportunity to admit my guilt but did not. Had I plead guilty I might have received whatever treatment was available at Atascadero. Because I did not plead guilty prior to December 31, 1981, that opportunity was lost forever.

The public defender made an appointment for me with a psychiatrist. I never got to read the results of his examination. There was a preliminary examination to determine if I would have to go to trial. In a matter of months I did sell my house and had money that I foolishly used to hire an attorney.

Michael Sands was considered to be an excellent criminal attorney who had successfully defended others who faced charges similar to mine. Once I did that the district attorney increased the charges to twelve counts.

The first trial ended in a hung jury. Only one person thought I was not guilty. The district attorney planned to try me again. This time it would be easier for them. All my cards were played. My witnesses would now be useless. In denying the charges I tried to shift the blame to Danny's mother. I had a witness come up from San Diego who had been a guest in my home during the period of time the molestations took place. He swore that Danny's mom wanted to marry me, that I refused, and that she was using her son to get back at me.

In retrospect, I guess I was sicker and more stupid than my imagination allowed. I also had a witness as to my character. Betty Gwiazdon, who had six children, testified that there was never any inappropriate behavior during the times that I visited her home. I really did not want to have Danny take the stand, but my attorney kept telling me it was the only way I could stay out of prison.

I have mentioned a few times already that I have been naive for much of my life, but once again I have to offer another example. I don't recall ever hearing the word pedophile yet I was being portrayed as one. The district attorney claimed I seduced Danny. I was shocked and startled to hear her make this charge. I was still not able to believe that I did anything wrong. But I was also curious. What was a pedophile and was I one? A major concern for me since my arrest was to try to understand what I did and why I did it.

Google and Wikipedia were not yet born, but today as I write this autobiography I am relying on both to convey information to my readers. One purpose of writing my life story is to educate readers of this disease and crime through this autobiography, even though it means baring my soul. Since 1981 I have not discussed most of what I am now writing with anyone. Perhaps some good can result. If just one child is not harmed in a similar manner, then the pain of this writing will have been worth the suffering and its goal will have been met.

The two questions I have been asking since 1981 are: What is the cause of pedophilia? Is there a cure?

As I write this thirty years later, I am relying mainly on Wikipedia. Although this source is criticized since anyone can post anything, information posted by scientists and professionals use citations and are deemed more reliable. I may take the liberty to comment so what is in italics is not my writing, but has been borrowed from Wikipedia. Readers may wish to access Wikipedia for citations and sources relied on in the following summary which represents the views of the experts as of 2011.

As a medical diagnosis, pedophilia (or paedophilia) is typically defined as a psychiatric disorder in adults or late adolescents (persons age 16 and older) characterized by a primary or exclusive sexual interest in prepubescent children (generally age 13 years or younger, though onset of puberty may vary). The child must be at least five years younger in the case of adolescent pedophiles. The International Classification of Diseases (ICD) defines pedophilia as a "disorder of adult personality and behaviour" in which there is a sexual preference for children of prepubertal or early pubertal age. The term has a range of definitions as found in psychiatry, psychology, the vernacular, and law enforcement.

According to the Diagnostic and Statistical Manual of Mental Disorders (DSM), pedophilia is a paraphilia in which a person has intense and recurrent sexual urges towards and fantasies about prepubescent children and on which feelings they have either acted or which cause distress or interpersonal difficulty. The current DSM-5 draft proposes to add hebephilia to the diagnostic criteria, and consequently to rename it to pedohebephilic disorder. Although most pedophiles are men, there are also women who exhibit the disorder, and researchers assume available estimates under represent the true number of female pedophiles.

No cure for pedophilia has been developed.

This purports to answer one of the two questions this autobiography poses – is there a cure for pedophilia?

There are, however, certain therapies that can reduce the incidence of a person committing child sexual abuse. In the United States, following Kansas v. Hendricks, sex offenders that are diagnosed with certain mental disorders, particularly pedophilia, can be subject to indefinite civil commitment, under various state laws (generically called SVP laws) and the federal Adam Walsh Child Protection and Safety Act of 2006.

So one therapy to reduce the incidence of child sexual abuse is indefinite civil incarceration for some! But that would work only for those who are caught and convicted and deemed to be a threat to society after a term in prison. They represent only the tip of this iceberg.

In common usage, pedophilia means any sexual interest in children or the act of child sexual abuse, often termed "pedophilic behavior". For example, The American Heritage Stedman's Medical Dictionary states, "Pedophilia is the act or fantasy on the part of an adult of engaging in sexual activity with a child or children." This common use application also extends to the sexual interest and abuse of pubescent or post-pubescent minors. Researchers recommend that these imprecise uses be avoided, as people who commit child sexual abuse *commonly exhibit the disorder, but some offenders do not meet the clinical diagnosis standards for pedophilia, and the clinical diagnosis for pedophilia pertains to prepubescents. Additionally, not all pedophiles actually commit such abuse.*

Law enforcement differs with the authorities and claims all pedophiles repeat sexual abusing.

I have been unable to find the basis on which law enforcement draw this conclusion. If that really is true then there cannot be a cure.

Pedophilia was first formally recognized and named in the late 19th century. A significant amount of research in the area has taken place since the 1980s. At present, the exact causes of pedophilia have not been conclusively established. Research suggests that pedophilia may be correlated with several different neurological abnormalities, and often co-exists with other personality disorders and psychological pathologies. In the contexts of forensic psychology and law enforcement, a variety of typologies have been suggested to categorize pedophiles according to behavior and motivations.

Even with thirty years of research there is still no exact cause conclusively established. My interest in finding the cause of pedophilia has not benefited from this research.

Nepiophilia, also called infantophilia, is not necessarily the same thing as pedophilia, and is used to refer to a sexual preference for toddlers and infants (usually ages 0-3).

Hebephilia partially overlaps with pedophilia as currently defined, and is used for individuals with a primary sexual interest in 11-14 year old pubescents.

Should I be termed an Hebephile instead of a pedophile?

The term paedophilia erotica was coined in 1886 by the Viennese psychiatrist Richard von Krafft-Ebing in his writing *Psychopathia Sexualis. The term appears in a section titled "Violation of Individuals Under the Age of Fourteen," which focuses on the forensic psychiatry aspect of child sexual offenders in general. Krafft-Ebing describes several typologies of offender, dividing them into psychopathological and non-psychopathological origins, and hypothesizes several apparent causal factors that may lead to the sexual abuse of children.*

Krafft-Ebing mentioned paedophilia erotica in a typology of "psycho-sexual perversion." He wrote that he had only encountered it four times in his career and gave brief descriptions of each case, listing three common traits:

1.The individual is tainted by heredity.

2.The subject's primary attraction is to children, rather than adults.

3.The acts committed by the subject are typically not intercourse, but rather involve inappropriate touching or manipulating the child into performing an act on the subject.

He mentions several cases of pedophilia among adult women (provided by another physician), and also considered the abuse of boys by homosexual men to be extremely rare. Further clarifying this point, he indicated that cases of adult men who have some medical or neurological disorder and abuse a male child are not true pedophilia, and that in his observation victims of such men tended to be older and pubescent. He also lists "Pseudopaedophilia" as a related condition wherein "individuals who have lost libido for the adult through masturbation and subsequently turn to children for the gratification of their sexual appetite" and claimed this is much more common.

In 1908, Swiss neuroanatomist and psychiatrist Auguste Forel wrote of the phenomenon, proposing that it be referred to it as "Pederosis," the "Sexual Appetite for Children." Similar to Krafft-Ebing's work, Forel made the distinction between incidental sexual abuse by person's with dementia and other organic brain conditions, and the truly preferential and sometimes exclusive sexual desire for children. However, he disagreed with Krafft-Ebing in that he felt the condition of the latter was largely ingrained and unchangeable.

The term "Pedophilia" became the generally accepted term for the condition and saw widespread adoption in the early 20th century, appearing in many popular medical dictionaries such as the 5th Edition of Stedman's. In 1952, it was included in the first edition of the Diagnostic and Statistical Manual of Mental Disorders. This edition and the subsequent DSM-II listed the disorder as one subtype of the classification "Sexual Deviation," but no diagnostic criteria were provided. The DSM-III, published in 1980, contained a full description of the disorder and provided a set of guidelines for diagnosis. The revision in 1987, the DSM-III-R, kept the description largely the same, but updated and expanded the diagnostic criteria. Some clinicians have proposed further categories, somewhat or completely distinguished from pedophilia, including "pedohebephilia," "hebephilia," and "ephebophilia" (though ephebophilia is not considered pathological). Other experts such as Karen Franklin consider classifications like hebephilia to be "pretextual" diagnoses which should not be considered disorders.

The ICD-10 defines pedophilia as "a sexual preference for children, boys or girls or both, usually of prepubertal or early pubertal age." Under this system's criteria, a person 16 years of age or older meets the definition if they have a persistent or predominant sexual preference for prepubescent children at least five years younger than them.

The Diagnostic and Statistical Manual of Mental Disorders 4th edition Text Revision (DSM-IV-TR) outlines specific criteria for use in the diagnosis of this disorder. These include the presence of sexually arousing fantasies, behaviors or urges that involve some kind of sexual activity with a prepubescent child (age 13 or younger, though puberty may vary) for six months or more, and that the subject has acted on these urges or suffers from distress as a result of having these feelings. The criteria also indicate that the subject should be 16 or older and that child or children they fantasize about are at least five years younger than them, though ongoing sexual relationships between a 12-13 year old and a late adolescent are advised to be excluded. A diagnosis is further specified by the sex of the children the person is attracted to, if the impulses or acts are limited to incest, and if the attraction is "exclusive" or "nonexclusive".

Many terms have been used to distinguish "true pedophiles" from non-pedophilic and non-exclusive offenders, or to distinguish among types of offenders on a continuum according to strength and exclusivity of pedophilic interest, and motivation for the offense. Exclusive pedophiles are sometimes referred to as "true pedophiles." They are attracted to children, and children only. They show little erotic interest in adults their own age and in some cases, can only become aroused while fantasizing or being in the presence of prepubescent children. Non-exclusive pedophiles may at times be referred to as non-pedophilic offenders, but the two terms are not always synonymous. Non-exclusive pedophiles are attracted to both children and adults, and can be sexually aroused by both, though a sexual preference for one over the other in this case may also exist.

Neither the ICD nor the DSM diagnostic criteria require actual sexual activity with a prepubescent youth. The diagnosis can therefore be made based on the presence of fantasies or sexual urges even if they have never been acted upon. On the other hand, a person who acts upon these urges yet experiences no distress about their fantasies or urges can also qualify for the diagnosis. Acting on sexual urges is not limited to overt sex acts for purposes of this diagnosis, and can sometimes include indecent exposure, voyeuristic or frotteuristic behaviors, or masturbating to child pornography. Often, these behaviors need to be considered in-context with an element of clinical judgment before a diagnosis is made. Likewise, when the patient is in late adolescence, the age difference is not specified in hard numbers and instead requires careful consideration of the situation.

Ego-dystonic sexual orientation (F66.1) includes people who do not doubt that they have a prepubertal sexual preference, but wish it were different because of associated psychological and behavioral disorders. The WHO allows for the patient to seek treatment to change their sexual orientation.

Debate regarding the DSM criteria

The DSM IV criteria have been criticized simultaneously for being over-inclusive, as well as under-inclusive. Though most researchers distinguish between child molesters and pedophiles, Studer and Aylwin argue that the DSM criteria are over-inclusive because all acts of child molestation warrant the diagnosis. A child molester satisfies criteria A because of the behavior involving sexual activity with prepubescent children and criteria B because the individual has acted on those urges. Furthermore, they argue that it also is under-inclusive in the case of individuals who do not act upon it and are not distressed by it. The latter point has also been made by several other researchers who have remarked that a so-called "contented pedophile"-an individual who fantasizes about having sex with a child and masturbates to these fantasies, but does not commit child sexual abuse, and who does not feel subjectively distressed afterward-does not meet the DSM-IV-TR criteria for pedophilia, because this person does not meet Criterion B.

A large-scale survey about usage of different classification systems showed that the DSM classification is only rarely used. As an explanation, it was suggested that the under-inclusiveness, as well as a lack of validity, reliability and clarity might have led to the rejection of the DSM classification.

Ray Blanchard, in his literature review for the DSM-5, noted the objections and proposed a general solution applicable to all paraphilias, namely a distinction between paraphilia and paraphilic disorder. The latter term is proposed to identify the diagnosable condition, which meets both Criterion A and B, whereas an individual who does not meet Criterion B, can be ascertained, but not diagnosed, as having a paraphilia. The current proposals for the DSM V will also resolve the current overlap between pedophilia and hebephilia by combining both diagnosis in a single new diagnosis called Pedohebephilic Disorder. This new diagnosis would be equivalent to the ICD-10 definition of pedophilia that already includes early pubescents.

O'Donohue, however, took the issue in a different direction, suggesting instead that the diagnostic criteria be simplified to the attraction to children alone if ascertained by self-report, laboratory findings, or past behavior. He states that any sexual attraction to children is pathological and that distress is irrelevant, noting "this sexual attraction has the potential to cause significant harm to others and is also not in the best interests of the individual."

In 1997, Howard E. Barbaree and Michael C. Seto, disagreed with the American Psychiatric Association's approach, and instead recommended the use of actions as the sole criterion for the diagnosis of pedophilia, as a means of taxonomic simplification.

In a 1993 review of research on child sexual abuse, Sharon Araji and David Finkelhor stated that because this field of research was underdeveloped at that time, there are "definitional problems" resulting from lack of standardization among researchers in their use of the term "pedophilia". They described two definitions, a "restrictive" form referring to individuals with strong and exclusive sexual interest in children, and an "inclusive" definition, expanding the term to include offenders who engaged in sexual contact with a child, including incest. They stated that they used the wider definition in their review paper because behavioral criteria are easier to identify and do not require complex analysis of an individual's motivations.

Although what causes pedophilia is not yet known, beginning in 2002, researchers began reporting a series of findings linking pedophilia with brain structure and function: Pedophilic (and hebephilic) men have lower IQs, poorer scores on memory tests, greater rates of non-right-handedness, greater rates of school grade failure over and above the IQ differences, lesser physical height, greater probability of having suffered childhood head injuries resulting in unconsciousness, and several differences in MRI-detected brain structures. They report that their findings suggest that there are one or more neurological characteristics present at birth that cause or increase the likelihood of being pedophilic. Evidence of familial transmittability "suggests, but does not prove that genetic factors are responsible" for the development of pedophilia.

Could the cause have a genetic component?

Another study, using structural MRI, shows that male pedophiles have a lower volume of white matter than a control group.

Functional magnetic resonance imaging (fMRI) has shown that child molesters diagnosed with pedophilia have reduced activation of the hypothalamus as compared with non-pedophilic persons when viewing sexually arousing pictures of adults. A 2008 functional neuroimaging study notes that central processing of sexual stimuli in heterosexual "paedophile forensic inpatients" may be altered by a disturbance in the prefrontal networks, which "may be associated with stimulus-controlled behaviours, such as sexual compulsive behaviours." The findings may also suggest "a dysfunction at the cognitive stage of sexual arousal processing."

The 2008 study suggesting a dysfunction at the cognitive stage of sexual arousal processing seems to be sound. Could it be that the nun who yanked me off the toilet while I examined my penis initiated the start of such a dysfunction in my arousal processing? **I keep flashing back to my childhood as I read the findings of the researchers hoping to find an answer.**

Blanchard, Cantor, and Robichaud (2006) reviewed the research that attempted to identify hormonal aspects of pedophiles. They concluded that there is some evidence that pedophilic men have less testosterone than controls, but that the research is of poor quality and that it is difficult to draw any firm conclusion from it.

Pedophilia can be described as a disorder of sexual preference, phenomenologically similar to heterosexual or homosexual orientation because it emerges prior or during puberty, and because it is stable over time. These observations, however, do not exclude pedophilia from the group of mental disorders because pedophilic acts cause harm, and pedophiles can sometimes be helped by mental health professionals to refrain from acting on their impulses.

Prevalence and child molestation

The prevalence of pedophilia in the general population is not known, but is estimated to be lower than 5% based on several smaller studies with prevalence rates between 3% and 9%. "Most sexual offenders against children are male, although female offenders may account for 0.4% to 4% of convicted sexual offenders. On the basis of a range of published reports, McConaghy estimates a 10 to 1 ratio of male-to-female child molesters." It is believed that the true number of female pedophiles is underrepresented by available estimates, and that reasons for this may include a "societal tendency to dismiss the negative impact of sexual relationships between young boys and adult women, as well as women's greater access to very young children who cannot report their abuse," among other explanations.

The term pedophile is commonly used to describe all child sexual abuse offenders, including those who do not meet the clinical diagnosis standards, which is seen as problematic by researchers, as most distinguish between child molesters and pedophiles. A perpetrator of child sexual abuse is commonly assumed to be and referred to as a pedophile; however, there may be other motivations for the crime (such as stress, marital problems, or the unavailability of an adult partner). Child sexual abuse may or may not be an indicator that its perpetrator is a pedophile. Offenders may be separated into two types: Exclusive (i.e., "true pedophiles") and non-exclusive (or, in some cases, "non-pedophilic"). According to a U.S. study on 2429 adult male pedophile sex offenders; only 7% identified themselves as exclusive; indicating that many or most offenders fall into the non-exclusive category. However, the Mayo Clinic reports perpetrators who meet the diagnostic criteria for pedophilia offend more often than non-pedophile perpetrators, and with a greater number of victims. They state that approximately 95% of child sexual abuse incidents are committed by the 88% of child molestation offenders who meet the diagnostic criteria for pedophilia. A behavioral analysis report by the FBI states that a "high percentage of acquaintance child molesters are preferential sex offenders who have a true sexual preference for [prepubescent] children (i.e., true pedophiles)."

A review article in the British Journal of Psychiatry notes the overlap between extrafamilial and intrafamilial offenders. One study found that around half of the fathers and stepfathers in its sample who were referred for committing extrafamilial abuse had also been abusing their own children.

As noted by Abel, Mittleman, and Becker (1985) and Ward et al. (1995), there are generally large distinctions between the two types of offenders' characteristics. Situational offenders tend to offend at times of stress; have a later onset of offending; have fewer, often familial victims; and have a general preference for adult partners. Pedophilic offenders, however, often start offending at an early age; often have a large number of victims who are frequently extrafamilial; are more inwardly driven to offend; and have values or beliefs that strongly support an offense lifestyle. Research suggests that incest offenders recidivate at approximately half the rate of extrafamilial child molesters, and one study estimated that by the time of entry to treatment, nonincestuous pedophiles who molest boys had committed an average of 282 offenses against 150 victims.

Some child molesters - pedophiles or not - threaten their victims to stop them from reporting their actions. Others, like those that often victimize children, can develop complex *ways of getting access to children, like gaining the trust of a child's parent, trading children with other pedophiles or, infrequently, get foster children from non-industrialized nations or abduct child victims from strangers. Pedophiles may often act interested in the child, to gain the child's interest, loyalty and affection to keep the child from letting others know about the abuse.*

Psychopathology and personality traits

Several researchers have reported correlations between pedophilia and certain psychological characteristics, such as low self-esteem and poor social skills. Cohen et al. (2002), studying child sex offenders, states that pedophiles have impaired interpersonal functioning and elevated passive-aggressiveness, as well as impaired self-concept.

They hit the nail on the head. Sounds like he is describing me!

Regarding disinhibitory traits, pedophiles demonstrate elevated sociopathy and propensity for cognitive distortions. According to the authors, pathologic personality traits in pedophiles lend support to a hypothesis that such pathology is related to both motivation for and failure to inhibit pedophilic behavior.

According to Wilson and Cox (1983), "The paedophiles emerge as significantly higher on Psychoticism, Introversion and Neurotocism than age-matched controls. [But] there is a difficulty in untangling cause and effect. We cannot tell whether paedophiles gravitate towards children because, being highly introverted, they find the company of children less threatening than that of adults, or whether the social withdrawal implied by their introversion is a result of the isolation engendered by their preference i.e., awareness of the social approbation and hostility that it evokes".

Studying child sex offenders, a review of qualitative research studies published between 1982 and 2001 concluded that pedophiles use cognitive distortions to meet personal needs, justifying abuse by making excuses, redefining their actions as love and mutuality, and exploiting the power imbalance inherent in all adult-child relationships. Other cognitive distortions include the idea of "children as sexual beings," "uncontrollability of sexuality," and "sexual entitlement-bias."

One review of the literature concludes that research on personality correlates and psychopathology in pedophiles is rarely methodologically correct, in part owing to confusion between pedophiles and child sex offenders, as well as the difficulty of obtaining a representative, community sample of pedophiles. Seto (2004) points out that pedophiles that are available from a clinical setting are likely there because of distress over their sexual preference or pressure from others. This increases the likelihood that they will show psychological problems. Similarly, pedophiles recruited from a correctional setting have been convicted of a crime, making it more likely that they will show anti-social characteristics.

While not causes of pedophilia themselves, comorbid psychiatric illnesses - such as personality disorders and substance abuse - are risk factors for acting on pedophilic urges. Blanchard, Cantor, and Robichaud (2006) noted about comorbid psychiatric illnesses that, "The theoretical implications are not so clear. Do particular genes or noxious factors in the prenatal environment predispose a male to develop both affective disorders and pedophilia, or do the frustration, danger, and isolation engendered by unacceptable sexual desires - or their occasional furtive satisfaction - lead to anxiety and despair?" They indicated that, because they previously found mothers of pedophiles to be more likely to have undergone psychiatric treatment, the genetic possibility is more likely.

These experts also appear to suggest that a genetic basis is a factor.

Treatment

No cure, but lots of swings and misses as the following attests.

Although pedophilia has yet no cure, various treatments are available that are aimed at reducing or preventing the expression of pedophilic behavior, reducing the prevalence of child sexual abuse. Incarceration followed by the recidivism rate should tip the balance toward treatment, but it does not. Treatment of pedophilia often requires collaboration between law enforcement and health care professionals. A number of proposed treatment techniques for pedophilia have been developed, though the success rate of these therapies has been very low.

Cognitive behavioral therapy ("relapse prevention")

Cognitive behavioral therapy has been shown to reduce recidivism in contact sex offenders.

According to Canadian sexologist Michael Seto, cognitive-behavioral treatments target attitudes, beliefs, and behaviors that are believed to increase the likelihood of sexual offenses against children, and "relapse prevention" is the most common type of cognitive behavioral treatment. The techniques of relapse prevention are based on principles used for treating addictions. Other scientists have also done some research that indicates that recidivism rates of pedophiles in therapy are lower than pedophiles who eschew therapy.

Behavioral interventions

Behavioral treatments target sexual arousal to children, using satiation and aversion techniques to suppress sexual arousal to children and covert sensitization (or masturbatory reconditioning) to increase sexual arousal to adults. Behavioral treatments appear to have an effect on sexual arousal patterns on phallometric testing, but it is not known whether the test changes represent changes in sexual interests or changes in the ability to control genital arousal during testing.

Applied behavior analysis has been applied with sex offenders with mental disabilities.

Pharmacological interventions

Medications are used to lower sex drive in pedophiles by interfering with the activity of testosterone, such as with Depo-Provera (medroxyprogesterone acetate), Androcur (cyproterone acetate), and Lupron (leuprolide acetate).

Gonadotropin-releasing hormone analogues, which last longer and have fewer side-effects, are also effective in reducing libido and may be used.

These treatments, commonly referred to as "chemical castration", are often used in conjunction with the non-medical approaches noted above. According to the Association for the Treatment of Sexual Abusers, "Anti-androgen treatment should be coupled with appropriate monitoring and counseling within a comprehensive treatment plan."

Limitations of treatment

Although these results are relevant to the prevention of reoffending in contact child sex offenders, there is no empirical suggestion that such therapy is a cure for pedophilia. Dr. Fred Berlin, founder of the Johns Hopkins Sexual Disorders Clinic, believes that pedophilia could be successfully treated if the medical community would give it more attention. Castration, either physical or chemical, appears to be highly effective in removing such sexual impulses when offending is driven by the libido, but this method is not recommended when the drive is an expression of anger or the need for power and control (e.g., violent/sadistic offenders). Chemical and surgical castration has been used in several European countries since World War II, although not to the extent it was *employed in Nazi Germany. The program in Hamburg was terminated after 2000, while Poland is now seeking to introduce chemical castration. The Council of Europe works to bring the practice to an end in Eastern European countries where it is still applied through the courts.*

In law and forensic psychology

In law enforcement circles, the term "pedophile" is sometimes used in a broad manner to encompass a person who commits one or more sexually-based crimes that relate to legally underage victims. These crimes may include child sexual abuse, statutory rape, offenses involving child pornography, child grooming, stalking, and indecent exposure.

One unit of the United Kingdom's Child Abuse Investigation Command is known as the "Paedophile Unit" and specializes in online investigations and enforcement work. Some forensic science texts, such as Holmes (2008) use the term to refer to a class of psychological offender typologies that target child victims, even when such children are not the primary sexual interest of the offender. The FBI, however, makes a point of acknowledging preferential sex offenders who have a true sexual preference for prepubescent children.

Civil commitment

In the United States, following Kansas v. Hendricks, sex offenders that can be diagnosed with certain mental disorders, including pedophilia, can be subject to indefinite civil commitment. In Kansas v. Hendricks, the US Supreme Court upheld as constitutional a Kansas law, the Sexually Violent Predator Act (SVPA), under which Hendricks, a pedophile, was found to have a "mental abnormality" defined as a "congenital or acquired condition affecting the emotional or volitional capacity which predisposes the person to commit sexually violent offenses to the degree that such person is a menace to the health and safety of others," which allowed the State to confine Hendricks indefinitely irrespective of whether the State provided any treatment to Hendricks.

In United States v. Comstock, this type of indefinite confinement was upheld for someone previously convicted on child pornography charges; this time a federal law was involved-the Adam Walsh Child Protection and Safety Act. The Wash Act does not require a conviction on a sex offense charge, but only that the person be a federal prisoner, and one who "has engaged or attempted to engage in sexually violent conduct or child molestation and who is sexually dangerous to others", and who "would have serious difficulty in refraining from sexually violent conduct or child molestation if released". Neither sexually violent conduct nor child molestation is defined by the Act.

Child pornography

Child pornography is commonly collected by pedophiles who use the images for a variety of purposes, ranging from private sexual uses, trading with other pedophiles, preparing children for sexual abuse as part of the process known as "child grooming", or enticement leading to entrapment for sexual exploitation such as production of new child pornography or child prostitution.

Pedophile viewers of child pornography are often obsessive about collecting, organizing, categorizing, and labeling their child pornography collection according to age, gender, sex act and fantasy. According to FBI agent Ken Lanning, "collecting" pornography does not mean that they merely view pornography, but that they save it, and "it comes to define, fuel, and validate their most cherished sexual fantasies." An extensive collection indicates a strong sexual preference for children and the owned collection is the single best indicator of what he or she wants to do. Researchers Taylor and Quayle reported that pedophile collectors of child pornography are often involved in anonymous internet communities dedicated to extending their collections. Pedophile online community bulletin boards often contain technical advice from experienced child pornography offenders assisting new users with protecting themselves from detection.

Societal views

Pedophilia and child sexual abuse are generally seen as morally wrong and abnormal by society. Research at the close of the 1980s showed that there was a great deal of misunderstanding and unrealistic perceptions in the general public about pedophila (La Fontaine, 1990; Leberg, 1997). However, a more recent study showed that the public's perception has gradually become more well-informed on the subject.

Misuse of medical terminology

The words "pedophile" and "pedophilia" are sometimes used informally to describe an adult's sexual interest or attraction to pubescent or post-pubescent teenagers and to other situations that do not fit within the clinical definitions. The terms "hebephilia" or "ephebophilia" may be more accurate in these cases. This was especially seen in the case of Mark Foley during the congressional page incident. Most of the media labeled Foley a pedophile, which led David Tuller of Slate magazine to state that Foley was not a pedophile but rather an ephebophile.

Another erroneous but unfortunately common usage of "pedophilia" is to refer to the actus reus itself (that is, interchangeably with "sexual abuse") rather than the medical meaning, which is a preference for that age group on the part of the older individual. Even more problematic are situations where the terms are misused to refer to relationships where the younger person is an adult of legal age, but is either perceived socially as being too young in comparison to their older partner, or *the older partner occupies a position of authority over them. Researchers recommend that these imprecise uses be avoided.*

<u>*Pedophile advocacy groups*</u>

During the late 1950s to early 1990s, several pedophile membership organizations advocated age of consent reform to lower or abolish age of consent laws, and for the acceptance of pedophilia as a sexual orientation rather than a psychological disorder, and the legalization of child pornography. The efforts of pedophile advocacy groups did not gain any public support and today those few groups that have not dissolved have only minimal membership and have ceased their activities other than through a few websites.

<u>*Anti-pedophile activism*</u>

Anti-pedophile activism encompasses opposition against pedophiles, against pedophile advocacy groups, and against other phenomena that are seen as related to pedophilia, such as child pornography and child sexual abuse. Much of the direct action classified as anti-pedophile involves demonstrations against sex offenders, groups advocating legalization of sexual activity between adults and children, and Internet users who solicit sex from minors.

High-profile media attention to pedophilia has led to incidents of moral panic - particularly following reports of associated pedophilia associated with satanic ritual abuse and day care sex abuse. Instances of vigilantism have also been reported in response to public attention on convicted or suspected child sex offenders. In 2000, following a media campaign of "naming and shaming" suspected pedophiles in the UK, hundreds of residents took to the streets in protest against suspected pedophiles, eventually escalating to violent conduct requiring police intervention.

In short, in 1981 at the time of my crime and trial, there was no known cause and no known cure for pedophilia, or its cousin diseases, although the researchers since then offer intriguing hints at both. Unfortunately, as I write this autobiography thirty years later, the experts are no closer to finding either the cause or cure. I believe I may have discovered both as it relates to me.

When I committed my crime it was considered a disease controlled by incarceration at Atascadero State Hospital. When I was convicted a year and a half later in 1982 it had evolved to a crime punished by incarceration at California State Prisons. The Department of Correction has changed its name and today in 2011 they are the Department of Correction and Rehabilitation. But with California on the verge of bankruptcy there are no funds for rehabilitation.

Very little money is spent trying to find either the cause or cure. Millions and millions of dollars are spent by law enforcement in the name of public safety and most of that is wasted. In spite of the severe and increasingly stiffer criminal penalties, the incidences of child abuse continue to sky-rocket. I was never interviewed about my crime or my past while I was incarcerated or since I was released.

You may have had enough of my commentary. Let us get back to the story of my life.

I spent the time after my first trial in El Dorado County, in Mt. Aukum, living on Dorian Wright's property. Growing marijuana was a felony then. The concept of medical marijuana had still not been developed. I no longer worked for the Southern Pacific railroad because I was fired as soon as they learned I was arrested. So I grew marijuana.

In late April, my dear friend Dorian Wright had received the seeds he purchased from Russia, via an ad in a magazine from a company in Denmark. The seeds arrived by United Parcel from Seattle. I read a few books on how to grow, nurture and harvest the plants. An old chicken coop sans chickens was used as a greenhouse to start the plants. While they were popping up in April, I was digging holes - one hundred and twenty five of them. Each was the size of a five gallon paint bucket. I mixed chicken manure and sand with the native soil. I dug a trench to house an electric cable and another for the water pipe. I lived in a small trailer and that is how I spent the summer of 1982 awaiting my second trial.

I stalled my second trial by getting a number of extensions of time as I wanted to be around to harvest my crop. I was growing 110 plants for Dorian and 15 for me. I was able to focus on producing quality plants and in late September I began to harvest and sell some early buds. My lawyer Michael Sands was considered an expert attorney. He consumed most of my money from the sale of my house. And he was just as competent absorbing my new revenue stream from the sale of marijuana.

I had considered disappearing and toward that end in lieu of a birth certificate I obtained my baptismal certificate from St. Ambrose Catholic Church in Schuylkill Haven. Although doing that reflected my opinion of my fate, that move was the extent of my thoughts of going underground.

Prior to the harvest I met a lady -Terry Greenfield- whose son had been molested. I never met him, nor did I ask her about him. She appeared to be understanding of my predicament and interested in me and my future. We had sex, something I really needed and something that was missing from my life for such a long time. I would have settled for a loving relationship, but you take what you can get.

The trial lasted five days. It looked bad from the start. I was not able to get my witnesses to return and testify (lie) on my behalf. I listened to my expert attorney whose primary advice as he sent me to the stand was "Don't let that bitch put you in prison." He was referring to the district attorney whose specialty was convicting child molesters.

I had a last weekend of freedom while the jury was out. I spent it in a Pollock Pines bar dancing and getting drunk with Terry. We had gotten close, so I thought. I had asked her to take charge of my crop which was worth about $15,000 when sold. Dorian's brother in South Lake Tahoe was able to sell all that we grew. On the first Monday morning in November I heard the verdict: Guilty. I was convicted on eight counts for the crime of oral copulation that took place on three different dates between July 15, 1981 and August 8, 1981. Sands did not show up but sent an intern attorney instead. I lost my freedom. I was handcuffed and remanded to the Sacramento County Jail.

It would take another six weeks before I was sentenced. The district attorney was demanding I get six years. My attorney was arguing for probation. And the probation department was recommending three years. The maximum sentence that could be imposed was eight years.

Judge Babich, a rabid Catholic who would attend church services during lunch every day, let his religion get in the way of his search for justice when it came time to sentence me. While in the county jail I had written him a letter and explained that I was molested at *St. Joseph's House for Homeless and Industrious Boys*. That was a big mistake, as he took offense at my defaming the Catholics and blaming them in part for my behavior. In 1982 the truth about Catholic priests molesting boys had not been made public yet. Babich sentenced me to 19 years and 8 months. He mentioned that there were no mitigating circumstances to justify a lower sentence.

It happens to a lot of convicts. Once a long sentence is handed down, the girlfriend or the wife of a convict abandons her boyfriend or husband. Terry was no exception. She had been visiting me often in the county jail. On the night I was sentenced she made her decision not to continue her relationship with me. She did not tell me. She just did not show up. When Dorian learned of this, he went to her home and took all the marijuana that she had. I had an El Camino truck worth a few thousand and she had already sold that.

Over the Christmas holiday, I was awaiting transportation to Vacaville, the Department of Correction's reception center.

Being convicted of child molestation carries with it a sentence of a different kind in addition to what the court hands down. Convicts consider all sex offenders as the lowest scum on earth. They are a target of beatings, stabbings and often death. It was not too much of a problem in the county jail as the security there was such that shanks, or hand-made knives, were not commonplace. About the only possession an inmate could have was a toothbrush less than three inches long and a pencil, the size that golfers use which is also less than three inches. But state prison was an altogether different place.

Just like in the county jail, the Vacaville reception center guards made you strip off all your clothing, and before you put on their orange jump suit, you had to bend over, grab the cheeks of your ass and spread them so the guards could see if you were hiding anything up there, like drugs or weapons. I spent six weeks in Vacaville.

Someone suggested that if you knew how to type it would be easy to volunteer for a job. As that would offset the boredom, I volunteered and lucked out. I got a "job" as 104-B clerk. What this job entailed was reviewing the main document that listed personal information about an inmate, specifically his crime or crimes, and transferring that information to other documents.

The clerk's job was also to update information on the form. It was not long before I found my 104-B form. I changed my crimes - PC 288 - Child Molestation to PC 245C, Aggravated Assault with a deadly weapon on a Police Officer. In a comment box on the form, I typed: "inmate should be considered dangerous and mentally unstable".

When February arrived I departed Vacaville for Folsom State Prison. In Vacaville every inmate is categorized or given points which determines the type of prison, or level, an inmate is to be sent. Inmates assigned a Level One usually had just a few years and were considered low risks. Level Four, on the other hand, were high risk. Inmates assigned to this level had generally been sentenced to life with or without the possibility of parole. Most were considered dangerous and many had been convicted of multiple murders, and would never see freedom again. Folsom prison was a level four prison and I was classified as a level four inmate.

Other factors used to determine what level an inmate merited were considered in addition to the sentence. High school graduate or marital status was used. If you did not graduate or were not married, you received additional points. Had I thought about it I would have lied on both counts and may not have had enough points to be sent to a Level Four prison. But I did not, so it was off to Folsom for me.

The prison bus arrived at Folsom after dark. When inmates are transferred they wear a chain around their waist, and handcuffs on their wrists are connected to the chain. This restricts arm movement. Cuffs around the ankles with short chains connecting them also restricts leg movement. These were all removed after we entered R&R,

the place in every prison from which inmates are either received or released. Released! It would be almost twenty years before I would be in that category. The reality was starting to sink in.

A little history from the public domain is in order to put my new home into perspective for the reader.

Folsom State Prison is located near the city of Folsom, 20 miles northeast from the state capital of Sacramento. Opened in 1880, Folsom is the second-oldest prison in the state of California after San Quentin and was the first in the country to have electricity.

Folsom was one of the first maximum security prisons, witnessing the execution of 93 condemned prisoners over a 42-year period. It is possibly best-known in popular culture for two concerts performed at the facility by musician Johnny Cash in the late 1960s.

The mailing address is Represa, CA 95671. Represa (translated as "dam" from the Spanish language) is the name given in 1892 to the State Prison post office because of its proximity to a dam on the American river that was under construction at the time. (This dam was replaced in 1955 by the Folsom Dam.)

There are no dormitories within the Folsom State Prison's secure perimeter, and prisoners are housed in one man cells, but due to overcrowding there are two inmates to a cell. This was accomplished by adding an upper bunk.

There are five housing units within the secure perimeter, including the original two-tiered structure, named Building 5. Unit 1 is the most populous cellblock in the United States, with a capacity of nearly 1,200 inmates on four five-tiered sections. It is named Building 2.

All cells include toilet, sink, bunks and very little storage space for inmate possessions. There are two dining halls, a large central prison exercise yard, and two smaller exercise yards. The visiting room includes an attached patio as well as space for non-contact visits where visitors are separated from inmates by thick Plexiglas windows and communication is by using closed circuit telephones.

California's second-oldest prison has been long known for its harsh conditions in the decades following the California Gold Rush. Construction of the facility began in 1878 on the site of the Stony Bar mining camp along the American River.

The prison officially opened in 1880. Inmates spent most of their time in the dark behind solid, boiler plate doors in stone cells measuring 4 feet by 8 feet. The doors had 6 inch eye slots. Air holes were drilled into the cell doors in the 1940s, and the cell doors are still in use today.

After the State of California took sole control of the death penalty in 1891, executions were held at Folsom and at San Quentin State Prison. Folsom's last execution was held on December 3, 1937; after that date, all executions occurred at San Quentin.

Folsom State Prison was the first prison in the world to have electric power, which was provided by the first hydroelectric powerhouse in California. The nearby quarry provided granite for the foundation of the state capitol building and much of the gravel used in the early construction of California's roads.

Folsom State Prison was one of America's first maximum-security prisons; a total of 93 prisoners were hanged here between December 13, 1895, and December 3, 1937.

California's vehicle license plates have been manufactured at the prison since the 1930s. Other prison industries include metal fabrication and a print shop.

Folsom was built to hold 1,816 inmates. In 1968 each prisoner in Folsom lived in his own cell. Almost every one of the prisoners was in an education program or learning a trade. According to the National Corrections Oversight Coalition most prisoners who were released did not return to prison after being released. The cost of housing prisoners "barely registered" in the state's budget.

In 1983 Folsom was overcrowded, having 2,645 inmates. There were two inmates in almost every cell. The cost to house each inmate tripled. There were very few education programs and even fewer opportunities to learn a trade. Many prisoners who were released returned to the prison system within two years.

As I write this autobiography, Folsom is now even more overcrowded, and most of its prisoners who are released are returned to prison after being released. The cost to house an inmate for one year is now $50,000. A new prison was constructed next to the existing structures and that is overcrowded too. Called The New Folsom Prison, residents of the original prison are housed there. The old or original Folsom State Prison is now used to house only level one inmates, mostly parole violators who have only a year to serve that year.

In 1937, a warden of Folsom State Prison, Clarence Larkin, was stabbed during an escape attempt and died from his wounds.

During the 1970s and 1980s violence at Folsom peaked, when the Aryan Brotherhood and other prison gangs made prisons increasingly dangerous. The establishment of Secure Housing Units did not do much to control gang-related violence. The first was setup at Folsom. Later SHUs were established at Pelican Bay State Prison and California State Prison, Corcoran.

An inmate doing time in SHU stayed in his cell twenty-three hours a day and had an hour to exercise outdoors by himself or to take a shower. He can shower twice a week and visit the exercise yard for an hour on the other five days. He had to be in handcuffs between his cell and the yard or shower and was escorted by two guards.

In 1982, the year before I arrived, there were 65 serious stabbings that required hospitalization. And there were six deaths by stabbing. The number of deaths doubled in 1983. Twelve inmates died from stabbings. The number of serious stabbings more than tripled. These stabbings were serious enough to require the inmates to be transferred to a county hospital.

Folsom State Prison was made known to the outside world by country music legend Johnny Cash. Cash narrated a fictional account of an outlaw's incarceration in his song "Folsom Prison Blues" (1956). In addition, Cash performed two live concerts at the prison. The first was in 1966 and the most famous live concert was at the cafeteria on January 13, 1968, which was recorded as the album At Folsom Prison. Cash later said of the Folsom State Prison inmates "they were the most enthusiastic audience I have ever played to." The "Folsom Prison Blues" single from that album was #1 on the country music chart for four weeks.

Folsom State Prison has been the location of a number of feature films, including Riot in Cell Block 11, Heat, American Me, The Jericho Mile, Another 48 Hours, Diggstown, parts of Walk the Line (a biopic of Johnny Cash), and Inside the Walls of Folsom Prison, which was the inspiration for Cash's song. The television drama 21 Jump Street also featured Folsom State Prison when Johnny Depp's character Tom Hanson was imprisoned for murder.

Notables who served time at Folsom include Sonny Barger of the Hells Angels, Edward Bunker, Eldridge Cleaver, Joseph Gamsky, aka Joe Hunt, of the Billionaire Boys Club and Glen Stewart Godwin, whose escape from Folsom earned him a spot on the FBI Ten Most Wanted Fugitives list. (He escaped while I was there.)

Others are Cameron Hooker, Rick James, musician Suge Knight, owner of Death Row Records, Timothy Leary,

Charles Manson, Erik Menendez, and Edmund Kemper, the co-ed killer.

Gangs in Folsom State Prison were numerous and varied, each differing in their power, influence, organization, and strategies. The more popular ones at Folsom include: the Mexican Mafia, the Aryan Brotherhood, the "Norteños"or Northern California Hispanics, and the "Sureños" or Southern California Hispanics.

The Aryan Brotherhood was formed in 1967, in California's San Quentin State Prison, and had grown from the Blue Bird Gang of the 1950s and 1960s.

Initially formed for the protection of whites against blacks in prison, the gang gradually moved to criminal enterprise. In prison, they strive to control the sale of drugs, gambling, and "punks," or male "unpaid" prostitutes. It is common knowledge that "Racial warfare comes second to business." The Aryan Brotherhood has carried out contract killings for the Mexican Mafia, but racist beliefs prevent members from consorting with African Americans, including even taking a cigarette or a candy bar from them.

The Aryan Brotherhood is reportedly governed by a 5 member steering-committee. Original members traditionally had to be at least part Irish, denoting the significance of the shamrock still worn today by Brotherhood members, but this tradition has waned. As testament to their commitment to white-cultural supremacy, their constitution states: "Our organization is a white supremacy group. No pretense is or will be made to the contrary."

The Aryan Brotherhood produced an offshoot in the 1970s called the Nazi Low Riders, which emerged in juvenile prisons under the jurisdiction of the California Youth Authority.

180

Released or paroled members have smuggled money or drugs into prison, including marijuana, cocaine, and methamphetamines. The creed by which the Brotherhood members operate under is: "I will stand by my brother. My brother will come before all others. My life is forfeited should I fail my brother. I will honor my brother in peace and war".

It was dark when our busload of fish, the term for new arrivals, left R&R and headed through the dining hall to our cells. The dining hall was separated from a hallway by an eight foot cyclone fence with barbed wire gracing its top. There was a gutter with water flowing next to the hallway. I saw a rat scurry by. What had I gotten myself into? It was like I had stepped back a century or longer.

The prison was on lockdown which meant there was a violent act, a stabbing or serious fight, and no one could leave their cell, not even for meals. The meals were delivered three times a day. Each meal was the same: a brown bag containing two balogna sandwiches with mustard on white bread, and an apple. I arrived in early February and the lockdown lasted until mid-March. My first "celly" was a Canadian, who told me he was in for bank robbery. I learned quickly that one inmate never asks another what his "beef" or crime was. That was a bit of a relief. One of the first acts I was called upon to perform was to be the lookout for him while he shot up with heroin.

Being on lockdown brought with it a sense of security, although it was very boring and the meals left a lot to be desired. Coming off lockdown was like a holiday coated with tension. Nevertheless, getting to go to the yard, to interact with other inmates, to get a little sunshine, all combined to make it feel like a treat.

The end of the first lockdown happened in mid-March, 1983. On the way to the yard someone mentioned "let's play pinochle" and four of us "fish" headed for the section of the yard where tables were located. I quickly found a table and four of us were just starting to play pinochle. One of the players whose nickname was CJ was my pinochle partner. I did not know him but had seen him at the Sacramento County Jail. I did not know his name other than he was called CJ.

An inmate appeared behind me to my left, reached across the table and stabbed CJ right in the heart. Within seconds a blast from a guard's rifle sounded, all the inmates immediately lay on the ground, an alarm was blaring, a few blue lights were blinking and the yard filled with guards.

We were back on lockdown. CJ was dead.

It took a while for word to get around. The reason CJ was killed was his beef. He had been convicted of child molestation. Inmates at Folsom took care of the records. When a new busload arrived, the records were scanned to see who had a sex beef. During the previous lockdown, my bus arrived. CJ was on that bus. CJ's record was apparently reviewed by custody clerks – inmates - and his death certificate was created. I was hoping my fake documents went unnoticed. Fear has a way of increasing when you do not have all the facts. Your mind creates strange scenarios.

Inmates often find God in their prison cell. I did. I felt so helpless and so alone. I had nowhere to turn. I asked God to protect me, to help me. I had not been to a church in a long time. I did not know how to pray. In spite of the thousands of Hail Marys and Our Fathers I chanted at *St. Francis Orphan Asylum*, I had no idea how to approach my creator. But I had to try. The guards offered no protection. I could not talk to other inmates. Maybe God's way of protecting me was to put the prison on lockdown.

During my first year at Folsom - 1983 - the prison was locked down for a total of 265 days. On the 100 days that it was not locked down, there were 212 stabbings that required hospitalization. And, there were 12 deaths. Stabbings or killings happened because of racial problems, drugs, debts or because the victim had a sex beef, either rape or child molestation. (Pall Mall and Camel cigarettes were the currency at Folsom)

Although I thought my 104-B form which I had altered at Vacaville probably kept me alive for the first year, it had to be the work of my creator. He had a plan for me but I did not know what it was.

Inmates, specifically the leaders of the gangs, got to know that another inmate had a sex beef because an inmate - the custody clerk-handled the 104-B forms. Gang leaders would be notified every time a busload arrived. They would then use the inmates with sex beefs in two ways. They would require those inmates' visitors to bring in drugs or other contraband. Or they would require those inmates to do their stabbings. They would be victims of stabbings if they failed on either account. Sometimes they were not used for either. Like CJ, they were just stabbed and many died.

Folsom housed almost twice the number of inmates for which it was built. There were more than 2,600 inmates and fewer than 1,000 had jobs. The sentencing rules favored those who worked. For every day one worked, his sentence was reduced by one day. This was known as half-time. For those who did not work, they received a lesser reduction of their sentence if they stayed out of trouble. Known as third-time, they received one day off for every two days of good behavior. If given an opportunity to work and they refused it, or if they got into trouble and ended up in SHU, they did not receive any reduction of their sentence. Inmates, who had life sentences with or without the possibility of parole did not qualify for half-time or third-time.

I was not able to get a job for my first year. Every inmate was re-classified once a year. If the inmate's points were reduced because the years of the sentencing were less, he might be transferred to a prison with a lower level. The counselors who did the reclassifying would not look at my paperwork for a year. But when my time to be reclassified arrived, the counselor found the error on my 104-B form and corrected it. Now inmates might learn of my beef and I felt it was only a matter of time before I would suffer a similar fate as the other inmates with similar beefs. Stress was my constant companion. Little did I know it then, but so was God.

Before I could get stabbed or killed, I got lucky and got a job as the Kitchen Sergeant's clerk. Now I would be entitled to half-time. One aspect of the job consisted of making cell moves. Another was my creating three lists every time the joint went on lockdown. One list would be of Blacks, one of Mexicans and one of Whites. One of the three lists of twenty-five inmates would be used depending on the reason for the lockdown. The "Whites" list would be used if the reason for the lockdown was Blacks and Mexicans were involved in a stabbing or fight. The Whites would then make the sandwiches for the duration of the lockdown. They would fix themselves great meals and got to bring a lot of good food back to their cells in the evening.

Needless to say, it was the Aryan Brotherhood who comprised the "Whites' list. They also "requested" cell moves. Whenever they wanted to stab someone, they would request a cell move for the future victim. The next morning when the cells were opened for breakfast, it took less than one minute for the stabbing to take place. The sound of the guard's rifle echoing inside the building would announce to all that the stabbing took place. It would be followed by another lockdown.

It would have been a simple matter for the prison administration to control the 104-B cards, and to prevent inmates from having access to them. But they did not, and the stabbings were part of the program. The law suits that followed contributed to the annual cost of $50,000 to house each inmate. It must have cost the CDC millions of dollars for their failure to protect inmates. The seeds to today's California 26 billion dollar deficit were being nurtured back then.

God was indeed watching over me during my stay. He had answered my prayer. And I was not aware that it was He who kept me alive.

Anyone in prison knows that all mail coming and going is read by guards. I received a letter from a prison in Susanville, Ca. It seems Ray Robinson, who had recently been named Citizen of the Year in Mt. Shasta, was convicted of molesting two young girls. In his letter he discussed our similar crimes. I immediately wrote back to him to remind him that the contents of his letters in the future could be detrimental to me. That he was in prison surprised me a little, but maybe it shouldn't have. In 1976 I had a couple of pre-teens staying at my house. Ray came by and convinced one of them to visit his house. Yes, he molested her. I recall him telling me her pubic hair was just as soft as that which accompanies fresh corn husk. Maybe that was another time I should have been a man, but in retrospect, I can admit I was not. I was just as sick as he was. And now we were both paying the price. Mine was more expensive. He was in a level one facility and he would not live with the constant threat to his life.

I did not make friends at Folsom. I learned by observing. Just like in the animal kingdom, if one looks weak, the others attack.

Every year each inmate file is reviewed and he is interviewed and then re-classified. In essence, he could be offered a chance to transfer to a lesser level prison. I was given that opportunity after I was at Folsom for two years. But I had a lot of juice or power by virtue of my job, so I declined. I felt it was better to stay where I knew the ropes than to have to learn them all over again somewhere else. Besides, I had a job and was getting half-time. If I were transferred to another prison I might not get a job and would only get one-third time credits.

I was in a standoff with the Aryan Brotherhood. Although I did not know if they knew my crime, as long as I was doing their bidding, I was relatively safe. I made it easy for them to carry out their stabbings by making the cell moves they wanted. I kept their members on the White's list for kitchen duty during lockdowns. They even treated me as human. Because many of them had jobs as cooks, they would actually make breakfast for me.

As I did not know if they knew my beef, I was reluctant to eat what they prepared thinking they might be trying to poison me. Another inmate, a Black, also worked for the Kitchen Sergeant. The first time I was given a breakfast, I turned around and gave it to the black inmate telling him I was not hungry. He did not die, so I assumed whatever they gave me in the future was not poisoned, or they did not know about my crime.

I had taught myself to paint using acrylics. I had a single cell, a fringe benefit of my job. I thought everything was going just fine. Although I had a job, it paid less than eight cents a day. I did not have enough money to buy materials for painting but used pieces of canvas and wood that other artists discarded. I created 5 inch by 7 inch paintings on canvas and sold them through the Folsom gift shop.

One day during 1985 one of the guards who worked with the Kitchen Sergeant told me: "The AB plan to kill you. They found out about your beef." Before his words sunk in he had taken me to the custody office where I met with a case worker who said I would be transferred in the morning to Tehachapi, a brand new prison east of Bakersfield.

I did not sleep that night. The bus was loaded very early in the morning while it was still dark. I did not breathe a sigh of relief until after the bus departed Folsom at eight that morning. The ride to Tehachapi was a welcomed relief. It was the first time I had seen the outside world in three years. The distance from Folsom to Tehachapi is three hundred and forty miles. The trip took nine hours. It was an enjoyable trip. Even the balogna sandwiches tasted good.

In contrast to Folsom, the brand-new Tehachapi prison was clean, the cells were much larger, and every inmate had a cell to himself. I was given the job as prison photographer. The stress that accompanied me for three years in Folsom seemed to vanish. God had kept me safe, even though I was unrighteous and had not been obeying His law for most of my life.

There was a room to be used as a darkroom in R&R. Because the prison was new, I had to order all the supplies including a camera, an enlarger, film, paper and the chemicals to process them.

The chemicals, film and paper arrived first along with the enlarger. There was a notice that the camera I ordered was on backorder and would not arrive for a few weeks. In the darkroom, I cut a roll of film and a sheet of paper into a one-inch diameter circle that would fit in the bottom of a film canister. In the cap, I made a very tiny hole with a needle. This was my pinhole camera. I loaded a few canisters with film or paper and brought them back to my cell. I proceeded to make photographs of things in my cell and of the grounds surrounding the prison. When I returned to the darkroom, I processed the film and paper and made enlargements. I did this to test the film, paper and chemistry, as well as to make sure I knew what I was doing before the camera arrived.

In a week I had a few dozen of the prints I had photographed and printed. Some were of the Tehachapi Mountains taken through the slit of a window in my cell. A guard came by one day, found the photographs and tried to charge me with attempted escape. Tehachapi was billed as escape-proof, so when the guards found the prints they jumped to the conclusion that I was preparing to escape. They did not buy my explanation that I was testing film, paper and chemicals. Sergeant Trimm, who was in charge of R&R, came to my aide by claiming he authorized me to do the testing. The charges were dropped.

As the prison photographer, I took photographs of everyone who came into the prison. There was contraband found on some arriving inmates and I had to make photographs to document it as this would be used as evidence at their hearings.

One arrival from San Quentin had an eight inch piece of aluminum with one end already sharpened. The other end was one inch by a quarter inch. The shank was folded or bent in half, coated with Styrofoam, and stuck up his ass. (When a match is held under a typical coffee cup, it melts the Styrafoam. He had methodically dripped it on his folded shank.) The metal detector did not detect it, but someone had snitched on him. So he was confined to a holding cell where the plumbing was turned off. The guards just waited until he pooped it out. I photographed the shank in stages as the guard removed the Styrafoam coating and revealed the shiny contraband. I was secretly rooting for the guards as I did not want to be on the receiving end of that shank.

In another instance, an inmate had hollowed out the heel of his boot and secreted heroin and a needle in it.

In yet another, a can of shaving cream had the bottom removed, its foam removed and replaced with drugs, and resealed. It came into the prison from an inmate's package from home.

In addition, there were a few stabbings or other injuries. A few stood out. In one case an inmate had what looked like a pinhole in the side of his neck. He was stabbed with a hard piece of wire. He was dead. The guards had wheeled him into R&R on a gurney so I could photograph his wound before they took him to the morgue.

Another guy was wheeled through R&R on his way to the hospital. He stopped for his photograph. His neck was cut from under one ear to under the other ear and all the insides were hanging out. He was smiling. I do not think he realized how gross he looked or how badly he was cut. And yet another guy was shot with one of those balls from a shotgun-like device. He had a bright red, swollen imprint of the impact in between his breasts. He was not breathing as I photographed his wound.

Tehachapi cost the state $93 million in 1985. That is why it was billed as escape-proof. Inmates generally think of ways to escape even when they do not have any intention to do so. I often did too. The Southern Maximum Security Complex at Tehachapi was "touted as the most advanced in the country," but was also "called a 'white elephant' and a 'Cadillac' because it took so long to build and cost so much.

Tehachapi is near the summit on Highway 57, east of Bakersfield, and the city and prison sit at about 4,000 feet elevation. For a few months in the winter it gets foggy. When it does, all the inmates are kept in their cells because they cannot be seen from the guard towers. The exception was the prison photographer whenever there is an incident that required photographic documentation. One foggy Sunday morning two inmates angrily tried to shave each other and made a bloody mess out in the dayroom. I was called out to photograph them and their "weapons". So I was locked in R&R for the few hours it would take to process the film and make prints. There was just one piece of glass between me and freedom and no one around to hear it break. Although there was a tower immediately outside, the fog rendered it useless. The glass would have been easy to break and I could be out, but what would I do if I got out? Needless to say, I did not break the glass.

Inmates are entitled to receive packages periodically from their friends or relatives. The prison maintains a list of approved items that can come into the prison in those packages. A couple of Vietnamese inmates had their relatives send in a package. Apparently the food in the package was not on the approved list as it contained a fish product or two and really stunk up R&R. Sergeant Trimm, whose job it was to open and inspect the contents of all packages for contraband, rejected the package.

I liked the two youngsters and suggested a way they could get their food past Trimm in the future. One of them worked in the laundry and visited R&R frequently to deliver blue jeans and white T-shirts, the prison uniform, and to take away the red jumpsuits inmates traveled in when transferring from other institutions.

My idea was to have another package sent in with what they wanted. Before it arrived they were to buy a box full of legal stuff from the prison store or canteen. I would hide what they bought in my darkroom, and when their package came in, I would swap the contents of both boxes. When they came by to pick up the dirty jumpsuits, I would put their contraband package in the cart used to transport the jumpsuits back to the laundry. This was done so the number of packages received did not differ from the number distributed.

It worked fine. And I did not give it much thought until they wanted another package of contraband. Inmates are allowed four packages a year. It also worked the second time.

The Super Bowl of 1986 attracted a lot of attention and interest. It was of interest to the guards in Tehachapi too. What I did not know was that an inmate who worked in the Secured Housing Unit (SHU) had a guard's uniform brought into the prison with the help of the two Vietnamese using the same procedure I used to import their contraband. The black inmate walked out during the guard's shift change as the Super Bowl was underway and all eyes were glued to TV screens. He managed to make it to the local bus station undetected and called his mother from there. He was serving a life sentence for murder and his mom knew him better than anyone. She called the authorities who went to the bus station and captured the first person to escape from the escape-proof prison. No authorities ever questioned me or the Vietnamese inmates, and apparently the escapee did not give them up.

California State Prison at Tehachapi was a lot less stressful than Folsom. Because it was new, inmates were single-celled. I was getting used to prison life and enjoyed my new surroundings. I had been incarcerated for more than four years and had a little more than fourteen years to go.

Correctional Sergeant Trimm and I had a slight ethical problem. He wanted me to use the prison darkroom to make prints and enlargements for his fellow correctional officers. Some of the photos bordered on pornography. Because he came to my aid when the contraband photographs were found in my cell, I made the prints and enlargements for him even though I knew what he wanted me to do was a bit illegal. But then this was just another instance where you could only tell the difference between guards and inmates by what they wore.

Every year each department of state government has money budgeted to them. In April word goes out that supply orders will be filled. In general the rule is you must order more than you ordered last year, even if it was not needed. This is the traditional waste in government politicians claim annually that they will get rid of. They never do. Because we were new to the budget, I used my creativity and ordered enough films, chemicals and papers to start my own business. I knew it would never be used but it would establish a baseline for future budgets. This built-in procedure by state workers surely contributes to the billions of dollars in debt the state of California is in at the time of this writing.

On today's news Governor Brown signed an executive order prohibiting most state travel. I wonder when he will get around to fixing the phony ordering and waste of supplies. If he was truly interested in resolving the budget problem, he would use zero-based budgeting. This would require justifying what was being ordered each year, and not just adding a percentage to what was ordered in the previous year.

Another new prison - named Richard J. Donovan - was built just east of San Diego. California Department of Corrections (CDC, now CDCR) thought it made sense to populate it with inmates who would not present a problem. Many from Tehachapi were transferred there, as I was. It felt good going to yet another new prison which would not be overcrowded. Unfortunately I did not get the job of photographer as it was already assigned to another inmate.

Because I was concerned about my part in the escape from Tehachapi, I sought out a high ranking officer to discuss my concern. After he assured me I would have total immunity, I gave him the details of my involvement. I did not want to be responsible for another escape or worse. It would be a simple matter to import guns and drugs into the prison using the same procedure.

I hadn't been at this new prison for two weeks when I received an official notice from the Board of Prison terms. In essence they review the sentences of all inmates to determine if the sentences inmates received were grossly disparate. I had never heard of this process. I was stunned when I read in the letter that they determined that that my sentence was three times longer than other inmates who had been convicted of similar crimes. I was ordered back to court in Sacramento for re-sentencing.

Babich, the radical Catholic judge, was now retired. And by now the truth about Catholic priests molesting boys all over the world was coming to light. He would not be my judge. Thank God. God sure answers prayers in interesting ways.

Transportation to Sacramento from San Diego was a strange experience. Normally a CDC bus is used but we rode in a van run by a company that contracted with CDC. The van stopped at various county jails and a few other state prisons, picking up and dropping off inmates. The trip took 32 hours. We slept sitting up. We stopped to get take-out from McDonald's three times.

My court appearance was very brief. I was overjoyed to hear that my sentence was reduced from 19 years and 8 months, down to six years. This was vindication that Babich was neither an honorable nor an impartial judge but a vindictive bastard who imposed a sentence not to fit the crime but to punish me for having the audacity to reveal my childhood molestation by superiors in his Catholic Church. I don't know why it was so difficult for Babich to believe me, He should have known that historically many leaders of the Catholic Church have spent much of the past two thousand years exploiting many of its members.

As I write this autobiography in 2011, the Catholic sex abuse cases are an ongoing series of scandals for the Catholic Church. The scandals related to sex crimes either committed or covered up by Catholic priests and bishops, and other members of religious orders, while under diocesan control or in Orders that care for the sick or teach children. These cases began receiving public attention beginning in the mid-1980s, shortly after my conviction. The attention led to criminal prosecutions of the abusers and to successful civil lawsuits against the church's dioceses and parishes where abuse was admitted to have occurred.

Sexual abuse of minors by the priesthood has received significant media attention in Canada, Ireland, the United States, the United Kingdom, Mexico, Belgium, France, and Germany. Additional cases have been reported to authorities throughout the world.

In addition to cases of actual abuse, much of the scandal has focused around members of the Catholic hierarchy who did not report abuse allegations to the civil authorities and who, in many cases, reassigned the offenders to other locations where the predators continued to have contact with minors and had opportunities to continue to sexually abuse children. In defending their actions, some bishops and psychiatrists contended that the prevailing psychology of the times suggested that people could be cured of such behavior through counseling. Members of the church hierarchy have argued that media coverage has been excessive.

In the United States, churches have paid more than $2 billion in compensation to victims. Abuse has not been limited to America.

In Ireland, reports into clerical sexual abuse have rocked both the Catholic hierarchy and the state. A nine-year government study, the Ryan Report, published in May 2009, revealed that beatings and humiliation by nuns and priests were common at institutions that held up to 30,000 children. The investigation found that Catholic priests and nuns for decades "terrorized thousands of boys and girls, while government inspectors failed to stop the abuse."

So I guess I wasn't the only one terrorized. It did put my criminal act into perspective. I re-live my acts of sexual abuse of my numerous victims frequently. I focus on my last victim. How much damage had I done to Danny? Was there anything I could do at this point in time to mitigate the psychological harm I caused him? At the time I was arrested, I wanted to pay for psychological help for him, but the court prohibited me from having any contact. My lawyer's advice was that it would be an admission of guilt.

In response to the widening scandal, Pope John Paul II emphasized the spiritual nature of the offenses as well. He declared in 2001 that "a sin against the Sixth Commandment of the Decalogue by a cleric with a minor under 18 years of age is to be considered a grave sin, or delictum gravius."

With the approval of the Vatican, the hierarchy of the church in the United States claimed to institute reforms to prevent future abuse including requiring background checks for Church employees and volunteers, while opposing legislation making it easier for abuse victims to sue the Catholic Church.

Perhaps Judge Joseph Babich has been rolling over in his grave each time the media reports another priest-child abuse tragedy, but I will bet that if he is, he has his fingers in his ears.

Now that I was re-sentenced, I had less than 13 months to serve. Because my points were now very low, I was reassigned to Vacaville, a level one prison. There was light at the end of my tunnel and it was not the headlight of a train. I would be released in October, 1988, just a month short of six years when half-time was taken into account.

Time flew by at Vacaville. That prison reminded me of *St. Joseph's House for Homeless and Industrious Boys*. The stress of the previous four years was now gone. Most of the inmates had so little time left to serve they were eager to get out and stabbing someone was not a priority for them.

Inmates either worked or were required to attend a class. I finally got assigned to a typing class. I could already type eighty words per minute so the class was both easy and boring. The civilian teacher, a beautiful Ms. Tam, was using IBM computers to teach the typing class. She had half a dozen Apple computers and asked me if I could figure out how they worked. She gave me permission to take the manuals back to my six-person dorm. In 1987 I had no idea what a computer could do, but I quickly taught myself to program one using Apple Basic.

A trick math question circulates that asks: which would you prefer - to work: thirty days for $10,000 or to work the first day for a penny, and the second for twice as much or two cents, and double that on the third and double it again on each subsequent day until you have worked thirty days?

After understanding just a little of the Apple Basic programming language, I wrote a six line program and sent the instructions to the printer. In seconds the printout showed how much was earned on each day as well as the sub-totals. The total for thirty days would be $10,737,418.23. The speed with which the computer came up with the answer sold me on computers.

I did not know or think much about what would be in my future but I now knew it would include computers.

I went on a diet to look healthy. I weighed 220 pounds in March, 1988, and by the time I left Vacaville I was down to 165. I had lost fifty-five pounds in seven months. But I did not look healthy. The skin hung from my arms and other places and looked like a series of cascading scrotums. Strangers were asking me if I were dying, or if I had AIDS.

The day arrived for me to depart Vacaville for freedom. I was driven by the guards to the Greyhound bus station and bought a ticket for Sacramento. It was a real rush handling money for the first time in almost six years. I called Dorian Wright, one of the few friends I made in law school. He was to meet me at the bus station in Sacramento.

Dorian was about 165 pounds when I last saw him almost six years earlier. He was now more than 210 pounds and his first words when he met me were: "We switched bodies."

When an inmate leaves prison there is a good chance he will re-offend and return to prison in a short while. Generally the inmate goes back to his neighborhood and hangs out with his old friends or "homeboys". Because a job will not be easy to find, the path he takes will generally lead to crime: burglary, robbery or selling drugs.

I did not have a neighborhood to return to, nor did I have friends or "homeboys". I was not a burglar or a robber, but I did have experience growing marijuana. I had no idea what I would do for employment. Dorian had an auto body repair business in Rancho Cordova, a city a few miles east of Sacramento. He had a partner John Heinz. The name of the business was KK Enterprises. I would be their only employee. I would be an independent contractor so they did not have to pay taxes, workers comp etc.

I knew nothing about repairing car bodies, so I got to do the mundane work: removing damaged or dented parts, installing new replacements. There was lots of masking and sanding and of course I kept the floors and toilets clean. John was dead set against hiring me, but Dorian prevailed. Heinz told me how low an opinion he had of all criminals.

Twenty-three years later in April, 2011, John Heinz made the news. Seems he lost his temper and left a message on a Muslim customer's phone. The sheriff's department was investigating him for a hate crime. I did not call to remind him that he was now a criminal, although I thought about it.

I noticed John spent a lot of time doing paper work, especially doing the books. I had purchased a used computer with my first wages. It was a laptop with two disk drives and a quarter of a megabyte of RAM - a pea brain as computers go. I found a bookkeeping software program. It created financial statements including balance sheets and income statements. John was not interested in my proving that my computer could save him a lot of time, but again, Dorian prevailed. Needless to say, the computer produced error-free results much faster than what John was able to do. It was another example of the proverbial tortoise beating the hare. After a few months using my program, KK Enterprises entered the computer age. And John never bothered thanking me for my contribution.

Inmates are on parole when the leave state prison and it is for a three-year period of time. My parole was in effect from my release date in 1988 until October, 1991. I was never visited by parole agents. The CDC obviously does not do a good job supervising parolees as the following 2010 news story of worldwide interest indicates.

On June 10, 1991, eleven year old Jaycee Dugard was abducted 150 yards from her home in South Lake Tahoe as she was walking to the bus stop. Her stepfather, Carl Probyn, was home. He saw a man and woman in a gray sedan make a sudden u-turn. He told police a woman grabbed the girl and pulled her inside the car.

More than a million flyers with the 11-year-old girl's picture were mailed out in the years immediately after she was kidnapped.

Parolee Phillip Garrido and his wife Nancy kept Jaycee in the backyard of their Antioch home for 18 years, hidden from the rest of the world in a series of sheds -- one made entirely soundproof. Garrido admitted to fathering her two children -- ages 11 and 15.

Although CDC parole agents had visited the Garrido residence frequently they never connected any dots. Garrido had been imprisoned in Nevada for kidnapping a young lady. He had imprisoned her in a makeshift bedroom and repeatedly raped her while forcing alcohol and drugs on her. When agents visited the Garrido home they accepted his statement that Jaycee was his daughter, even though he was a registered sex offender. She was helping him in a printing business he ran from his home.

Jaycee's fate finally changed on Monday, Aug. 24, 2009, when a University of California, Berkeley, female cop grew suspicious of Garrido after he came to campus with the two daughters, aged 15 and 11, looking for an event permit to distribute religious flyers.

"He was clearly unstable," Lisa Campbell, 40, the UC Berkeley manager of special events said at a press conference. And her mother mode went into gear when she watched Jaycee's 15-year-old stare "straight up in the air."

Campbell stalled Garrido, and asked him to return on Tuesday, Aug. 25. Meantime, she went to fellow UCBPD officer Ally Jacobs, 33, who ran a background check on Garrido and discovered he was a sex offender.

Ultimately the search of his residence revealed the hidden backyard within a backyard. The hidden backyard had sheds, tents and outbuildings where Jaycee and the girls spent most of their lives. There was a vehicle hidden in the backyard that matched the vehicle originally described at the time of the abduction. The tents and outbuildings in the backyard were placed in a strategic arrangement to inhibit outside contact. Neither of Jacee's children had ever gone to school; they had never been to a doctor. They were kept in complete isolation in this compound in the rear of the house. The CDC parole agents never suspected anything, and never inspected the back yard.

My only connection with my parole office was pathetic at best. I was asked to attend a weekly meeting along with a few others who had been convicted of child molestation. We were told to speak freely but if we revealed any crimes for which we were not convicted, we would be arrested and charged. One can just imagine how productive these meetings were. After about six weeks we were told the meetings were no longer necessary. I was never contacted by my parole officer after that announcement.

I did try to connect with a few former friends, but they reacted like I was radioactive. Just like dominoes, they fell away as I approached them. I could understand that inmates considered child molesters the lowest scum on earth, but I did not expect this reaction from people on the outside. It did say a lot about the friends I made. I did not need friends like that. Except for Dorian and his family, I was totally alone. Even though most people are of the opinion that if you do the crime and do the time, then you can re-join society. Well, that is another truism that is not true. So now the punishment for my crime was to resume after my incarceration.

Chapter Nine
Public Service: From Secretary to Analyst – 1988

Unless one has a conjugal visit from his wife, sex in prison is confined to homosexuals or involuntary man-on-man known as rape. I had no conjugal visits, nor did I have any visitors at all, and I had no sex for six years. I lived on Dorian's property in Mt. Aukum in a trailer until I had enough money to get an apartment. I rented an apartment at 14th and Q streets in downtown Sacramento and met a girl named Anna. Luck was with me as I had sex with her on the first day. She left in the morning and I never saw her again. She had been shooting crack cocaine, something I was unfamiliar with. Between her shooting drugs and my lack of sex for such a long time, we spent from eleven one night until sunrise having the best sex of my life. That day in 1988 would also be the last time I had sexual intercourse.

My earnings working at the body shop were providing me with just the basics. I was earning less than the minimum wage. Knowing I would never get ahead at KK Enterprises, I applied for a job with the state as a typist. I went to Los Angeles to take a test and scored high. By the time I returned to Sacramento I had two job offers which I rejected because they were in Los Angeles. I did not want to go to LA

I transferred my eligibility to Sacramento and immediately had two job offers in Stockton. One was with the San Joaquin County probation office. The other was with the Department of Health Services Office of Drinking Water. I interviewed with both on the same day, was offered a job with both immediately, and accepted the position offered by DHS. I was now a respectable Office Assistant Typist.

On the state's application, the question "Have you ever committed a felony" needs to be answered only if you are applying for a job in a state prison or one that is relevant or requires a background check. Most ex-felons seeking employment either lie to get a job or tell the truth and don't get hired, as most applications other than for state employment require that question be answered regardless of the position. Even county and city employment is barred to ex-cons.

It is no wonder that the recidivism rate is so high. Although it is common knowledge that one has paid his debt to society, it is really a myth. Society has its way of forgetting that the crime was paid for and they want revenge in addition. That is why society gets recidivism. That is why the prison industry is booming and the cost to house inmates is skyrocketing. Society gets what it pays for.

My starting salary as a typist was almost $1700 a month, a lot more than the minimum wage and I had benefits too: vacations, sick days and a dental and health plan. The commute from Sacramento to Stockton was more than 80 miles each day, but I enjoyed driving.

I was replacing a lady who retired. She had refused to learn to use the computer. I was more than eager to use it. On the first day of work, the four other employees, all engineers, were going to South Lake Tahoe for a three day conference. I asked what they would like me to do in their absence. They suggested I type address labels for the fifty-four water companies they regulated.

When they departed I wrote a small computer program that addressed envelopes. I only had to type each address once. My program would print that address on an envelope. I fed all three thousand envelopes - the entire office supply - into the printer. There was nothing else to do until they returned. When they returned and saw the six boxes of envelopes, all addressed, they were eager to learn how I did it and what else I knew about computers. Those were the days before such a feat was commonplace and available from Microsoft Word or other office software products.

Later when I was asked to type letters for the engineers, I chose instead to teach them how to use their computers. I would then be happy to proof-read and process the letters they sent to the water companies they regulated. So that left me with plenty of time which enabled me to focus on learning to program in other languages. The computers they had were IBM PCs, not Apples.

It was not long before I had the opportunity to use my computer skills. The Office of Drinking Water regulated any water company that had two hundred or more service connections or customers. Counties regulated those companies who had fewer than two hundred users like small motels. The state required the water companies to test the drinking water for organic and inorganic substances quarterly and to submit the results of the testing for each water source such as a lake, stream or reservoir. The state had contamination standards that could not be exceeded for each of the compounds. Whenever the water being tested failed to meet those standards, the engineers became concerned and ordered the water company to correct the problem. The results of the test were sent to the Stockton office on a daily basis.

The engineers would read the reports, and log the results whenever a well, reservoir or other water supply exceeded the allowable contamination. They would then require mitigation of the contamination. Each well or source had an identification number, like each American has a social security number. The engineers would look up the name of the water source and add the identification number and other related information to the test results. Sometimes they did not add the information correctly. What they were doing would be similar to the IRS getting a tax return and looking up the social security number from a master list and adding that to the return. Nothing could be more inefficient. A computer program could solve that problem.

The problem grew rapidly because the reports had been accumulating for months and the engineers were way behind in their paper work. This allowed for very little time for them to actually go to the water source to conduct random tests, which they were required to do. Stockton was one of three offices in the Sacramento region. There were nine regions in California and all had the same paperwork problem.

Without being asked, I wrote a program that was designed to be used by the laboratories conducting the tests for each water company. Essentially the labs would do the paper work the engineers were doing. In short, this meant compelling the water company to insist the labs use the program to generate a paper report with all the information filled in. And there would be no errors.

This freed the engineers from the drudgery that was wasting their time. The engineers would also receive a 5-inch floppy disk in addition to paper reports. If any substance on the report exceeded the state's standard, the program would alert the engineer by presenting the information on the computer screen as well as activating a bell sound.

I wrote only one program for only one of the required tests. I demonstrated this to the supervising engineer who quickly set up a meeting with the Regional Engineer. After I demonstrated the program, the Regional Engineer realized that his other offices had the same backlog and my program would get rid of their backlogs too.

Most businesses in 1988 still did not have a computer programmer on their employee roster. Most of their employees did not know how to use computers. So I was in the right place at the right time.

I was paid $.32 a mile for driving my own car, received $25 for meals each day I was away from home, and I was reimbursed for motel bills as I traveled to the labs in northern California introducing my software program.

When I was back in the office, I worked on two additional programs for the other tests that were required. Selling labs and water companies on using my programs kept me busy for a few years. I was on top of the world.

Water companies employ water treatment operators who have to be licensed by the state. There are five grades or levels with grade one being the entry-level step. The Department of Health Services Office of Drinking Water gives a test twice a year. If applicants fail the test they can visit with the regional engineer and discuss the questions they got wrong so they will be better prepared to take the test in the future. One person who failed the test came into the Stockton office and reviewed his test with the head engineer. Later, that engineer asked me to send the test to our headquarters in Sacramento. I did, after I made a copy of it.

I now had another opportunity to write a program, but this one would benefit me, not the state. I borrowed the questions and answers from that test and used the dBase III programming language to create software that gave the user the test questions and answers. I then advertised the software in an industry magazine. I sold it for $33.33 a copy and in the course of four months sold 150 copies through the mail in California. I also applied to take the exam myself. I had no intention of becoming a water treatment operator, but wanted to see how the test was administered.

Normally, the test could be completed in two hours. I finished it in fifteen minutes. I was aware that others in the gym taking the test must have thought that I just quit because I was turning in my test so early. It was easy to finish the test so quickly because in the process of writing the program I had asked and answered the questions hundreds of times in debugging the program.

I did not give that program much thought until one day I received a few requests by mail asking if I had the Grade Two software. Because I received so many requests, it dawned on me that the state used the same questions on the exam. Everyone who bought my program got all the answers correct.

I did not have questions and answers for a Grade Two test so I paid an engineer $500 to write me the equivalent of the Grade Two exam and used the same programs, but substituted the new questions and answers. I ran another ad but in a national magazine and started receiving orders from many foreign countries. In some cases I could not read the language so just tossed the letter. I really enjoyed programming computers. I also enjoyed the money I was making on the side. Although I was providing the answers to the questions, most water treatment plant operators knew their jobs. So my actions were not a threat to the public's health.

The state also required a monthly test to determine if the water was contaminated by E coli. Most E. coli strains are harmless, but some can cause serious food poisoning in humans, and are occasionally responsible for product recalls. E. coli are an ideal indicator organism to test environmental samples for fecal contamination. So if a cow takes a poop and contaminates a stream or lake, the test required by the state would call for action to rid the water of its contamination. This was another opportunity for me to write a program which produced the report, and did the complicated, required calculations correctly.

Of the various water providers our office regulated, one was the Calavaras County Fair Association. They learned of my programming skills when one of our engineers visited their site for an inspection of their water system. Their manager called me and asked if I would like to write a program for the upcoming Jumpin' Frog Jubilee contest.

One of America's most respected literary artists, Mark Twain, wrote about the jumping frogs of Calavaras County. In his story he had one contestant fill another's frog with buckshot so that amphibian wouldn't be able to win the contest. The county established the tradition of having visitors to their fair enter bullfrogs and give them a chance to compete by jumping from a round piece of felt, six inches in diameter. The contest was simple: add the total distance of three leaps. If your frog jumped further than the rest, you were the winner of a trophy.

I had previously attended the Calavaras County Jumpin' Frog Jubilee in 1972 as a Young Republican. We sat in the hot sun waiting for our frog's turn to jump. We thought we could keep our entrant cool so we placed him in our cooler along with our beer. When it came time for him to jump, he was rather stiff and did not move. We were disqualified.

So I was familiar with the event and accepted their offer to write a computer program. It was intended to prevent the same person from entering more than one frog. In addition, each entrant's distance would be calculated along with the position they finished. A computer could do this before the day was out and postcards would be generated and sent to all contestants in Monday's mail. Previously it took a week or longer to notify the contestants of their standings.

The fair was a two day event. The best frogs on Saturday competed on Sunday in the finals. I field-tested my computer program on Saturday and got up very early on Sunday to make some corrections and to add the finishing touches to it. I was on the stage in a secluded and enclosed area with my laptop. Some of the locals had gathered and were drinking coffee. They were not aware that I was within earshot. They were also having an interesting discussion that caught my attention.

The previous year, someone had entered an African frog that was half again as big as California frogs. Needless to say they could jump much further. This year there were a lot of African frogs and the local community leaders who ran the contest were concerned that California frogs would never again win. They devised and implemented a plan that would have earned a big smile from Mark Twain. The pillars of the community reduced the diameter of the green felt launch pad to five inches. That was good enough to disqualify most of the contestants who entered African frogs because they could no longer fit within the pad's boundaries. A frog from California was successful and so was my program for which I was paid $800. To my knowledge no one ever discovered the ruse.

I was invited to the next regional conference of the Office of Drinking Water in Lake Tahoe where I was pleasantly surprised. For writing the programs in use by the labs that were saving the three offices so much time and money, I received a plaque in recognition of my work. Getting recognition really felt good.

Our office had been using the reports my program generated and it no longer had a backlog. The regional office decided to introduce it to the Office of Drinking Water Headquarters so all nine regional offices throughout the state would benefit by using it. Headquarters had been taking the paper reports from each of the nine regional offices and were manually entering data into a mainframe computer. This required three full time clerks. It looked like I would get statewide recognition, but there was a storm on the horizon.

My social life was zilch. No friends, no women, no prospects. It was extremely difficult for me to move forward.

Just how does one convicted of child molestation make friends? I couldn't make friends prior to my conviction. The stigma of being an ex-convict and molester remained a tremendous barrier for me to having a social life. I made contact with whomever I believed was my friend before my conviction, and everyone - except Dorian - treated me like a leper.

I flashed back occasionally to my days in Folsom when life appeared to be over for me. The few times in my dark hours when I reached out to my creator and asked for help, He had come through. Maybe he had something in store for me. I thought I would explore religions to see if I could fit in. Perhaps my ulterior motive to get a social life this way doomed my pursuit of spiritual help from the beginning.

My job in Stockton was about to erupt in a volcano of anger.

When the Regional Manager, Bert Ellsworth brought my computer programs to the attention of the Office of Drinking Water Headquarters, the Chief of the organization was impressed and insisted the DHS Data Committee invite me to its next meeting. The Data Committee was headed by a chemist named Dave Storm. His interest was in running the main frame and hiring data entry clerks. I attended that meeting and later learned it was like a lamb going to slaughter.

David Storm, as a chemist and head of the data committee, set the contamination standards for the state. He also had a hobby as a computer programmer. He wanted to hire more than the three data entry clerks who were inputting the water tests data into a mainframe. As the paperwork backlog increased, that would justify his hiring more data entry clerks, but my program got in his way. When I showed up for the meeting I was asked to provide the committee with the source code used in my programs. I happily complied but thought it strange that I was never invited back to another meeting. It soon became apparent why I was excluded from future meetings.

Storm had hired a programmer from the University of California at Davis to take my source code and re-write the program using the programming language C++ which was a much more robust language. He had promised her a state job when she finished. Without a word to Bert or me, he sent his program named **Right On** to every lab in California informing them that only output from his program would be acceptable in the future. All labs would no longer be permitted to use my programs.

The state was experiencing a downturn in the economy and initiated a freeze on new hires. The writer of the **Right On** program who Storm promised to hire and did not, successfully filed a claim against the state and was ultimately awarded $50,000.

The state of California has a program to encourage money-saving ideas. It is aptly named the Merit Award. If an employee submits an idea which proves to save the state money and the idea is not a duty for which the employee was hired, the submitter gets a sizeable amount of money, usually ten percent of the savings for the first year.

Bert suggested I submit my programs in for a Merit Award which I did. The state organization that determines if an idea is meritorious sent the idea to the Office of Drinking Water for comments. They wanted to know if the idea was workable, if it saved money, how much, etc. They could then give me an award. But the person who was to reply with the answers to those questions and other relevant information was **David Storm**.

In his response he lied to the state stating that the program was not workable, it would not save any money, and he had previously looked at using computers to do data entry but it was not cost-effective. The state informed me that there appeared to be a conflict between the information I provided and the response from Storm. Nevertheless I did receive an award, but the monetary aspect was reduced to $150 because of Storm's response.

After this was settled, headquarters determined that I was not permitted to be traveling all over the state because I was only a typist. Previously both my boss in Stockton and his boss Bert Ellsworth thought it would be a good idea if I took classes on state time and be paid by the state in order for me to obtain a quick education in computer programming. But Storm urged the Office of Drinking Water headquarters to prevent me from attending class. They then determined that I was not eligible to have classes paid for by the state and these were cancelled. I was asked to give back the money they already paid for books.

It was difficult for me to believe that we both worked for the same state. I settled back to my job as a typist. The head of our office in Stockton was promoted and transferred to Sacramento. His position was filled by Joseph Spano one of the three engineers who worked in the Stockton office.

I generally liked Joe, even though he was a self-professed Christian and an active bigot. Not a day would go by when he wouldn't stop at my desk to tell me a racist or sexist joke. It would be one thing if he was kidding, but he was expressing his philosophy. I kept a tape recorder on my desk which I though was a more efficient way of taking notes for instructions. On a hunch, I started using it to record Joe's remarks. He was not only telling inappropriate jokes, he was defaming other state employees. Little did I know that the tape recordings of his remarks would come in handy one day.

Joe referred to the data committee in headquarters as the Collection Utility. They had a cubicle next to the training cubicle in Sacramento. Joe asked me to send a stack of papers to them. I scribbled the abbreviation C.U.N.T. on a yellow sticky note on the pile of papers to be sent to the *collection utility near training*. I affixed the note to the pile and later stuffed it all in a manila envelope. I inadvertently forgot to remove the sticky note before stuffing the papers into the envelope.

When those papers were received, the shit hit the fan in Sacramento. I was going to be reprimanded and punished. A meeting was set to take place in Joe Spano's office. This was his first opportunity to be management and was he ever.

He was 100 percent behind the organization and was pushing hard at the meeting to carry out headquarters demand that I be fired. It was general knowledge that a state worker has to kill his boss twice before the state worker would be fired. So here was a showdown between Joe Spano and a representative of Storm against me and my union representative.

After the charges were read I was asked if I wanted to plead guilty and accept the punishment. My union representative took a stab at a defense with a statement which did not impress Joe or headquarters' representative. It did not impress me either. I said I thought they would want to hear my tape recordings of Joe before I made a decision. Minutes into the tape, my union representative's attitude changed from pessimistic to optimistic, and finally he smelled victory. One highlight on the tape was that Joe used the same word I used in referring to the collection utility near training. His laughter on the tape neutralized my use of it on a piece of yellow paper. After the tape testified, I gave them a list of what I thought should happen to me: a transfer to Sacramento as I could no longer work

212

for a bigot; a promotion to Data Processor, as I believed I earned that title for what I gave the state; and a refund of the money I had used to purchase the books needed to attend the college classes. I stated these were non-negotiable, and should they reject any of my demands, I would send copies of the tape to the news media, to N.O.W., to the governor and everyone else who I thought might have an interest in hearing it.

They agreed to everything I demanded. I was to be transferred to the Sacramento Office managed by Bert Ellsworth.

While they were putting through my promotion and transfer, I was filling out job applications with other state organizations and taking tests to get on as many hiring lists as possible.

A week later no one was in the office except the recently hired engineer who was filling Joe Spano's old position. Someone from building maintenance came to our office and removed a piece of the floor in front of my desk to access electric wires. He left the screws lying on the floor. He then left the office for lunch. Seeing this as an opportunity, I picked up a stack of papers, went back to get a cup of coffee, and stopped by to get a signature from the new engineer in his office for one of his letter. As I returned to my desk only ten feet away, I stepped on the screws, pressing them into and cutting the linoleum, threw the coffee and stack of papers into the air, and "fell" making sufficient noise that invited him to the scene of me holding my head while laying on the floor. He determined that I had slipped on the screws. I complained of my "injuries" and he urged me to see a doctor, offering to call one. I said I would go to the hospital in Jackson.

I was off work for six weeks. Unemployment compensation paid me for the loss of wages and my hospitalization. I really did not want to work for Joe Spano any more so I was actually waiting to be called by one or more of the state agencies who had open positions for which I had taken tests.

I did not have to wait long. I was interviewed by the State Water Resources Control Board. The position was half time with the Labor Relations Manager for the Department and half time with its Medical Office. The job was in Sacramento. I was offered the job at the interview. I accepted immediately and I was now considered a Confidential Employee because I worked with secret information, including pay rates and social security numbers. I was also privy to employee grievances as the Labor Relations manager was the third level of review. This job did much for my ego. Here I was an ex-felon being viewed as a trusted employee. I believe this loophole has been closed and background checks are now required for this kind of a position.

And I really liked the job. Information Technology was just budding and most small organizations did not have an IT person on staff. Although my title was a Data Processor, I filled the Information Technology need informally. Because I was willing and eager to do anything dealing with computers I was considered a valuable asset. Perhaps the most exciting aspect of working for the SWRCB was they had a training program and encouraged lateral transfers into fields that were not dead ends, unlike typists and data processors. By the end of my first year I applied for the position of Staff Services Analyst. This was a position created for women who were stuck in dead end jobs, like typists and data processors. It enabled females to branch up and out. Working for Labor Relations I noted that all of the SSA positions were indeed occupied by females. How could I be turned down? Wouldn't that be gender discrimination against a male if I were not hired?

There was no need to make that argument as I was hired by the Board's Clean Water Program. They needed someone who could use a computer to track the leaking underground storage tanks. In California, there were more than 40,000 gas stations or similar facilities that had been leaking oil and gas and other toxic chemicals into the ground for decades. This was contaminating the state's drinking water supply. The Clean Water Program had the responsibility to oversea the clean-up of the leaks.

The United States Environmental Protection Agency passed The Clean Water Act, a law requiring the ground water to be cleaned up. The USEPA delegated the responsibility to the states and provided funding. California also taxed gasoline and gave additional funds to the SWRCB who would give grants to owners and operators of gas stations to clean up the leaks. My job would be to manage a database that would track the leaks and the stage of cleanup for each.

This job would be easy. Every time a station had a leak discovered, the county or city was required to fill out a form in triplicate and send one copy to the state. The state maintained a data base and used reports from that data to ask the legislature for funding as the problem was growing. But my job was not as easy as I initially thought. The state's record of the leaks did not reflect reality. Not every county or large city sent the information required by the state: those that did send the data did not necessarily send the *correct* data. So the state really had no idea how many leaking underground storage tanks were leaking, how many were fixed, and how many still had to be cleaned up.

The existing data base was not actually a data base but a collection of information in a spreadsheet. It was never maintained properly from its inception. I was eager to order new software and learn advanced database programming to correct the problem. In short order I created a database that pleased everyone. The biggest problem was in reconciling the data in our computer with the leaking sites in 58 counties and a number of larger cities. This meant I had to do a lot of traveling. And that also meant I could get per diem: money to eat three meals a day, and to be reimbursed for motel expenses. Ordinarily I would have stayed at Motel 6s, but just about every state worker I knew who travel stayed at $100 or more per day, first class hotels, so I followed suit.

It took until 2011 when Governor Brown finally looked at this waste of taxpayer money for the practice to be brought to a halt by allowing only essential travel.

From the start at SWRCB, I was treated with kindness and respect. As the manager of the Clean Water Program was heading out to the legislature to ask for more funding, I would prepare reports to justify the request. The IT field was interesting in this respect: when someone asked you a question, it meant they did not know the answer, and even when I did not know the answer, I could invent an answer. And I did that a few times. It gave me both time and the motivation to find the correct answer and to increase my knowledge.

My "knowledge" and eagerness was rewarded as I received a *Superior Accomplishment Award* along with a check for $250. The contrast between being a state employee working with the Department of Health Services and SWRCB was amazing. Working for SWRCB made it easy to let go of the rage created by Storm.

I became aware that I was actually becoming a state worker. When I started my career as a typist, I would arrive early, I would not take any breaks, I would take a short lunch hour, and I would leave late. No one bothered to say any thanks. Now, I was coming in late, taking many breaks, taking long lunch hours, working on my personal things while in the office, and leaving early. This was the *Superior Accomplishment* for which I was given an award? It is no wonder the public holds state workers in such low esteem. And it is easy to see why the state finds itself $20 billion dollars in the hole in 2011.

Prior to my run-in with Joe Spano and my transfer, I had moved from the small Sacramento apartment at 14th and Q Streets to a house I purchased in Ione, a very small town about forty miles east of Sacramento. I took a quick stab at publishing another newspaper, starting with just classified and display ads. The computer and printers made it much easier to self-publish. It was a booming success financially. I seemed to be doing everything right from a business standpoint. I had obtained a business license. I had taught myself bookkeeping in prison so I set up books to track my expenses and income, and I sold display ads on a thirteen week contract. I even printed a local telephone directory that was profitable due to the sale of display ads and I delivered a directory to every house in Ione.

I made a few contacts and was appointed to the Planning Commission. I was now commuting to Stockton from Ione instead of from Sacramento. There were quite a few churches in Ione, but I did not attend any so any opportunity for fellowship was lost. I invited my neighbors, a married couple with two kids, to participate with me in the newspaper venture. They were lifelong residents and their connections and reputation would be a sufficient contribution in lieu of an investment of capital. The husband in the family was talented and set out to make news boxes. His wife ran a dance studio in town. It seemed we were on a solid foundation so I converted the paper to a newspaper. I was back to taking photos which I really enjoyed. Along with writing, publishing also served to fill the void I was feeling.

The paper was well received, until the son of a friend of my "partners" was hospitalized. I wrote the story about his injury and that ended the newspaper. That family did not think the story should have been told. I did not see how I could continue while I had partners who would be my censors. They were adamant, so I folded the paper. Although I did not have the expertise to make friends, I had a lot of experience burning bridges behind me. This was yet another example.

I bought my first recreational vehicle, a 1989 Holiday Rambler. It was 32 feet long and I paid $12,000. I rented out the house in lone and moved into a mobile home park in West Sacramento, and lived in the RV. This coincided with my new job in Sacramento, so I no longer had to commute. I soon found a house in West Sacramento on Birmingham Avenue that was completely rebuilt. The reason it was rebuilt was that it had recently been a "crack house" and had been raided by the police who put quite a few gunshot holes in the walls and roof. Two brothers from Indiana bought it, rebuilt it and I offered to buy it before they even put it up for sale. I paid $90,000. It was a three bedroom house with one bathroom.

The couple who sold me the RV lied to me. They lied when they said it did not leak. The first rains in November proved it did. They also lied when they mentioned that their family of six stayed out camping for weeks at a time. It did not dawn on me to ask what they did for water. It had a fifty gallon supply of fresh water. That would mean that the family took showers, flushed the toilet, cooked, did dishes and drank a total of one and a half gallons a day - for six! It is true that you learn something every day. So is the admonition: buyer beware!

I was hooked on the RV lifestyle. It gave me the feeling of freedom. Someone once asked why I bought an RV and I replied that when I hear a knock on the door and notice that it is a bill collector, I just drive off. I planned to buy something bigger and better one day.

Sacramento gets cold and foggy in January and February. The state has two holidays in February. So I started taking "vacations" to Arizona to visit my friend Chip Fyn. I would tie together the holidays, a few weekends and a couple of sick days in order to spend a few weeks in the 75 degree climate that Arizona offers in February. On one such trip, the RV's engine seized up and stopped. I towed the RV on the California - Arizona border and called the Golden 1 Credit Union to have the RV they were financing fixed. They said I was no longer creditworthy. So I abandoned the RV, rented a car and continued my vacation to visit Chip and returned to West Sacramento. Before long I bought a newer, longer and better RV. I filed bankruptcy to get out from under my financial pressures.

No one for whom I worked at SWRCB knew of my past. I never discussed it and never needed to. That tranquility was about to be disrupted. I received a letter from the Department of Justice informing me that I had to register as a sex offender. I would have to go to the local police department once a year, every year for the rest of my life, within five days of my birthday. I would be fingerprinted and photographed. I had always believed that if you did the crime and did the time that was the end of it. I also believed that you had to have notice of the consequences of an act that is criminal and that a law adding an additional punishment was not lawful. This is known as an ex *post facto* law, or a law passed after the fact. Guess I was wrong on both counts.

During the years I was in prison the topic of child molestation dominated the airwaves and media. The public reacted angrily and vented their anger through legislation.

The Jacob Wetterling Crimes Against Children and Sexually Violent Offender Registration Act (the Wetterling Act) is a United States law that requires states to implement a sex offender and crimes against children registry. It was enacted as part of the Federal Violent Crime Control and Law Enforcement Act of 1994.

The Wetterling Act requires states to form registries of offenders convicted of sexually violent offenses or offenses against children, and to form more rigorous registration requirements for sex offenders. Furthermore, states must verify the addresses of sex offenders annually for at least ten years, and those offenders classified as sexually violent predators must verify their addresses quarterly for life. It also required state compliance by September 1997, with a two-year extension for good faith efforts to achieve compliance; non-compliance would result in a 10% reduction of federal block grant funds for criminal justice.

Under this law, states had discretion whether or not to disseminate registration information to the public, but it was not required. Congress amended the Wetterling Act in 1996 with Megan's Law, requiring law enforcement agencies to release information about registered sex offenders that law enforcement deems relevant to protecting the public. Also passed by Congress in 1996 was the Pam Lyncher Sexual Offender Tracking and Identification Act. This act requires the Federal Bureau of Investigation (FBI) to establish a national database of sex offenders to assist local enforcement agencies in tracking sex offenders across state lines.

The Wetterling Act was amended for the final time in 1998 with Section 115 of the General Provisions of Title I of the Departments of Commerce, Justice and State, the Judiciary, and Related Agencies Appropriations Act (CJSA). The CJSA amendment provided for greater discretion among states for procedures used for contacting registered offenders to keep their addresses updated. Also, the CJSA required offenders to register in a state other than their own if they were there for school, and required federal and military employees to register in their state of residence.

Megan's Law is an informal name for laws in the United States requiring law enforcement authorities to make information available to the public regarding registered sex offenders. Individual states decide what information will be made available and how it should be distributed. Commonly disseminated information includes the offender's name, picture, address, incarceration date, and nature of crime. The information is often displayed on free public websites, but can be published in newspapers, distributed in pamphlets, or through various other means.

At the Federal level, Megan's Law is known as the Sexual Offender (Jacob Wetterling) Act of 1994, and requires persons convicted of sex crimes against children to notify local law enforcement of any change of address or employment after release from custody (prison or psychiatric facility). The notification requirement may be imposed for a fixed period of time - usually at least ten years - or permanently.

Some states may enact registration for all sex crimes, even if no minors were involved. It is a felony in most jurisdictions to fail to register or fail to update information.

Megan's Law provides two major information services to the public: sex offender registration and community notification. The details of what is provided as part of sex offender registration and how community notification is handled vary from state to state, and in some states the required registration information and community notification protocols have changed many times since Megan's Law was passed. The Adam Walsh Child Protection and Safety Act supplements Megan's Law with new registration requirements and a three-tier system for classifying sex offenders according to their risk to the community.

The Supreme Court of the United States has upheld sex offender registration laws twice, in two respects. Two challenges to state laws (in Hawaii and Missouri) have succeeded, however.

John Walsh, Adam Walsh's father, is famous today for his TV role on America's Most Wanted which airs on Saturday nights in Sacramento and features wanted criminals. The show had a long run but was cancelled in 2011. He lobbied for additional legislation and succeeded. His six-year old son was abducted and murdered so he has dedicated his life to punish sex offenders.

The Adam Walsh Child Protection and Safety Act became law in 2007. This law implements new uniform requirements for sex offender registration across the states (however, these laws can differ in each state). Highlights of the law are a new national sex offender registry, standardized registration requirements for the states, and new and enhanced criminal offenses related to sex offenders. Since its enactment, the Adam Walsh Act (AWA) has come under intense grassroots scrutiny for its far-reaching scope and breadth. Even before any state adopted AWA, several sex offenders were prosecuted under its regulations. This has resulted in one life sentence for failure to register, due to the offender being homeless and unable to register a physical address.

Because of the act, all 50 states have now passed laws requiring sex offenders (especially child sex offenders) to register with police. Accordingly, the law requires that the offenders report where they take up residence upon leaving prison or being convicted of any crime.

In 2006, California voters passed Proposition 83, which will enforce "lifetime monitoring of convicted sexual predators and the creation of predator free zones." This proposition was challenged the next day in federal court on grounds relating to "ex post facto." The U.S. District Court for the Central District of California, Sacramento, found that Proposition 83 did not apply retroactively.

Patty Wetterling, the mother of Jacob Wetterling and a major proponent of the Jacob Wetterling Act, has openly criticized the evolution of sex offender registration and management laws in the United States since the Jacob Wetterling Act was passed, saying that the laws are often applied to too many offenses and that the severity of the laws often makes it difficult to rehabilitate offenders.

The constitutionality of registration laws has already been tested.

The registration laws have resulted in U.S. Supreme Court rulings. In two cases docketed for argument on November 13, 2003, the sex offender registries of two states, Alaska and Connecticut, would face legal challenge. This was the first instance that the Supreme Court had to examine the implementation of sex offender registries throughout the U.S. The ruling would let the states know how far they could go in informing citizens of perpetrators of sex crimes. The constitutionality of the registries was challenged in two ways:

There was an ex post facto challenge. In Smith v. Doe, 538 U.S. 84 (2003), the Supreme Court upheld Alaska's sex-offender registration statute   . Reasoning that sex offender registration deals with civil laws, not punishment, the Court ruled 6-3 that it is not an unconstitutional ex post facto law. Justices John Paul Stevens, Ruth Bader Ginsburg, and Stephen Breyer dissented.

And there was a Due process challenge. In Connecticut Dept. of Public Safety v. Doe, 538 U.S. 1 (2003), the Court ruled that Connecticut's sex-offender registration statute did not violate the procedural due process of those to whom it applied, although the Court "expresses no opinion as to whether the State's law violates substantive due process principles."

Registration laws have been contested in State Courts.

In Hawaii, in State v. Bani, 36 P.3d 1255 (Haw. 2001), the Hawaii State Supreme Court held that Hawaii's sex offender registration statute violated the due process clause of the Constitution of Hawaii, ruling that it deprived potential registrants "of a protected liberty interest without due process of law." The Court reasoned that the sex offender law authorized "public notification of (the potential registrant's) status as a convicted sex offender without notice, an opportunity to be heard, or any preliminary determination of whether and to what extent (he) actually represents a danger to society."

In the state of Missouri many successful challenges to sex offender registration laws have occurred because of a unique provision in the Missouri Constitution (Article I, Section 13) prohibiting laws "retrospective in their operation."

In Doe v. Phillips, 194 S.W.3d 837 (Mo. banc 2006), the Supreme Court of Missouri held that the Missouri Constitution did not allow the state to place anyone on the registry who had been convicted or pleaded guilty to a registerable offense before the sex offender registration law went into effect on January 1, 1995, and remanded the case for further consideration in light of that holding. On remand, the Jackson County Circuit Court entered an injunction ordering that the applicable individuals be removed from the published sex offender list. Defendant Colonel James Keathley appealed that order to the Missouri Court of Appeals in Kansas City, which affirmed the injunction on April 1, 2008. Keathley filed an appeal with the Supreme Court of Missouri.

In response to these rulings, in 2007, several Missouri State Senators proposed an amendment to the Missouri Constitution which would exempt sex offender registration laws from bar on retrospective civil laws. The proposed amendment passed the State Senate unanimously but was not passed by the Missouri House of Representatives before the end of the 2007 legislative session. The same constitutional amendment was proposed in and passed by the Missouri Senate again in 2008, but also was not passed by the House of Representatives by the end of that year's legislative session. As a result, the decisions of the Missouri courts prohibiting the retrospective application of sex offender laws remained intact.

The Missouri Supreme Court ruled on Keathley's appeal (Doe v. Phillips now styled Doe v. Keathley) on June 16, 2009. The Court held that the Missouri Constitution's provision prohibiting laws retrospective in operation no longer exempts individuals from registration if they are subject to the independent Federal obligation created under the Sexual Offenders Registration and Notification Act (SORNA), 42 U.S.C. 16913. As a result, many offenders who were previously exempt under the Court's 2006 holding in Doe v. Phillips were once again required to register.

On January 12, 2010, Cole County Circuit Judge Richard Callahan ruled that individuals who plead guilty to a sex offense are not required to register under Federal Law and thus are not required to register in Missouri if the date of their plea was prior to the passage of the Missouri registration law.

Missouri also has a number of laws that restrict the activities of persons required to register as sex offenders, several of which have also been challenged as being retrospective in their operation. On February 19, 2008, the Supreme Court of Missouri held that a law prohibiting registered sex offenders from residing within one thousand feet of a school was retrospective in operation as applied to registered sex offenders who had resided at a location within such a distance prior to the enactment of the law. Another exception to the school-residence proximity requirement was handed down by the Court on January 12, 2010 in F.R. v. St. Charles County Sheriff's Department. In this case, F.R. was convicted prior to the enactment of the law and the Court held that, as such, he was not required to abide by the restriction. Consolidated with F.R. was State of Missouri v. Charles A. Raynor, in which the Court found that Raynor was not required to comply with R.S.Mo. 589.426, a law restricting the activities of registered sex offenders on Halloween. It should be noted that, in both F.R. and Raynor, the ruling applies only to the named party.

So the nation and the states clamped down and hard. But even proponents of registration laws think the laws may have gone too far.

Many believe that sex offender registration has become a self-defeating process. In the effort to register as many people as possible for sex-related crimes, the sex offender registry has grown exponentially with too many people for law enforcement to effectively manage. In many states, the sex offender lists even include people arrested for visiting prostitutes, underage teenagers who engaged in consensual sex with each other, and minors who emailed or texted nude photos of themselves to their friends.

After registering for the first time, I wondered if my employer and my co-workers would be given information about my past.

Ray Robinson was released from prison in Susanville a few years before I was released. Even though he had received the Businessman of the Year award prior to his conviction, the folks in Dunsmuir and Mt. Shasta did not welcome him home. He received a number of death threats for molesting the two local young girls and the California Department of Corrections decided to send him to Oregon. I re-connected with him and visited him and his new wife Kathy in Eugene on a few occasions. Ray tried to convince me that he was not guilty but it was clear to me he was in denial. Where I took the position that I did not want anyone to know about my crime and my past, he wanted everyone to know about his. But he wanted to let them know he was not guilty. I knew better. And so did he.

Ray had an interest in railroading as a hobby. He became active and tried to get a small town in the suburbs of Eugene to build a commuter railroad. He established lots of connections with politicians and almost succeeded in getting the railroad built but an executive with Nike stopped him in his tracks when he threatened Ray with public humiliation. He said he would make sure the newspapers ran an article pointing out that he was a child molester. Ray dropped his plans for the commuter train. He later moved to Deadwood, near the Oregon coast and proceeded to build his own hobby railroad. Over the years as his close friends found out about his past they abandoned him. But Ray had a way of obtaining new friends. He used his park-like property and railroad as a lure.

About six months before I was released from prison I contacted the Salvation Army in an effort to locate my brother Nick. They have excellent resources to find "lost" people. It had been more than thirty years since I last saw Nick. Lo and behold they found him. He wrote to me and told me he had been working for Hughes Aircraft as an engineer but was on disability and would not be returning to work.

He almost did not respond to the Salvation Army inquiry about me. He remembered my middle name as Michael and I was using Anthony. When a Catholic is confirmed at about eight years of age - supposedly confirming their vows they made as an infant when baptized - they select a middle name. A nun at *St. Francis Orphan Asylum* had a list of names and when she asked what name I wanted I said Anthony. She said that name is already taken and assigned the middle name Michael to me. When I finally reached the age of reason I changed my middle name to Anthony because I wanted my initials to read S.A.M.

Nick lived north of San Luis Obispo near the coast of California. I planned to visit him when I was released. But it took about a year before I could afford the trip. He lived on forty acres in a house he built by himself. Actually, the house portion consisted of a bathroom, a small bedroom, and a kitchen-living room combination all less than 350 square feet. The rest of the structure - 2,000 square feet - was like a garage or warehouse.

I was eager to know if I had any nieces or nephews. Nick had been married and divorced three times but had no kids. He was quick to point out that the problem was the women he picked out. "It was their fault we got divorced." I tried to suggest that we both might have had problems establishing relationships but he was not about to listen. Something caused him to marry three times and for me to remain a bachelor.

Nick was into guns and rifles. When I finally visited him he gave me a tour of his arsenal. He had three machines he used to load his own ammunition. He told me he had more than one hundred pistols and rifles. He confided in me that the day would come when he would be part of a militia as he did not like which way the country was headed. I was not about to ask how he would be able to shoot more than one gun or rifle at a time, but did not.

Nick and I talked about Dad, and about the orphanages. He still had a hatred for Sister Francis, but he never was able to express why. He told me that some orphans were part of a psychological experiment dealing with dominant and submissive siblings. He said the nuns were instructed on how to treat siblings and to report the results. Perhaps that is why we were never close.

Nick told me he was never beaten with the green stick but knew I was. Maybe he was the submissive one and I was the dominant sibling and the green stick was used to level the playing field. He surmised that some of my beatings may have been part of the experiment. As he was two years older than me, his memory helped me re-construct parts of my childhood. One thing we both learned after a few get-togethers: we did not seem to like each other. We were brothers in name only.

Even though he lived almost four hundred miles away, I had visited him three times and wanted to have him visit me. He had lots of excuses why he could not: no gas money, no reliable car, didn't want to leave his place unguarded. I offered to fill his tank up, or to buy round trip bus or train tickets.

It became clear he had a reason not to visit but he was not letting me in on it. One day I called him and told him I bought a computer for him. His response: when are you going to bring it down? I said you have to come up to get it. He did. He spent overnight and was in a hurry to return. I guess the no gas or unreliable excuses were overcome because he was getting something for nothing.

On my last visit to his home we were having a discussion about the past we shared. Out of the blue he asked: Do you know why I am still pissed off at you? I was startled, shocked, and curious so I replied. "No. Why?" He proceeded to tell me that after our dad died I chose to hang around with my friends and did not acknowledge him as the head of the family. I was caught off guard and got a bit pissed off myself. I could not believe that he was holding against me something I didn't do when I was eleven years old. He had been mad at me for more than forty years and I did not know the reason.

But that revelation convinced me there was no way we had a future. I got up without saying another word and even though it was late in the evening I got into my RV and headed north.

He eventually moved to Idaho and the only way I knew that was when I googled his name and saw that he renewed his radio operator's license with the FCC which published a list on the internet.

So it was clear to me that I had relationship problems. No friends, no relatives anymore, no girl friend, only co-workers. The West Sacramento police did not notify my employer or my co-workers of my registration requirements. They did not notify my neighbors either.

Nevertheless I did generate a few relationships. I managed to date two different ladies who worked at the SWRCB during the same period. Neither knew I was dating the other. I took each of them to visit Ray and Kathy in Oregon where we camped out. One was into giving and getting oral sex. Fortunately she was not into intercourse. I had a medical problem that was about to surface that stopped me from this activity. The other lady was quick to point out that her days of having sex had expired. Neither relationship bloomed.

As the twentieth century was nearing its end, I found myself as lost and confused as I had been for more than half the century. I had both a house and an RV. There was no one to invite into my home. There was no one to accompany me in my RV when I took a trip. I could count my friends on one hand and had fingers left over. Chip Fyn lived in Arizona and Ray Robinson lived in Oregon. Dorian Wright lived in Mount Aukum, California. But a change was in the air.

In the mid-90s Sacramento was gaining a large number of Russian immigrants. With the fall of the Soviet Union in 1991 and the subsequent transition to free market economy by means of shock programs came hyperinflation and a series of political and economic crises of the 1990s, culminating in the financial crash of 1998. By mid-1993 more than 39% of Russians were living in poverty, a sharp increase compared to 1.5% of the late Soviet era. This instability and bleak outcome prompted a large new wave of both political and economic emigration from Russia, and one of the major targets became the United States, which was experiencing an unprecedented stock market boom in 1995-2001.

The major group of post-Soviet immigrants was the political refugees, persons who claim persecution or reasonable fear of persecution in Russia. In 1990, 50,716 citizens of the former USSR were granted political refugee status by the United States. There were 38,661 in 1991, 61,298 in 1992, 48,627 in 1993, 43,470 in 1994, and 35,716 in 1995, with the trend steadily dropping to as low as 1,394 refugees accepted in 2003.

For the first time in history, Russians became a notable part of illegal immigration to the United States, the most common example being mail-order brides. Russian women would advertise themselves in international marriage agency with the express purpose to marry Americans to become citizens. Nearly half of all mail-order brides to come to the United States in 1996 originated from Russia and Ukraine Together with illegal immigration, the influence of the Russian Mafia became prominent in the United States.

A notable part of the 1991-2001 immigration wave consisted of scientists and engineers. Faced with extremely poor job market at home coupled with the government unwilling to index fixed salaries according to inflation or even to make salary payments on time, they left to pursue their careers abroad. This coincided with the surge of the hi-tech industry in the United States, creating a strong brain drain effect. According to the National Science Foundation, there were 20,000 Russian scientists working in the United States in 2003, and the Russian software engineers were responsible for 30% of Microsoft products in 2002.

The Soviet Union was a sports empire, and many prominent Russian sportspeople found great acclaim and rewards for their skills in the United States. Examples are Maria Sharapova, Alexander Ovechkin, Alexandre Volchkov, and Andrei Kirilenko. Nastia Liukin was born in Moscow, but came to America with her parents as a young child, and developed into a champion gymnast in the U.S.

The U.S. communities with the most residents born in Russia in the mid-90s included West Sacramento with 4.3% and East Yolo with 4.3%. North Highlands had 1.5%. I noticed a lot of these immigrants as I shopped in the West Sacramento Raley's, the local grocery store.

When I was in Biloxi, Mississippi, in 1960, I had a yearning to learn the Russian language. I enrolled in a class on-base but after a few weeks I learned I was transferring to California. That was the end of the class and my interest in the language was put on hold.

Now Russians were opening stores and I found a fruit and vegetable store that posted the names of its products in both English and Russian. This was an opportunity for me to resume learning the language. I had always enjoyed reading Russian literature so I had a natural liking for Russian history and their people. I did not go for the propaganda the US government had been cranking out against Russians since World War II. I had so many reasons not to trust authority and not trusting our government was also justified for so many reasons.

One Saturday morning as I was going from aisle to aisle in a small store in West Sacramento trying to read the

Russian words, I decided to ask a customer if she knew anyone who could teach me the Russian language.

"Excuse me ma'am, do you know anyone who would be willing to teach me Russian," I asked rather quickly. "KOLAAHHH,!" She shouted. I was alarmed. What did she mean? What did I say that prompted this reaction?

From another aisle came a young, good-looking, silver-haired fellow who approached me. The lady said something to him in the Russian language. He looked at me so I repeated my question. He nodded his head. It appeared that he understood what I was asking. Somehow we exchanged written addresses and he agreed to meet me at 7:30 pm on the following Monday to discuss my pursuit of the Russian language.

I showed up on Monday evening at their apartment at 7:30. It was near Auburn and Watt in North Highlands. I knocked on the door a few times before I was convinced there was no one home. I thought to myself: these Russians were rude, standing me up.

I have never locked my keys in my car in my life, but God apparently had me do it this time. I called Triple A to come and unlock my car. It took about forty minutes before they showed up. As the tow truck came up the street, I noticed it was followed by a small, older car that was loading with a family of six. Sure enough, Nick and Marina Klimov were in the front. They had been at my home in West Sacramento. They probably wondered why I wasn't there. Maybe they thought I was a rude American who stood them up.

I soon learned they did not speak much English. I also realized that it was more important for them to learn English than it was for me to learn Russian. And finally I learned that "Kola" was the affectionate or diminutive form for Nicolay.

Chapter Ten
Adopted by Immigrants - 1998

As I write this today, January 3, 2011, Timothy was born to Nick and Marina's daughter Yelena and her husband Stanislav. This is their third grandchild. Timothy has an older sister Nellie, and an even older brother Benjamin. I have now known the Klimov family for a dozen years. And knowing them has been the most wonderful gift of my seventy years.

After the locked car incident and the confusion on who was to meet with whom where, I found myself spending lots of time at the Klimov apartment. Nick and Marina had four children: Yelena, Sergey, Slava and Valeriy. They ranged in age from twelve to six. All were going to school full time and were learning English quickly. They had been in America for about one year.

Nick had decided to emigrate from Russia due to religious persecution. As refugees they were given a little financial help from the government. In short order Nick and Marina leaped over the language barrier and he found a job delivering the Sacramento Bee newspaper. To say the family was tight-knit would be an understatement. Nick had his entire family stuffed in a small foreign car at 3 am every morning to deliver newspapers before delivering his wife and children to school.

Over time, I had the privilege to meet many of their friends and noted quickly that Russians had the same quality and character that early Americans had, but that modern Americans have lost long ago: integrity, ingenuity and the desire to work hard. And I was to find out very soon that their hearts were loaded with love.

I found myself visiting with them most evenings after super and spending four or five hours, helping them with their English assignments. I knew they did not have much spending money so on weekends or holidays I would invite them to see sites such as the redwoods on the Northern California coast or Yosemite National Park. I was not learning much Russian but one of the first words I did learn was "pah-dar-key" which means gifts. As each of the Klimovs had their birthday, I bought a present or two and there was a party. When Christmas came, it filled my heart to be in a position to buy presents for all of them. Videos were made of these happy times and are sure to be cherished by them as they grow older.

Soon we mutually adopted each other. The reason this time has been the best time of my life is that they made me feel so much a part of their family. I never had a family, so the experience was both joyful and fearful. I don't recall any friends every saying they loved me before. First Valeriy said it. Then Marina did. I started to believe it because of the way they all treated me. Actions do speak louder than words. At every meal and especially at picnics which included their extended family members (where sometimes as many as twenty persons were present) Marina always prepared a plate for me first. I was not used to such attention, but it was heartwarming. I had a lot to learn about being loved and how to love.

The word love was absent even in the relationships I had with Janice Kling and Judy Nelson, the former I was engaged to for forty-eight hours, and the latter I lived with for almost two years. Maybe I was not the lovable kind. But the Klimov family oozed with love for each other. I never met such a family. Nick and Marina would not think of going anywhere without including every member of their family. And one place they went together often was to church.

They were Baptist and attended a small church in West Sacramento. They invited me and because it was such a pleasure to be in their company I accepted and going to church with them became a regular Sunday activity.

In Folsom prison even when I recognized that I could not make it without divine help, I did not have a serious interest in attending church. Although prior to meeting the Klimov family, I did make a few attempts. When I got out of prison I sought out the Salvation Army in Sacramento because they found my brother. So I did some volunteer work for them. I seized on the opportunity to write a computer program that enabled The Salvation Army to track the families who were given a turkey and other food for the Thanksgiving and Christmas holidays. Some families gave two or three addresses so they could get more food. My program was intended to discover and prevent this fraud.

I also attended the Salvation Army church services for four consecutive Sundays. I sat in the back pew and must have looked out of place with my long hair and beard. The preacher noticed and mentioned to the congregation that they should make newcomers to their service feel welcomed. He repeated this suggestion on each of my visits, but none of the parishioners even bothered to say hello to me. So I stopped attending. No fellowship was to be had for me in that army.

Some time later I visited a bishop in the Mormon Church in West Sacramento to see if I could get some spiritual fulfillment there. When I mentioned my past he was quick to let me know I would not be welcomed because The Latter Day Saints included many families with children. I did not know if the reason was because I was in prison or because of why I was in prison. I suspected the latter. I accepted his rejection without comment. I was getting used to the reaction people had to child molesters. Perhaps the Book of Mormon differs from the Bible? Although I had not read the Book of Mormon, I wondered if it mentioned that Jesus died for everyone's sins and that the second greatest commandment requires that we love one another.

Jehovah's Witnesses visited my home months after that rejection so I took them up on their invitation to attend their services. I started reading their brochures and publications such as The Watchtower and actually became spiritually interested, perhaps because their booklets were well-written. One of the elders befriended me and brought to my attention that their church had a need for computer services so I was happy to provide my programming skills. I spent more than one year attending their services. I even attended one of their annual, national conferences which were held in the Cow Palace in San Francisco where many thousands attended.

One day out of the blue one church member checked the Megan's Law database which tracks all registered sex offenders. She quickly divided the parishioners into those who immediately hated me and those that didn't by revealing what she found in the database. The elder and other church leaders started citing biblical verse to try to dissuade the haters but to no avail. My reaction was different than when I was told I was a dime a dozen. I actually thought of going into their Sunday service with a tank of propane and a lighter to try to convince them that I was not sick. But instead I just stopped attending their service. The elder visited my home to try to convince me to return but instead I convinced him I had a history of not going where I was not welcomed. I felt safe in continuing my lifelong habit to just run away.

I needed to understand why and how a religious organization could be so divided on the subject of child molestation. I spent many hours researching their official position from sources including their monthly magazine The Watchtower, as well as from their critics, and summarize it in the following paragraphs.

The Jehovah's Witness organization has not been immune to molesters within their congregations. This may have been what prompted the member of the local congregation to host her witch hunt. The leadership of Jehovah's Witnesses has a disciplinary system that applies to all congregation members who commit child abuse, rather than only to members in positions of authority. Their policy states that child sex victims be immediately protected from further abuse, and that abusers be prevented from finding additional victims. If allegations of child abuse are deemed to have a sound basis, an internal judicial committee is formed, and the accused individual is relieved of any positions of responsibility in the congregation.

Anyone found to have sexually molested a child and failing to demonstrate repentance is to be disfellowshipped from the congregation. If an accused individual denies wrongdoing, but later due to evidence presented in a court of law, it is proven that he or she was involved in child abuse, the individual is disfellowshipped.

Because I was not yet a member, I did not have to suffer the disgrace of being disfellowshipped.

I learned this from the elder who befriended me and who attempted to quell the disturbance of his flock. An abuser who is judged repentant by a committee of elders is given a public reproof. It is announced to the congregation that the named individual has been reproved, though the nature of their crime is not stated. Some time later, a talk is given to the congregation, discussing the type of sin and the need to be on guard against it; the reproved individual is not named in connection with this talk.

For a considerable period of time, a reproved individual is not permitted to participate in meetings by commenting in group discussions or making presentations from the platform. They are immediately debarred from serving in any appointed position in the congregation, usually for life.

In a fax sent by Jehovah's Witnesses' Office of Public Information to the producers of the BBC's Panorama television program, it stated that at least twenty years must have passed before an individual who committed an act of child sex abuse could even be considered for appointment to a responsible position in the congregation, if ever.

My crime had occurred twenty years earlier.

Former child molesters, including those who molested children before becoming Jehovah's Witnesses, those eventually reinstated into the congregation after being disfellowshipped, and those who were deemed repentant, are subject to a number of restrictions, which normally remain in place permanently.

A 1997 Watchtower article stated: "For the protection of our children, a man known to have been a child molester does not qualify for a responsible position in the congregation. Moreover, he cannot be a pioneer or serve in any other special, full-time service. Former sex offenders may not offer public prayers, read paragraphs during congregation studies, or be given even minor responsibilities in the congregation, such as handling microphones or distributing literature in the Kingdom Hall, and the person's home may not usually be used for congregation meetings."

Apparently the Jehovah Witnesses worship differently or maybe they translate God's intentions differently.

Wikipedia notes that according to the Watch Tower Society spokesman, J. R. Brown, "sex offenders are not permitted to participate in the congregation's house-to-house preaching, unless accompanied by a responsible adult." Commenting on the effect of these restrictions, Jehovah's Witnesses' legal representative, Mario Moreno, stated that these restrictions alert members that the individual "lacks spiritual maturity."

If a former child abuser moves to another congregation, elders from the previous congregation must send a letter to the body of elders in the new congregation, outlining the offender's background and whether the abuser is still under the restricted privileges. Other members of the new congregation are not formally made aware of the abuser's past.

In August, 2001 victims of abuse within the Jehovah's Witnesses congregation used the legal system to get justice. They did so because the society required it members to turn inward with any problems, to pray, and to ignore the mandatory requirement to bring the abuse to the attention of the police.

The Jehovah's Witness victims created a webpage - *Silentlambs.org* - to benefit victims of abuse, and the following information on their home page features a report of a lawsuit.

"Victims of child molestation have served a lawsuit against the Watchtower Bible and Tract Society, the corporate entity that controls the organization of Jehovah's Witnesses. The law firm of Reinhardt and Anderson, in Saint Paul, Minnesota, is filing the first of several lawsuits in behalf of victims who have been injured by the Watchtower's policy of ignoring reported child sexual abuse.

The organization of Jehovah's Witnesses is a closed society that requires its members to turn inward to the organization with any problems, rather than seek outside help. This practice conflicts with laws requiring the reporting of suspected child abuse. Victims' attorney Jeff Anderson states: 'Child sexual abuse is not tolerated anywhere else. With the onset of the laws protecting children such as neighborhood notification laws and mandatory reporting statutes, the days when child molesters enjoyed a cloak of silence are past, except within the organization of Jehovah's Witnesses. This church seems to think they are above the law and the rules do not apply to them. This case is simply about making Jehovah's Witnesses understand they have the same rules as everyone else when it comes to protecting our children.'

Jehovah's Witnesses are accused of creating an organizational policy that, in the opinion of victims, has shielded child molesters, while continuing to harm victims. It is alleged that when a victim comes to the church elders to report child sexual abuse by a church member, Watchtower has instructed the elders to require the victim to present proof of the sexual abuse before the victim is to be believed. According to church policy, the proof can include two eyewitnesses to each act of abuse. Failure to present such proof can result in the victim being ostracized and shunned by elders and the congregation for false accusations against a member.

Anderson states: 'The very nature of child sexual abuse is that it rarely happens in the presence of others. Child victims of sexual abuse are especially traumatized as the perpetrators often threaten them into silence. Jehovah's Witnesses policy is no different. The victims do what they are supposed to do, go to the church, and the church turns against them.' Victims claim that elders often do nothing to prevent known child molesters from having contact with children, including requiring all church members to solicit Watchtower literature on the doorsteps of unsuspecting residents.

The first lawsuit will be filed in Nashua, N. H., where Jehovah's Witness church member, Paul Berry is alleged to have repeatedly sexually molested his stepdaughter and his daughter, starting when they were three years old. When the girls' mother went to the church elders with her suspicions of abuse, the elders told her she should be a better wife, and to pray more about the situation, ignoring New Hampshire's mandatory child abuse reporting statute. The abuse continued and Berry was ultimately criminally convicted for the abuse of his stepdaughter and was sentenced to 56 years in prison. The same church elders, who initially received the mother's reports of abuse several years earlier, spoke to the judge at Berry's sentencing hearing and maintained their belief in his innocence."

The stories of many victims can be found at www. silentlambs.org which is run by the non-profit organization Silentlambs, Inc., founded by a former Jehovah's Witnesses elder, William H. Bowen of Calvert City, Kentucky. He acknowledged that the organization offers resources, healing and closure to victims of child molestation. Nevertheless in referring to his letter of resignation dated December 31, 2000, to the Watchtower, Bowen states, "I felt compelled to resign as pastor of my local congregation in protest of internal policies that shield sex offenders and hurt children. When the church promotes child molesters to positions of leadership and requires them to call at the homes of the unknowing public that is bad policy."

The religion that takes first prize for shielding child molesters is the Catholic Church. Their history of protecting pedophiles and ignoring abuse victims is well documented. On May 18, 2011, the US Conference of Bishops in a $2,000,000 study reported that only 4 percent of the 65,000 instances of priests abusing children involved pedophiles.

They used victims under the age of ten to determine if a priest was a pedophile. (Critics argued that the age should have been from 10 to 16, not under 10) That study also claims the Catholic requirement of priests not being permitted to take wives - celibacy - did not contribute to the large number of molestations. They noted in their report that other denominations that require celibacy and abstinence from sex agreed with their findings. Neither did homosexuality the report claimed, although most of the victims cited in the study were boys. The study concluded that the reason for the molestations were the sexual revolution of the sixties. Victims' advocates claimed the report was more of the same lies that the church has been hiding behind even though they have paid out more than $3 billion dollars as a result of litigation.

So my attending the Baptist service with the Klimov family was not based on my spiritual needs, although it turned out that I did find spiritual solace. It was, however, a place where I could personally commune with my God and I could be with people who loved me. They were living the biblical commandment found at 1 John 3:23 "And this is His commandment, that we should believe on the name of His Son Jesus Christ, and love one another,"

But a question haunted me: what would the Klimov family do if and when they learned of my past?

It has been difficult making friends since my release from prison, even though my crime made it very easy to lose virtually all of the "friends" I had prior to my arrest. Although I did establish tentative relationships with co-workers and that brought satisfaction to my existence and employment, my personal friends outside of the Klimov circle could be counted on one hand with fingers left over.

It is necessary to restate a summary of my friendships other than with the Klimov family. First would be Dorian Wright from Mount Aukum, California, then Ray Robinson from Deadwood, Oregon, and finally Chip Fyn from Apache Junction, Arizona. How many other people can summarize their friends on one hand with fingers left over at the age of sixty-nine?

All three were ex-felons. Dorian got busted when we were in our first year of law school for building a false fuel tank that was used to bring cocaine into the US from

Mexico. He understood a little of what I faced coming out of prison and was a great help in providing me with employment in KK enterprises, his auto body business when I was released.

Ray Robinson had been convicted of molesting two young girls in Mount Shasta in the early eighties and had served a little less time than I had. Because of death threats from Dunsmuir and Mount Shasta residents prior to his being released, he was allowed to parole to Oregon where he attended a program that was designed to prevent his re-offending, or at least attempt to provide him with psychological tools and tips to prevent him from creating more victims. He had bought a beautiful piece of paradise near Deadwood, Oregon, and pursued a life-long dream of building a hobby railroad. Ray was an expert at manipulating people to do his will so he had a lot of so-called volunteers help with the task of re-building a house and turning a 73 year old cow farm and dumpsite into a wildlife preserve for his railroad. When finished, he invited strangers he befriended to spend a few days camping out and riding the railroad. He encouraged them to bring their children. Ray claimed he told everyone of his past criminal history, but he still maintained that he was not guilty. He felt comfortable being in denial.

Chip Fyn had evolved from carving life-size wooden statues in Pollock Pines into using a computer to draw and color every aircraft ever designed, and sell them on DVDs worldwide. He calls Arizona his home and lives with Annie a few years his senior in an RV. One of Chip's sons was arrested before he was twenty-one years old and spent almost twenty years in an Arizona prison for child molestation. Chip's felony was using jumper cables and connecting them from PG&Es electric wires to provide power to enable him to grow marijuana plants inside a gutted travel trailer in which the bottom was removed.

So my list of friends might qualify for the shortest list in the record books, but now it appeared that I had actually made friends whom I could treasure, and from whom I could learn a lot. These friends would also be my family. I was quickly becoming a Klimov and it felt so good.

Periodically, I would visit Ray and his wonderful wife Kathy. Kathy had been a victim of child molestation herself. I could not understand why she would marry someone she knew had been convicted of child molestation. She also had six children. I had met her former husband and their kids - all grown up - and we all had a cordial relationship during my visits when any of them were at the Deadwood property. I even brought the Klimovs to campout on Ray and Kathy's property for a few days one summer.

I generally visited Chip and Annie in February, In Arizona, when I took vacations.

So as the century was about to turn, I enjoyed the job I had at the State Water Resources Control Board and I especially enjoyed my newfound family. Nick was so amazing. Whenever he detected I had a problem or a special need, he rushed in to solve it or to fill it. On a few occasions I had automobile problems and he dropped whatever he was doing to fix them. Although the house I bought was three bedroom with one bath, when I decided I wanted to expand it by enlarging one bedroom, adding another, and adding a second bathroom, he did all the work. He never asked for a cent. He was so talented. I often laugh at how he would get me out of his hair by suggesting I go into town to get an insignificant tool, or whatever, and when I returned he had finished what he was working on. I realized he did not really need the tool, so my tool collection grew.

Marina was equally amazing. She knew how to run a household, how to host parties, picnics and dinners, and especially how to raise her children. She was a true love machine. Hers were the most obedient kids I had ever encountered. I had a problem with the Russian language in that I would interpret their lively discussions with each other as arguments or fights. But I was wrong. Russians use their voices like Italians use their hands. When I would think the kids were being disrespectful to Marina by speaking loudly, I would attempt to discipline them by demanding they obey her. But they playfully laughed off my interruptions of their discussions. They were really so loving toward each other. I had a lot to learn about their culture and about their language.

I finally looked at my large, empty house and suggested the Klimovs move in. Although this was a great idea in that it would give them an opportunity to save money for their own home one day, it was a great big mistake on my part because I did not know how to behave like a member of a family. I guess I had a touch of manipulation in me.

Russians do something so few Americans do. They remove their shoes before entering their homes. This makes so much sense. Why drag in dirt and dispense airborne diseases and discolor the carpeting? So after moving into my house, there would always be a half dozen pairs of shoes outside my front door.

I have generally been super careful not to get injured, unless on purpose, especially since I have diabetes and injuries take a very long time to heal. On one or more occasions I had problems navigating past the shoes upon entering or leaving my house. I would take the time to line the shoes up, one row to the right and one row to the left of the front door. I did not want to twist an ankle or worse. I tried to explain this to the kids, but I was not successful in communicating my concern of getting injured. Every time I came home, the shoes would be scattered in front of the door.

I also have a temper and at times cannot find my ability to control it. One day I actually did twist my ankle and went into a rage. I ranted and raved, threw the shoes into the flower beds, and stormed off into my room. I refused to talk to any of the Klimovs. Nick tried desperately to resolve the problem. I remained adamant with my silence.

During the course of our one-way discussion, finally out of frustration, Nick announced that moving in was the stupidest thing he had ever done. When I returned from work they were all gone. They moved. I suddenly felt my heart crack. What had I done? There is a saying that "you only hurt the ones you love." Now I knew what this meant. Once again, I was all alone. I had walked away from so many confrontations. This was the first time I experienced the loss of a relationship from the losing end.

I don't actually recall how we got back together. But we did. I was relieved. I had never learned to say I am sorry, even when I knew I was wrong. But I would have to learn. I would have to pay close attention to my behavior in the future. I did love the Klimovs. I did not know how to show it. All my life I had been buying friends. This family was not for sale. They were genuine. I was beginning to learn what they already knew so well: how a family worked.

Nick had been going to American River College where he was getting schooled in computers. He finally graduated with two degrees, but employment in that field became next to impossible. His graduation coincided with the collapse of the dot com bubble and the massive exportation of IT jobs to India and other foreign countries.

The SWRCB did hire interns, and our Clean Water Program was about to interview college students for open positions. I encouraged Nick to apply and he did and was hired.

Marina had two sisters in the Sacramento area, Alla and Inna. Inna had previously emigrated with their families and had been working at Raleys for a few years, so Marina applied for a job and was hired by Raleys.

Yelena and the boys were flying through high school. They did not participate in things like sports or other extra curricula activities. They had their church activities to keep them busy. They learned the English language very quickly. I was especially impressed with Valeriy, the youngest boy. He was so self-disciplined. He would have his homework finished before he arrived at his home.

I had an opportunity to often bring one or more of them home from school. They never rode the school bus. Mom wouldn't allow it. She was too much in charge of their lives and always concerned for their safety. At times on the way home we would stop at a fast food place like Carl's Jr. I enjoyed my role as their grandfather, as I was a few decades older than Marina and Nick. I playfully referred to Marina as Mom, and Nick as Papa. I am not sure I have a logical explanation for this. It felt and sounded good as I never remembered calling anyone mom or papa.

I was still helping them at times with their schoolwork. Marina and Nick were now well in command of enough English to get by with their homework and needed very little help. Slava and Sergey didn't need too much help. Valeriy needed none. Yet I would make myself available should any of them need any help. I was happy to be in the position to be helpful.

Invariably as I was about to leave their home for mine at eleven in the evening, Yelena would ask softly: "Steve, could you help me"? "When is it due" I would ask, even though I knew the answer. "Tomorrow" she sheepishly smiled. I would quickly ascertain what needed to be done, and realizing there was not enough time to help by teaching her how to write, I would write the paper myself and at the same time give an overview explanation of what I was writing.

Nick was one of seventeen children in his family. One of his sisters, Luba, and her husband Ivan, along with their five children, were also living in the Sacramento area. As they were both going to college they chose to live in an apartment.

Marina was one of eighteen children in her family. I went with Nick and Marina to the airport to welcome to the US, her sister Alla, her husband Sergey and their three children. The Soviet Union lost so many of its males during World War II; I think the government encouraged large families.

I reaped the benefits of such a large, extended family. When any number of them got together, there was always frequent and pleasurable laughter and sheer joy.

Whenever I had a problem, at the mere mention of it, Nick sprang into action and solved it for me. I recall having a Ford van and there was a water leak in a small radiator wedged in the back of the glove compartment. It was part of the heating system. Ford wanted to charge me $375 to fix it and it would take three days. Nick fixed it at no charge within six hours.

When I bought my house in West Sacramento there was a moratorium on room additions because the section of town I lived in was the only area still on septic tanks. The health department said the ground was too contaminated and the city was going to hook everyone up to sewers in the near future. Noting that I wanted to enlarge my home, Nick did most of the work. His adding a bathroom, enlarging one bedroom, and adding another bedroom tripled the value of my house. I could not imagine ever being able to repay him.

One time the septic tank stopped working. Nick hand-dug most of my backyard to determine the reason it was not working and proceeded to fix it.

I could not ask for a better friend. He was so intelligent and talented. Nick would give anyone the shirt off his back, whether you needed a shirt or not.

As the year 2000 was on the horizon, one task I had at the SWRCB was to make sure all the computer programs were Y2K compliant. Fortunately for me, Nick was working as an intern for a different department on the floor below mine and it was comforting to know that I could run any problem I encountered by him for a solution.

The Y2K scare had most businesses including governments purchasing new equipment and software that was Y2K compliant. This was the beginning of the dot com bust as most businesses also started to hire foreign labor brought over on work visas. Businesses continued to outsource most IT jobs. This essentially dried up employment in the IT field. Nick had obtained two college degrees just in time to find out no one was hiring.

Marina was such a dedicated mother. She was the proverbial mother hen who took her job of protecting her brood very seriously. She even extended her care to me. Not a day would go by when she would not telephone to make sure I was ok. She included me in on all of her family's activities. It was such a warm feeling to be wanted, to be cared for, and to be loved. In my opinion, she could easily be nominated for Mother of the Century and win.

I had only been hospitalized or needed medical attention seven times in my entire life. I could barely recall having my tonsils removed. I remember getting an ice cream to sooth my throat while I recovered. I also remember having been circumcised. Actually, I only remember my swollen penis while examining the black stitches that held my foreskin in place.

I already mentioned as a teenage runaway getting smacked behind my left ear trying to defend my timid friend from some idiots. This was when I went on my own to a hospital and faked fainting in order to get some attention and moved to the front of the line.

In 1969 while playing football at American River College, I tore the lateral meniscus in my left knee and spent a month getting surgery and rehabilitation at the hospital owned by Southern Pacific Railroad.

It wasn't until I faked slipping on the screws in 1994 that I was to visit another hospital. I lived in Ione, about forty miles from Stockton, where I worked for the Office of Drinking Water. Small rural towns did not have good medical care. Instead of seeing a doctor I saw a pseudo-medicine man at a clinic in Plymouth a few miles away. He apparently gave me pills which I reacted to and which ultimately hospitalized me. He told me to drive to the hospital in Jackson about twenty miles away to get an x-ray for my office "slip and fall". Before I got to the hospital my body, and especially my face, was burning so much that I stopped at a gas station and dipped a rag into the container used to wash windows and washed my face to cool it off.

The doctor-wannabe gave me Amoxicillin which is used to treat certain infections caused by bacteria, such as pneumonia; bronchitis; gonorrhea; and infections of the ears, nose, throat, urinary tract, and skin.   It is also used in combination with other medications to eliminate H. pylori, a bacterium that causes ulcers. Amoxicillin is in a class of medications called penicillin-like antibiotics. It works by stopping the growth of bacteria. Antibiotics will not work for colds, flu, and other viral infections. Why did this quack give me this medication? I do not know but had I known then what I know now I would have sued him. My medical complaint was that I was dizzy from a fall.

When I arrived at the hospital I was admitted immediately. In a day or two it was determined that I had a rare reaction to amoxicillin known as Stevens-Johnson

Syndrome (SJS). All my skin was shedding. The nurses were changing my sheets four times a day. They had referred to me as the snake. I had a severe reaction to amoxicillin. I did not know it at the time but it could have been fatal. God was once again watching over me. Perhaps the reaction was punishment for my faking an injury.

There were two more times I was hospitalized.

It was approaching Christmas and I was planning to put a tree up and decorate it. I had moved a sofa from the living room toward the dining room. In the dining room I had a fancy table that was oval shaped and made of three-quarter inch thick, grey glass. It rested on four black, metal legs which were attached to each other as a single unit.

As I shoved the sofa I did not see that it moved the legs, but the glass top stopped moving when it reached the wall. The legs kept moving. This left the glass top teetering on the leg structure.

In a little while my cell phone rang. As I picked it up from the dining room table and recognized the voice of Marina Klimov, I turned around and started to rest my butt on the edge of the table. The glass top cracked...then broke. I went to the ground. The cell phone dropped. As I went down the broken glass dug into my back at waist level. I kept falling. The cut into my back got bigger. Sitting on the floor, I reached behind me and I grasped what felt like a wet banana hanging off my back. It was about six inches long and about an inch thick. The top of the chunk of meat and skin was still attached to my body. It tapered to a point where the busted glass entered my skin.

Blood was everywhere. I could not find my phone which flew out of my hand. I got up and walked across the street to my neighbors. With a bloody hand I banged on their door. Fortunately it was Saturday and they were home. "Call 911", I asked. I didn't need to explain as I was so bloody and they later told me I was as white as a ghost. I was losing a lot of blood by the time an ambulance arrived. The last thing I heard was an EMT state loudly: "He is losing blood pressure!"

I do not recall the ride to the hospital, but when I woke up there were about twenty doctors, interns and nurses gathered around. They were listening to a doctor discuss my injury. I soon focused on one person in the crowd. It was Nick.

Apparently he raced over after I dropped the phone. He lived about twelve miles from me. He found out from my neighbor what had happened. He then raced to the hospital.

Along with my neighbor, Nick cleaned the kitchen, removed the broken glass table, and later delivered a beautiful, round, wooden oak table.

I never learned how he got into that hospital among all those medical folks, but over the years it still brings a smile to my face when I recall it.

It took a few days to begin to recover from the 58 stitches. Nick and Marina brought the entire family to visit. Later when I was released, they devoted their time and energy to getting me home and were in constant attendance until I was able to take care of myself. What would I have done without the Klimovs, without my family?

The most recent hospital visit came when I learned I had prostate cancer in 1999. This is a type of cancer that can sometimes be ignored because it is slow growing. Most males will get prostate cancer but are likely to die of something else first. But prostate cancer can be a threat if it is growing fast and spreading. Mine was.

I was told by my doctor to go to Sutter Medical Center in Sacramento which owns a great reputation for dealing successfully with various cancers. The first doctor was so eager to perform surgery he established a date and made an appointment before our discussion concluded. When I declined and informed him I wanted to see what other options were available, he quickly told me his wife was a specialist in administering chemotherapy. I couldn't get out of his office fast enough.

I went home and got on-line to do some research and chose the Mayo Clinic as my expert source. I read in the news that the famous South African President Nelson Mandela, and the mayor of New York, Rudy Giuliani, had both recently had a procedure for their prostate cancer called Brachytherapy.

So I do not misinform my readers, I will paraphrase from the Mayo Clinic website. Brachytherapy is an advanced cancer treatment. Radioactive seeds or sources are placed in or near the tumor itself, giving a high radiation dose to the tumor while reducing the radiation exposure in the surrounding healthy tissues. The term "brachy" is Greek for short distance. Brachytherapy is radiation therapy given at a short distance: localized, precise, and high-tech. There were two choices available for me: High-Dose Rate and Permanent.

With High-Dose Rate Brachytherapy, thin catheters are first placed in the tumor. The catheters are then connected to an HDR afterloader. This machine contains a single highly radioactive iridium pellet at the end of a wire. The pellet is pushed into each of the catheters one by one under computer control.

The computer controls how long the pellet stays in each catheter, and where along the catheter it should pause to release its radiation. With a few well-placed catheters in the tumor, HDR brachytherapy can provide a very precise treatment that takes only a few minutes. After a series of treatments, the catheters are removed, and there are no radioactive seeds left in the body.

Permanent brachytherapy, when used for prostate cancer, the radioactive material is placed in your body permanently. The radioactive material may be placed by hand or with the help of a computerized machine. You may feel pain during the placement of radioactive material, but you shouldn't feel any discomfort once it's in place.

This was my choice. Surgery, chemotherapy and external beam radiation had too many adverse side effects.

Brachytherapy allows doctors to deliver higher doses of radiation to more-specific areas of the body, compared with the conventional form of radiation therapy (external beam radiation) that projects radiation from a machine outside of your body. Brachytherapy may cause fewer side effects than does external beam radiation, and the treatment time is usually shorter with brachytherapy.

The patient's body will emit low doses of radiation from the area being treated at first. Usually the risk to others is minimal and may not require any restrictions about who can be near you. In some cases, for a short period of time you may be asked to limit the length and frequency of visits with pregnant women or with children. The amount of radiation in your body will diminish with time, and restrictions will be lifted.

In 1999 this procedure was considered experimental and it took some selling by the doctors to convince Blue Cross to allow it and to pay for it. They succeeded and Blue Cross paid.

I was brought to the hospital in Roseville by my dear friends the Klimovs at 6 am. They waited around until the procedure was over. They had me home in West Sacramento, thirty miles away, at 10 am.

I was knocked out during the procedure and when I woke up I was given tweezers, a very small lead container, what looked like a number two coffee filter, and a plastic container for my urine. I also had a tube in my penis which emptied into a quart-sized, plastic bag that would store my urine. I was given instructions -when the plastic bag was filled - to pour my urine thru the filter and note if any rice-size, radioactive pellets came out. If they did, I was to use the tweezers and put them into the lead container and return them to the hospital on Monday.

None did.

When I visited the doctor and was having eye-to-eye contact conversation with him, he calmly pulled my pants down and before I could process what he was doing, he did it. He quickly yanked the tube out of my penis. It was like painful sex. I let out a yell and produced a big smile simultaneously. He just as quickly told me that if he had explained what he was about to do and how painful it would be, I might seriously object. I thanked him for his expert and professional care.

I visited a dentist even fewer times than I visited hospitals. I do recall brushing my teeth in *St. Francis Orphan Asylum*, but do not recall doing so at St. Joseph's. Needless to say the consequence was prematurely rotten teeth. When I worked at Gimble's at the age of 15, I had a serious and painful toothache. I heard a commercial ad on the radio from a dentist whose office happened to be close to where I worked. So I visited him during my lunch hour. This was yet another of my big mistakes.

He hurt me so much I never visited another dentist for four decades. The reason his price of $5 was so affordable was he did not use much Novocain, if any.

In Folsom State Prison dental care was not to be had. The prison was built for a few thousand prisoners and twice as many were housed there. An inmate could request a ducat or permission slip to visit the dentist, but the backlog was such that I never got a response to any of my requests.

So, I pulled my own teeth. Removal was not professional as I did not have tools. I used a paper clip. Every day I would work the offending and throbbing tooth out of my gums. Slowly and painfully they came out, pieces of tooth at a time or one tooth at a time.

When I left the prison system I only had about eleven teeth left. In prison I learned to hide the gaps between my teeth by not smiling. As each tooth was removed not smiling became easier as there was so little for me at which to smile.

Dorian had a good friend Jeff Herndon who was a great dentist and had a practice in Quincy, a small town about 120 miles north of Sacramento. One day he visited Dorian's body shop when I was working there. Dorian introduced me to him. Jeff promptly checked inside my mouth. I informed him of my initial dental experience in Philadelphia in 1956 and the accompanying pain, as well as the lack of an opportunity for dental care while incarcerated.

We quickly established a relationship and over the next year he pulled my remaining teeth and fitted me with false teeth. Because I worked for the state and had dental insurance, he ultimately installed both upper and lower dentures. For the past twenty years I have used the dentures and have never had either a complaint or a tooth problem. Because of the false teeth and various improvements in my lifestyle and employment, I could smile again.

It would be remiss of me not to mention again my visits to psychiatrists. When I joined the Air Force, during basic training I failed to be clean shaven one morning. A drill sergeant was screaming in my face and asked why I had stubble on my face. I explained, loud enough for my peers to hear, that someone stole my radio. He asked what a radio had to do with my failure to shave. I thought

I was being funny by joking that my razor was on top of the radio. He did not share my humor and made me do twenty-five pushups and then ordered me to see the base psychiatrist. Nothing much came of the visit.

When I was arrested in 1981, my first attorney, a public defender, made an appointment with a psychiatrist for me. I never had an opportunity to read the report he received and he never got to use it in court, because I hired Michael Sands, a private attorney. It could have contained useful information.

Almost ten years later when I started working for the state, I made an appointment with a psychiatrist to try to determine why I molested Danny and what I should do to prevent re-offending. We had a number of sessions and I thought we were making progress. Unfortunately, this occurred at the same time my problem with Joe Spano arose. The state, because they were paying the bill for my visits, obtained information about the sessions I had. They then proceeded to use it to research my criminal past. I guess the confidentiality I thought existed did not. They did not get to use the information against me because my tape recording of racist Joe stopped them in their tracks.

Enough of my experiences with the medical professions: it is with pleasure that I resume writing about my beloved Klimovs.

I first met Yelena, the oldest of the Klimov children, when she was 12. I was impressed with how she mimicked her mother and watched over her three younger brothers. In their first apartment Yelena's room was the walk-in closet. It was private and separated from her brothers' sleeping area with a curtain. She kept her room so neat and guarded her privacy like a tigress. I had never seen a closer relationship between anyone than the relationship Yelena had with Marina. Yelena was a mother-in-training at that early age. She also had a very loving relationship with her father.

Sergey, the oldest of the boys, was the happy one. He had a smile all the time. He was bright and intelligent and too independent for his age. He and I had a few arguments. He seemed to want to exercise his independence at an early age. He could already use the English language to hurt someone and he did this to me on a few occasions. Generally I ignored him. But my reaction to one particular insult he flung at me over the telephone was to threaten to kill him. All of my life I knew that my bark was a better weapon than my bite. I hung up. The phone rang again within a minute. I heard Yelena defending her brother and trying to find out what had happened. Although I was almost fifty years older than the four Klimov children, I was learning a form of sibling rivalry.

Slava was the serious one, although he too had a great sense of humor. He was also very intelligent and I noted he was very sensitive. He was so generous with his time and talent and distinguished himself early as a born leader. He sprung to leadership roles in both the church's youth group and at their summer camps. As I write this today he is visiting the Ukraine along with Valeriy, sharing the word of God with those underprivileged children and helping to organize and host summer camps. Slava has the biggest heart. He is contemplating and studying for the nursing field and already has an EMT certificate. His future customers will be in good hands.

Valeriy was the youngest at seven years of age. He was like a puppy dog, and everyone loves a puppy. I remember fondly his helpfulness, especially when Nick or Marina had mail or a document that they wanted me to help them interpret and understand. I needed reading glasses and seldom carried mine with me. Valeriy would sense my problem and would produce a magnifying glass so I could read. He had an uncanny ability at a very early age to perceive things that should only have been within the purview of someone three times his age. He was the first to say 'I love you' to me and he would then assure me that 'we all love you.' I have suffered from depression for much of my life. He had the ability then to know that what he had to say was a cure for my down moments.

Over the years I was able to bring one or all of the Klimov boys home from school, especially after my retirement as I had plenty of free time. I can still recall one discussion with Valeriy about his future. I noted as we would stop for junk food he was discovering money and what it could do, so I planted a seed in his mind. I explained to him what a CPA (Certified Public Accountant) did and how much money they made. As I write this, Valeriy is in college majoring in accounting with his sights set on that profession. He will make a great CPA.

All of the boys were musically inclined, just like their father who could play the accordion, the piano and the guitar. They also had good singing voices, almost as good as Marina's who always sounded angelic when she sang. Most Russians I met enjoy singing. I especially enjoyed the times Marina, her extended family and visitors would sit around the living room singing.

Russians love to sing as a group, whether in a living room or around a campfire. I really enjoyed those late evening sessions when we camped out. None of the other campers complained so I think they enjoyed the singing too.

Sergey picked up a guitar in his early teens and impressed himself when he learned his first chord. He insisted I listen to him. He did this too frequently and I finally told him "when you are good I will let you know." It did not take him long to become very good. And, I was quick to let him know that he was very good.

Slava tried his hand at the alto sax. That is a difficult instrument to learn. Slava, big hearted as he is, gave the instrument to a friend.

I bought Valeriy a child's accordion when he was about eight years old but he never did anything with it. In his last years of high school, though, he decided he would learn to play the piano. I offered to pay for lessons but he said he wanted to teach himself to play by ear. Today, he is an excellent pianist. He and Sergey play every Sunday at church.

Marina sacrificed and paid for piano lessons for Yelena when she was twelve. The sound of music in the Klimov's home is just one of so many reasons wherever they call home is such a comfortable and warm place.

One thing all the Klimov children had in common stood out. They were totally obedient to their parents. They learned the fourth commandment well and practiced it every day. I often observed how my childhood was so opposite to theirs. Although I knew of the fourth commandment, I did not adhere to it. How could an orphan honor his mother or father? I was so glad to be a part of their family and to see how it worked.

One day I noted that Nick was sad and I quickly discovered why.

He had been searching for a house to buy and found one. The dot com bust was underway before Nick graduated so a job in the IT field was out of the question, even though he obtained two IT degrees. Nick had so much talent and experience as a mechanic. He quickly landed a job with a steel fabricating plant as their main mechanic. Nick found a house he wanted to buy but not being able to come up with a down payment was what made him depressed.

In communist Russia people borrowed from each other instead of from a capitalist bank. Housing was provided by the Soviet government so the concept of a mortgage was unheard of.

Nick went to his many friends to borrow the money, but his friends could not lend him the money. It was not that they did not want to, but they were all in the same boat. Most Russians did not have saving accounts and struggled to provide housing for themselves as they learned a new language and culture.

Fortunately, I was saving money for my upcoming retirement. I never had much of a value system so I had never saved money in my lifetime. Saving money was new to me. I had more than twelve thousand dollars saved. Financial experts would laugh at this miniscule amount. They boldly claim one needs hundreds of thousands of dollars for retirement but I believe the basis for that claim is simply their justification for the excessive fees they charge for their exaggerated advice.

A few years earlier I had put up three hundred dollars and showed Nick and Marina how to get a secured credit card with Bank of America to establish credit. Marina did the books in the Klimov household and she made sure to use the card every month but to pay off the balance every month. A year later, Bank of America increased their credit line and returned their security deposit which Marina gave to me. Their credit was established.

Marina's sister Inna had immigrated to America a few years earlier with her husband Peter and their four children. They owned a house. Marina had another sister Alla, who along with her husband Sergey and their three children, arrived in America a few years after Nick and Marina. They later bought a house. Nick had a brother Mike and his wife Svetlana who had a daughter and younger twin girls. They owned a house.

So when Nick and Marina hosted a dinner in their apartment, it was packed with a dozen adults and almost two dozen kids. It was always a happy time as there was so much laughter and never any arguments. There was always a lot of food and I learned in a hurry to like Russian and Ukrainian dishes. Marina's family came from the Ukraine. I enjoyed being part of this merriment, but Nick and Marina needed a house. They would convert it into a happy home. I parted with enough money that they were able to use as a down payment.

Within a year, the value of the house increased significantly, most of it was due to their sweat equity. I never asked but they produced the money I gave them for the down payment before the end of the first year.

Nick mentioned he had a brother Leonid in Russia, who wanted to come to the United States but was unable to enter as he and Marina did - as persons who were subjected to religious persecution. Leonid would need a sponsor, someone who could convince the US Justice Department that he and his family would not be a burden to government. I quickly volunteered to be that sponsor. I filled out an application on Leonid's behalf. The US government wanted to know how much money I earned and if I was willing to support Leonid's family for at least two years.

As I was approaching retirement my salary was almost four times as much as when I started working for the state. I was earning $6,500 a month! For the past ten years I received either a promotion or a merit raise twice a year. I started as an Office Assistant and was promoted to Data Processor, Office Technician, Staff Services Analyst, and finally to Information Systems Analyst. Each position had five steps. If there were no screw-ups you were entitled to a merit raise every six months.

I earned enough money to be a sponsor and as I owned a home in West Sacramento for the past ten years and would make it available to Leonid and his family at no cost to them, the application was approved.

Leonid arrived with his three sons - Alex, Roman and Vitali, and the youngest in their family, 15 year old Svetlana. They quickly filled my house and it became a home. Leonid was highly skilled in installing tile and quickly became employed. Roman had expertise with computers and had no problem earning money. Alex and Vitali had a range of interests and were also employed within a few weeks. Svetlana was finishing high school.

I owned an RV and was preparing to do a lot of traveling when I retired. I gave Leonid my Ford van so his family had reliable transportation.

Now I had an extended family too. Marina's mom and dad had also come to the US. They were both in their eighties and although they spoke virtually no English, we enjoyed each other's company with the help of Nick and Marina's translation.

There was one thing that haunted me from the first day I met Nick and Marina. One day they would have to learn of my criminal past. In the beginning it was not much of a problem because I could not tell them due to the language barrier, so I kept putting it off. Although the kids learned English very quickly, my past was something I could not discuss with them because of their youth and the subject matter. I did mention briefly without giving any details that I had been to prison. One day Sergey told me he had learned about the Megan's Law database in school. I dreaded what I expected him to say next. But he never accessed the database and my secret was temporarily safe.

No one at the SWRCB ever knew of my past. I had acquired a sixth sense in Folsom and was constantly aware of any external threat. The mere fact that an inmate innocently pointed in another person's direction was enough for that person to feel threatened and then act to prevent the perceived threat. I could hear in 360 degrees for hints that someone knew why I was incarcerated. I carried this skill with me into the workplace at the SWRCB.

One of the benefits of retirement would be to escape the stress of my past being discovered. The penal code I was convicted of was PC 288. Those numbers haunted me after my release from prison. The simple act of seeing a price tag at Walmart with those numbers reminded me of my past. Thirty years later as I exercise at 24 Hour Fitness on the treadmill and see the calories, time, or distance presenting those numbers, I am jolted back to 1981.

I often wonder how my victim relives my crime. From the start the court forbade me from making contact with him, an order which I assume is still in effect. He would be forty-three years of age now. Could there be such a thing as closure available to him should we have a chance meeting at this late date? He had a dysfunctional family which may have been as bad as me having no family as I grew up and was his age. I do hope he has been able to survive my criminal act and has been able to make a loving family for himself.

As for me, I have had the pleasure and benefit of being part of a loving family by way of informal adoption for the past dozen years. In knowing the Klimovs there have been so many enjoyable experiences. One in particular warms my heart. I watched Yelena mature from childhood. I guess she was a senior in high school when Stas Gorobchuk showed up at the Klimov home. He was very good looking, possessed superior intelligence and knew with precision that he wanted Yelena for his wife. He was a member of the same church that the Klimovs attended in Carmichael. The Baptist church in West Sacramento was taken by the City under the eminent domain laws to enlarge the city library a few years ago. We all attended Grace Family Church.

Stas was the perfect gentleman when he visited Nick and Marina. Yelena's younger brothers Sergey, Slava and Valeriy - still in their teens - really liked Stas who was half a dozen years older than Sergey. They ribbed and teased Yelena as younger brothers have a tendency to do. She reacted by declaring that she did not like Stas. But her blushing gave up her true desires and intention. Soon, she was praying for a sign to indicate if her future would be blessed by having Stas as her husband.

When a couple decides to become engaged in the Baptist church, they pray and ask for God's blessing or a sign of His approval. When their prayers are answered they then make an announcement in front of the entire congregation. Thereafter they are permitted to be in each other's company - even alone.

Yelena's blushing was enhanced with her beautiful smile whenever she and Stas were together. It was matched by the wide-open eyes of Stas as he followed her every move. They enjoyed a wonderful engagement and set a date. Stas had reliable employment in the computer technology field. But Marina, the ever watchful and cautious mother, decided that Stas had to get a real job. Marina had watched in pain as Nick spent so much time and energy obtaining two college degrees in the technology field only to see the dot com bust and so many jobs disappear or to be exported to India. Nick had settled for a job as master mechanic in a building products manufacturing factory. Marina insisted the wedding be postponed until Stas got a real job.

To put Marina at ease Stas took a job as a cross-country truck-driver and got to see a lot of America. He saved most of his earnings during the following six months, and finally nothing stood in his way of marrying Yelena. They had a wonderful wedding and were blessed in due time with the birth of Benjamin, who added immensely to their joy, and to mine. Marina became a happy babooshka or grandmother, and Nick became a dotting daydooska. And I too became a vicarious grandfather - in spirit. I was surrounded by love, by family, and it was growing quickly. For once in my life I was happy.

Next came Nellie. She was another unique blessing. Her birth prompted Stas and Yelena to buy their own home. Stas was a dedicated father, and as Yelena had learned so much from Marina, she became the ideal mom. I have never witnessed anyone pay so much attention to their children as she does.

As I now write this autobiography, they are once again blessed with Timothy. Today, at the age of seventy, I am part of a very large and heartwarming family. I considered my quest for a family to be complete. But there was more to come.

I saw firsthand the glue that held both families so close together: it was the teachings of their church. In the dozen years that I had known the Klimovs I observed their total commitment to their faith. It dominated their lives and they lived by the most important commandments in the bible: After being asked by the scribes what is the most important law, Jesus answered and said the first is ... thou shalt love the Lord thy God with all thy heart, and with all thy soul, and with all thy mind, and with all thy strength. The second is this; Thou shalt love thy neighbor as thyself." (Mark 12:30-31)

And I am a beneficiary of that commandment, their love. It is my most valuable treasure.

Chapter Eleven
Retirement - 2004

The Golden Years can come as a shock. Throughout one's life a universal observation is that people stop working, retire, and within a few years, die. On the other hand, there are people who have lived a very long time past their retirement date, and some maintain a perpetual smile and are obviously enjoying themselves. Others are beset with so many health problems they may wish they were dead. So what did I have to look forward to?

For the last five years of my career with the state, I anticipated traveling and making photographs when I retired. I started to accumulate everything I would need to make photographs, process the film, and make prints. I even contemplated making a few extra bucks selling my prints. I had purchased a beautiful, cherry wood 4x5 camera. It had a twenty three inch bellows. (This is the kind of camera one sees where the photographer is under a black cloth, making lots of adjustments, and pressing his thumb against the shutter release) I purchased new Nikon lenses, from very wide angle to telephoto. I also purchased a state of the art darkroom.

Within the last six months of my employment, one of the department heads asked me to look into digital cameras and to make a recommendation so they could purchase one. I was able to survey what was on the market from the simple, inexpensive units to the very complicated and expensive cameras. In the process of field testing them I quickly discovered that digital cameras would be the wave of the future and they would soon replace film cameras. They could do just about everything I could do with a large format camera and were much less expensive to use as there was no cost for film or processing film. Prints could be made on a printer instead of in a darkroom. I made recommendations for the department and then purchased for myself a high-end, Nikon digital camera. I then proceeded to put all my film camera and darkroom equipment on eBay. I even made a profit.

One of the first trips I took upon retiring on April 1, 2004, at the age of 63, was to Yosemite National Park. I spent a week and took thousands of digital photographs. I picked the best few hundred and offered a CD of them on eBay for under $10 plus a few bucks for shipping. I actually sold a few dozen under the label *MizeraGraphs*.

I then took a trip to both The Grand Teton National Park and Yellowstone National Park in Wyoming. I lived in the parks for a few weeks in early May and I really enjoyed the tranquility and beauty. As I had been an avid walker for the past ten years, I especially enjoyed the excitement of walking in the near proximity to the bison and grizzly bears every day. Retirement was going to be golden in more ways than one.

I also put a *MizeraGraph* CD on eBay of both the Tetons and Yellowstone. They too were selling well. Closer to home I spent time at Bodie State Park, a wonderful ghost town east of Yosemite, and continued creating CDs. Periodically I would search eBay to see what my competitors were doing and did I receive a jolt. Someone in Hong Kong who had purchased my CD of Yosemite was now offering it on a DVD together with a number of other photographs made by other photographers on eBay and for half the price of my CD. He was claiming they were his original photos.

Fighting him would have been a lesson in futility and frustration, so I did not. But I had to find a way to prevent anyone from stealing my work and claiming it as theirs. This led to my creation of Panoramagraphs. I would scan the horizon and make a series of overlapping photographs.

I would then stitch them together using software. The result would be a super wide panoramic view. Making photographs this way allowed me to offer very wide prints eight feet wide and larger.

I made a panoramagraph from Twin Peaks, the highest point in San Francisco, which stretched from the Golden Gate Bridge on the left to the Oakland shipyards on the right with Market Street and the San Francisco skyline in the middle. It could be printed twenty-two feet wide and the detail was spectacular. I planned on marketing it later to an expensive hotel or restaurant. In the event the anticipated big earthquake changed the skyline, I would have a detailed record of what San Francisco looked like before the quake.

I was soon traveling to Utah, Oregon, South Dakota and Arizona and photographing majestic landscapes, seascapes, and the deserts. I did a series of Mount Rushmore from every angle and even made panoramagraphs at night when it is bathed in powerful spotlights, a scene most people never see.

I did not offer my digital negatives but would offer prints of my work on canvas, and for much more than the price I was getting for CDs. Now no one could steal my work and pass it off as his or hers.

My focus would be on making photographs. Marketing them would come later. I was interested in the first half of my dream: traveling and using my West Sacramento home as a base of operations. But a minor nightmare became a roadblock.

It seems that a new neighbor discovered the Megan's Law database and printed my photograph and information about my crime and distributed it to all of my neighbors. That anonymous neighbor left a copy in my mailbox. Accessing the state database became a crime if one used the database to distribute the information.

I reported this to the West Sacramento police and their attitude was what I expected. Although it was a crime to do what the new neighbor did, they said they could not determine who it was. That, of course, was bullshit. Anyone who accesses any database can easily be determined and located through the computer's IP address. Seems the police enjoy selective enforcement instead of law enforcement. It is interactions like this between the general public and officers of the law that explains why respect for law enforcement dwindles daily.

Leonid and his family had found a new home so I contacted a property management company to rent my house while I resumed traveling. But first I needed a new home base. I searched eBay for land in Oregon. I quickly found a lot in Christmas Valley for sale. It was a third of an acre and undeveloped.

Christmas Valley is an unincorporated community in Lake County, Oregon. The community was named after nearby dry Christmans Lake, east of the present town site and the site of the former Lake post office, which ran from 1906 until 1943. Real estate development around a planned community by M. Penn Phillips, called Christmas Valley, started after World War II. Christmas Valley post office was established in 1963 as a rural station of Silver Lake.

Christmas Lake, Christmas (Lake) Valley, and nearby Peter's Sink and Peter's Creek were named for pioneer stockman Peter Christman, who grazed his cattle there and had a house at Silver Lake, eighteen miles to the southwest. These names were applied as early as September 29, 1877, when they were referred to by former Oregon Governor John Whiteaker in a letter to the editor of the *Eugene City Guard*. Whiteaker himself had an interest in the fossil beds at nearby Fossil Lake, and ranching interests in the area as well.

In 1961, developer M. Penn Phillips laid out the town site, including its fanciful holiday street names such as Candy Lane, Mistletoe Road, Comet Street, Vixen Street, etc. It also included the Christmas Valley Airport, a water system, a golf course, a lodge, rodeo grounds, and an artificial lake originally named Christmas Valley Lake and now called Baert Lake.

Phillips aggressively promoted the community in California to young, would-be farmers and retirees; often providing free bus tours and flights, and marketing the potential of the land as green and readily farmed. The company quickly sold out the parcels, and despite Phillips' claims that the community would soon have more than 5,000 residents, few actually moved there. In 1966, in an Oregon Tax Court decision about tax valuation of Christmas Lake property, Judge Edward Howell opined, "the land, at least in its present condition, is arid, dusty, windy, isolated, [and] subject to temperature extremes." In the early 1970s, the Phillips company faced lawsuits about misrepresentation of the property and the Phillips era is usually considered a scam.

Fifty years later I was able to purchase a lot for $2500.

Christmas Valley is about one hundred miles east, as the bird flies, from Crater Lake, one of Oregon's spectacular sights. I liked it. There was a view for a hundred miles in all four directions. The summers were naturally air conditioned. The closest town or city was Klamath Falls 135 to the southwest, and Bend 115 miles to the northwest. Lakeview, the capital City of Lake County is 105 miles to the southeast. It is a remote location.

I had a local contractor put in a semi-circular driveway on my eighty by one hundred and eighty foot lot. I planned to eventually develop the lot. I soon found out that the eighty foot frontage on the gravel road was not quite wide enough for my thirty-eight foot RV, especially when I was towing my 16 foot trailer. So I put the lot back on eBay for sale and it went fast for $3,600 to someone from San Francisco. He indicated that he would hold it for a few years. I sold it on monthly payments which allowed me to continue to live on it. I was now ready to travel again.

I decided to visit Chip Fyn who was living mostly in Apache Junction, Arizona, fifty miles east of Phoenix. Aside from my Klimovs, I was down to three original friends: Dorian Wright in California, Ray Robinson in Oregon, and Chip Fyn in Arizona.

There was an RV show south of Phoenix that advertised free hot dogs so Chip, Annie and I brought Chip's two terriers to the show and gave them all the hot dogs they could eat. Toward the end of the day, we thought we would look at some of the really expensive RVs, a few were for sale for between half a million and a million dollars. We worked our way down to those selling for a quarter of a million and I got hooked on a 2006 Monica Knight. It was forty feet long and had four slide-outs, which made it look like a house inside. We were the last ones to leave the show. I kept holding out with the salesman until I got a deal. The dealer gave me $30,000 for my Winnebago which could not have been worth a third of that. I would owe $195,000. What expensive hot dogs they were. But, now I was ready to travel. It was north to Alaska.

It was late April when I headed for Alaska. I wanted to drive the AlCan, as the Alaska-Canadian highway is known. First, I stopped in Oregon to visit Ray Robinson and his wife Kathy. I really liked Kathy and actually felt sorry for her as she was having problems with Ray's drinking.

Ray liked going to garage sales and whenever I visited, Kathy I would accompany him and buy useless things. On one particular visit years earlier, Ray scheduled visits to about thirty sales. Kathy and I were both exhausted, so late in the day we expressed a joint opinion that we did not want to continue "sale-ing". Ray became furious, accusing me of conspiring with his wife to deny him of a simple pleasure. I departed for California the minute I could get back to my RV.

Months later, I received a Christmas card from Ray which contained a bitter note declaring that he did not know if he wanted me for a friend. It took another year or so until he casually invited me to visit. I did. I took it all with an extra large grain of salt. This was still the Ray who would give you the shirt off his back unless you needed a shirt. He obviously needed someone to manipulate and I was an easy target. Had it not been for my desire to visit Kathy, I would have left Ray in a lurch, and in retrospect I should have.

The trip to Alaska had me wide-eyed. I departed in May just as the road was thawing out. The forty foot Monica was such a pleasure to drive. It had a big diesel in the back so it was very quiet behind the wheel, and oh so comfortable. The AlCan was a unique highway. So many people warn you about it being gravel all the way, clogged with traffic in both directions, and no one has ever made the trip without losing one of more headlights and their windshield. My windshield was enormous and in one piece. It made viewing the scenery a delight. A panoramic view of Canada and Alaska for a few thousand miles will refresh anyone's soul.

Proposals for a highway to Alaska originated in the 1920s. Donald MacDonald dreamed of an international highway spanning the United States, Canada and Russia. In order to promote the highway, Slim Williams originally traveled the proposed route by dog sled. Since much of the route would pass through Canada, support from the Canadian government was crucial. The Canadian government perceived no value in putting up the required funds to build the road. The only part of Canada that would benefit was not more than a few thousand people in the Yukon.

However, some route consideration was given. The preferred route would pass through the Rocky Mountain Trench from Prince George, British Columbia to Dawson City before turning west to Fairbanks, Alaska.

The attack on Pearl Harbor and beginning of the Pacific Theatre in World War II, coupled with Japanese threats to the west coast of North America and the Aleutian Islands, changed the priorities for both nations. On February 6, 1942 the construction of the Alaska Highway was approved by the United States Army and the project received the authorization from the U.S. Congress and President Franklin D. Roosevelt to proceed five days later. Canada agreed to allow construction as long as the United States bore the full cost, and that the road and other facilities in Canada be turned over to Canadian authority after the war ended.

The official start of construction took place on March 8, 1942 after hundreds of pieces of construction equipment were moved on priority trains by the Northern Alberta Railway to the northeastern part of British Columbia near Mile 0 at Dawson Creek.

Construction accelerated through the spring as the winter weather faded away and crews were able to work from both the northern and southern ends; they were spurred on after reports of the Japanese invasion of Kiska Island and Attu Island in the Aleutians. On September 24, 1942 crews from both directions met at Mile 588 at what became named Contact Creek, at the British Columbia-Yukon border at the 60th Parallel; the entire route was completed October 28, 1942 with the northern linkup at Mile 1202, Beaver Creek, and the highway was dedicated on November 20, 1942 at Soldiers Summit.

The needs of war dictated the final route, intended to link the airfields of the Northern Staging Route that conveyed lend-lease aircraft from the United States to the Soviet Union. The rather impractical, long route over extremely difficult terrain was chosen.

When I made my trip, the highway was generally in great shape. It was mostly paved and gravel in just a few places. There were some problems though. The winter is cold in Canada and the temperature does crack the highway. Sometimes drivers get a warning with a little red flag left by the Canadian highway maintenance crew. Sometimes you know there is a problem because the painted yellow line has a break or gap, or disappears. Sometimes there is nothing to warn you and you can bounce out of the captain's chair if you are not wearing your seat belt.

Only the last five hundred miles of the 2500 mile highway was rough. Sometimes the road just disappeared and you had to drive through mud for a few miles. But there was very little traffic in May. Another complaint was that there were flocks of mosquitoes. Perhaps I was a little early for them, but did not have that bad experience.

One enters Alaska in a tiny town named Tok. Of course there is an international border. I was a little apprehensive. Doing research before I left the lower forty-eight, I noted that Canada was very strict about allowing criminals into their country. One blogger mentioned that even if you had a traffic ticket twenty-five years earlier, the Canadian border guards would prevent you from entering the country. I had selected a very small border crossing in the most western part of the US border, west of Vancouver. I did not have a problem entering Canada. But at Tok I was concerned that on my return trip I might be prevented from re-entering Canada. What would I do with the RV? How would I get back to the United States?

Always guided by my criminal mind, I decided that if I could not get back across the border, I would torch the Monica, collect a little insurance money for my equity and fly back to the US and buy another RV.

I made it to Alaska, and headed west to Fairbanks. For the past thousand miles on the Alcan Highway, there were few opportunities to pull off the highway to make photographs. The few towns were small and hundreds of miles apart. There was a lot of wildlife including black bears, grizzly bears, moose, wild horses and a lot of smaller critters. I was so eager to get to Alaska I regret that I did not spend much time touring Canada.

My stay in Fairbanks was a different story. I was a genuine tourist. The first trip I took was on a paddlewheel boat. It cost $25 but was a great buy. Alaska has so many bush pilots and we were treated to a demonstration of a few of their skills. One flew by the paddlewheel boat slowly within forty feet as the tour guide gave us a lot of information over a loudspeaker about bush pilots. The pilot demonstrated how his plane with pontoons could land and take off on the water. Another pilot's plane had huge tires and he demonstrated how he could take off and land from very short "runways" on the shore.

We docked at an Alaskan Indian village and got off the boat. There were various demonstrations by local Indians on how they lived, especially how they caught salmon.

I stayed at a Walmart Super Store that night and it was the most interesting Walmart I have ever camped out at. Fairbanks gets very cold in the winter and motorists generally have electric heaters to keep their engines warm so they can start their vehicles in the morning. (Those who don't have motor block heaters keep their engines running all night) Walmart had electric sockets that RV-ers were invited to use. There was also a sign with a map showing where the local RV parks were located, along with an invitation to use them. This was by far the friendliest visit to a Walmart I ever experienced. I did make use of one of the parks.

I had made reservations to camp out at Denali National Park, halfway between Fairbanks and Anchorage. I also wanted to ride the Alaska railroad which connected Alaska's two largest cities. The next morning I parked at the new depot and boarded the train for Denali, where I would have a two hour layover before catching the return train back to Fairbanks. It was a breathtaking trip. Alaska is still a pioneer country and the train will stop to pick up or allow passengers to get off in the middle of nowhere. I even made use of the dining car and the food and service was outstanding.

I spent my layover hiking in Denali. The return to trip to Fairbanks was just as beautiful. One of the most interesting things about being in Fairbanks was the daylight. There was no nighttime in early June. At midnight it was still light and I had to remind myself to go to bed. Waking up a few hours later it was still light. The residents of Fairbanks celebrate by playing a baseball game throughout the night without lights, of course.

The next morning I drove to a town named North Pole, about fifty miles north of Fairbanks. It had a great outdoor spa fed by natural mineral springs. Although it was almost summer, there was no problem with snow on the roads, but the snow-capped mountains were always a visual treat.

I did a little more touring such as visiting a terminal of the Alaska pipeline and a few museums, but I was eager to get to Denali.

Denali National Park is unique for a lot of reasons. One is the road in the park. It is brown gravel and is ninety miles long. It terminates at Mirror Lake at the apparent foot of Mount McKinley, or Denali as it is now called. The mountain is usually covered with clouds and visitors may have to wait a few days until they get to view it. Some never do.

Visitors to the park cannot drive their personal vehicles around the park, except to and from the campground where they must have a reservation. There are a number of shuttle buses that are in use and are scheduled about a half hour apart for most of the day. It cost $30 for a pass and it was good for the five days I camped. On the first day I took the shuttle and headed west to see some of the park and its wildlife. A problem arose almost immediately after the first grizzly bear was spotted. The driver stopped and everyone on the bus moved to the side of the bus where the bear was visible in order to make photographs. I did not want to compete with the elbows and to try to make photographs through the windows, so I got off the shuttle at my first opportunity.

As the shuttle bus departed, it left me surrounded by silence standing all alone among the tremendous mountain ranges. This was Alaska!

I had my camera on a monopod which doubled as a walking stick. I started walking downhill. On my right was a steep drop into a valley about five-hundred yards below. To my left was thick brush more than six feet tall and it covered the steep uphill grade. The gravel road led straight ahead of me for the next hundred yards before it turned to the left and was out of sight. There was no sound except for the wind and the only movement was the clouds which obscured Denali's top three thousand feet. I meandered ahead for about sixty yards when suddenly a grizzly cub appeared. It stopped dead in its tracks and was quickly joined by two more curious cubs and their mother. Only forty yards separated us. We made eye contact immediately.

I remembered reading a brochure which warned of grizzlies and explained what to do if one encountered one. The written words were now ringing in my ears: Don't make eye contact! Mine were the size of silver dollars as I kept them glued to the bears. I stopped walking and suddenly heard a loud, fast thumping sound. It was my heart pounding. The little cinnamon cubs were staying close to mom who was glaring at me as her six hundred pounds moved closer to me like a short pendulum back and forth.

She was on the left edge of the road, next to the six-foot high brush, and I was on the right edge close to the steep drop into the valley. I could not turn and go back up the road, and running was out of the question as grizzlies can run thirty miles an hour, more than twice as fast as the fastest human. I decided quickly that if the grizzly started to charge me I would take my chances by stepping off the road and slide down to the valley floor. I reasoned that I would drop my camera and its monopod on the road as I departed so a shuttle driver would be put on notice to look for one of his former passengers.

But brochure notwithstanding, I kept my eyes glued to mom and her babies. It suddenly dawned on me that I had come to Alaska to photograph bears so I reached with my right index finger and pressed on the camera's shutter release, aiming the lens as I slowly rotated and aimed the camera on the monopod toward them. Mom gave me a break. She soon entered the thick brush and her babies obediently followed. Actually, God gave me that break and that beautiful experience.

Suddenly the silence returned, except for my heartbeat which was deafening. I did not move a muscle while listening intently to the brush. Would she be using the bushes to get closer to and attack me? After a few minutes and as the sound and speed of my heart lessened, I checked to see what kind of photographs I had. They were great. This was Alaska!

I repeated my shuttle rides on each of the next four days. I disembarked to experience the remoteness and wildness of Alaska. On one more occasion I found myself within fifty yards of another grizzly. She was along a creek and I thought I was hidden by trees. She stood up, looked around and sniffed the air. Thankfully, I had not taken a bath in a few days so I must not have smelled like something good to eat. The trees did not hide the smell of me.

I had crammed a lot of Alaska into such a short time. In retrospect I should have stayed for the summer, but I had already told Ray I would be back in time to attend his annual Meadows Party. This was an event on his property where he invited as many of his acquaintances as possible to help in the construction of his private railroad. He called them work parties. A lot of railroad hobbyists showed up every year as I often did.

The return trip found me heading south toward Anchorage, but I turned east and then north instead of entering Alaska's largest and most populated town. I traveled back toward Tok and wondered again if I would have a problem getting back into Canada and then back into the state of Washington.

Canada is such a beautiful country. The few people I met were very friendly. It was still strange converting kilometers into miles and liters into gallons. Although the money was very similar, a Canadian dollar converted into a little more than an American dollar. I used my visa card for most of the trip so I would have a record of my expenditures and actually received a pleasant surprise when I finally received my visa bill. The trip cost less than I had calculated because of the difference in the exchange rate.

I was on the last few hundred miles of the AlCan and there was virtually no traffic. My mind floated back to the admonition that no one ever travels the highway to Alaska and back without getting a cracked windshield or busted headlights. Within seconds I observed a crack develop at the base of my windshield and it zigzagged upwards for about sixteen inches. There was no vehicle going in the opposite direction and none had passed me. I was not on a gravel road. My broken windshield completed my trip to Alaska.

I had no problem entering the US and my deductible for the windshield was a mere hundred dollars. My insurance paid almost $1,200 because it was a large one piece windshield. I had made arrangements by phone to have the windshield replaced in Washington. Now it was off to visit Ray and Kathy and attend the Meadows Party.

Ray's wife Kathy and I had a very close relationship, probably because I knew Ray for about forty years and he and I both had spent time in prison for similar crimes, except he had molested two young girls. Kathy felt she could talk to me. On this visit she expressed concern about Ray. He had a safe in his office in the barn and had inadvertently left it open. Kathy happened to notice the open safe and glanced in. She found newspaper advertisements, the kind department stores run which feature young children modeling clothing, swimming wear or underwear. These ads depicted pre-teen models scantily dressed. Apparently Ray was still hooked after twenty years.

Kathy and I both expressed the fear that he might re-offend with one or more of the children of visitors to their residence. Although we both were concerned, neither of us confronted him. We both kept an eye on him however as he drove off in his Gator with a young girl sitting in the front next to him. Although we both knew he was still in denial, we hoped he would not re-offend.

My traveling took me down the coast of Oregon and as I was retired and now never in a hurry I explored every little town and the places in between. On the way to California, I would drive down highway 101 instead of Interstate 5. This allowed me to spend days hiking along the Avenue of the Giants and visit the redwoods.

It was always a pleasure stopping and visiting my Klimov family in Sacramento before setting off again on my travels. Nick has a brother Michael who is married to Svetlana and they have three children. Although they had purchased a home in the Sacramento area, the housing market or bubble was beginning to burst. They purchased a less expensive home in North Carolina and planned on abandoning the more expensive house. As they were packing a large rental truck, I joked with them about bringing back to North Carolina whatever they could not fit into the truck. Sure enough, they could not fit in the kid's bikes, the rototiller and other items, so that gave me an opportunity to take a trip across country.

My Monica Knight motor home was 42 feet and the trailer I towed was sixteen feet, a total of 58 feet. Diesel fuel was $3.27 a gallon when I departed California. Six months later when I arrived in Charlotte it was $4.91. As my RV was getting less than 7 miles per gallon, I vowed to get rid of the RV upon my return. I took three months to go east, stayed a month and it took two months to get back to California.

Chip was camping out at Mount Lassen about one hundred miles north of Sacramento when I started my trip so I put them on the top of my list and I spent three days with him and Annie on my way east.

After a few days I stopped by Christmas Valley before heading to Nevada. Before leaving Sacramento and while using my computer a pop up ad informed me that I could easily qualify for a credit card so I applied and was shocked to see the card in my post office box in Christmas Valley. The limit was only $500 and they were billing me in advance for various charges before I used it once. There was still an available balance of more than $300. I would teach them who was greedy. That balance allowed me to fill up the RV a few times as I started my trip. I had no intention of paying for the credit extended to me by the greedy credit card company. I was still not observing the commandment that required me not to steal. I had broken most of the commandments most of my life. Why should I stop now?

I had filed for bankruptcy three times in the previous thirty years. The first time I filed under Chapter 13, otherwise known at the wage earner's plan. Essentially, the court gets its fee as does the attorney. In exchange all creditors are told they would lose any interest, penalties and fees and would receive a little something each month out of whatever I paid the court. After that filing I never made any payments to the trustee and neither the court nor any creditor ever came after me.

After I was released from prison and started working for the state, I had established good credit. I was keeping current with my bills and had financed an RV with the Golden One Credit Union, an institution which serviced state employees. What ruined my credit was what Golden One Credit Union told me when the RV engine broke on a vacation trip to Arizona. I needed more credit. They declined telling me I was over-extended and therefore not creditworthy. So I abandoned the RV, maxed out my Visa issued by Golden One to rent a car to finish my vacation.

On my return I maxed out the rest of my credit cards. I then stopped paying on all of them and three months later filed Chapter 7 bankruptcy. I did not look at these transactions as stealing, but as working within the system. I had seen businesses do much the same thing frequently so I did not view my behavior as immoral. I owned a house in Ione and the Golden One had the mortgage on that too. Had they helped me when I was in need when my RV broke down, they may not have lost so much money on the second mortgage and the visa card, in addition to the balance owed on the RV.

For the next seven years I operated on a cash basis. It is amazing how, after one files for bankruptcy, credit card companies make it so easy to establish credit again, which I did. After seven years I was able to finance another RV and finally a house in West Sacramento. I went into retirement with financial obligations for a $195,000 RV, a house with an exaggerated appraised value and mortgage of $315,000, and nothing in either stocks or savings.

On the other side of my ledger I had income from a monthly social security check for $1170 and a monthly pension check from CalPERS, the state employee's retirement system, for $1985.

My trip east with a trailer full of Mike's belonging was a great adventure. It was the epitome of freedom. It was September when I left Christmas Valley and I ran into snow before leaving Oregon. But that was because I was in the high desert. The Nevada desert was different. No weather concerns but it bordered on boring. The sweet-smelling air and unique solitude are the prizes one gets when spending time in places like Nevada's deserts. I did encounter a wild burro who was just as surprised to see me stopping my motor home and chasing him for a photograph.

I spent a few days on the Bonneville Salt Flats in western Utah. This is where the land speed records are set. It is a strange place. The salt that was left behind when Lake Bonneville evaporated many, many years ago looks like snow. When one walks on it there is a crunching sound also similar to old snow.

In a Walmart parking lot in Salt Lake City I met a fellow who had a large truck with the word **Simplicity** painted on the side and back. Turned out that was his "church." He preached from the back of it. He had added a little steeple to the roof. Chimes hung inside the steeple. Whenever there was any movement inside the truck, or when the wind blew outside, the chimes offered soft music. He had observed the photos of my panoramagraphs on the side of my trailer. He had knocked on my RV door to inquire what it would cost him for me to make something he could affix to the outside of his truck. I suggested making a panoramagraph of the inside of his truck, which I did for him gratuitously. It was a challenge but it was one of the most interesting panoramagraphs I ever made.

In the southwest corner of Colorado I visited Dinosaur National Park. I did not have a schedule and never heard of this park, but I stayed there for three days. There were so few visitors to this park. I enjoyed hiking in solitude. The elevation stays well above 4000 feet across Oregon, Nevada, Utah and much of Colorado, so the air is so clean and crisp. There were so many small towns in Colorado on my way to the Rocky Mountain National Park and I visited as many as I could. As I enjoy walking, I would mark off a two mile stretch of road, then park and walk back to where I knew the two mile mark was. So I walked four miles and observed both sides of the road in a different part of the country every day. Retirement was a real pleasure.

I did get snowed-in at a state campground in the western part of Rocky Mountain National Park. My RV had four slide-outs and I extended them every night. The RV was as big as a one-bedroom house when the slide-outs were extended. In the morning as I tried to retract the largest slide on the driver's side I realized too late that I had a problem.

It had snowed about four inches overnight. As I retracted the slide I was not aware of the motor grinding, or that the snow on the awning was being compressed. By the time I became aware that the slide was not being pulled in properly, the teeth on the gears of the motor that moved the slide broke off. With the help of a few other RV campers, I removed the caked snow and we pushed the slide in manually. I was unable to extend it for most of the rest of the trip. Although the RV was less than eight months old, getting it repaired under the warranty was a hassle because I would have to drive to New Mexico. So I did not bother to have it fixed.

I waited for six days at that campground for the snow on the roads to be plowed. Each night it snowed a little more. Not wanting to wait any longer for a snow plow, I decided to enter the park from the east, which meant I had to drive about 250 miles around the southern border. But the trip was worth it. There are so many herds of elk to photograph in the park, but I did not observe any other wildlife, aside from a strange bird or two.

It was downhill to Kansas and I got to experience some of the wild thunderstorms that are common to the middle of the country. I prayed that I would not experience a tornado. The days following allowed me to observe and experience the life style of small town America. Although I headed east on a major highway, I always made it a point to do a few side trips everyday to accommodate my walking habit and to breathe in some local culture.

Visiting the giant arch in St. Louis is much different than just seeing photographs of it. The arch is massive, akin to the Golden Gate Bridge. Photos don't do either justice.

One highlight of my trip was spending time with the Amish in Kentucky. They create a lot of things for sale such as beautiful handcrafted furniture. Visitors can watch them work behind glass. They also make something that looked like a cabbage face doll, but there were no eyes, or mouth, or nose. This reflects their religious conviction that prohibits making images, I was told.

The weather was wet and foggy so I missed most of the fall colors in Smokey Mountain National Park in Tennessee. As I exited the southern part of the park and headed east, I was treated to some spectacular fall colors going east through the hills and dales of North Carolina.

North Carolina, especially Charlotte, was most enjoyable. Mike took his oldest daughter, but had left his two younger twins and wife behind, as he headed back to Russia, so I became part of this family. We attended church, went out for pizza, and did some sightseeing.

As I departed Charlotte and as I had never been to a real swamp, I made it a point to spend time at one in South Carolina. I took back roads through Georgia and Alabama to see a lot of these states. One of Kathy's sons, Greg, was stationed at an army base in Alabama so he and I spent a few days together.

I drove through Florida and Mississippi, stopping at Biloxi where I had spent ten months in the Air Force. I enjoyed my time on the Gulf of Mexico before heading north through Louisiana.

The devastation of Hurricane Katrina was still in evidence five years later. Katrina was a Category 5 Storm with winds up to 175 miles an hour, but weakened to a Category 4 before making landfall below New Orleans in Plaquemines and Saint Bernard Parishes. The storm, however, weakened the levee system which broke in several places [one place - the Industrial Canal - was weakened by a barge which rammed into it.] and over 90% of New Orleans was flooded.

Katrina also devastated the Mississippi Gulf Coast and caused damage on the Alabama Gulf Coast. The official death toll is 1697; however, Columbia geo-physicist and earth scientist John Mutter believes that the number is "well in excess of 2000." I was able to make a vistagraph of what was the equivalent of the Confederate White

House in Biloxi. It was in the process of being restored from Katrina's wrath.

After traveling north through Louisiana, it was west through Texas. I have been through Texas half a dozen times and have always found it boring. One would think that I would know enough to go through Oklahoma instead.

My rig had three excellent rear view cameras and a seven inch TV screen to monitor who was on either side of me or behind me, but the monitor stopped working and I planned to have it fixed in New Mexico.

Although I never made any plans on this trip, every day I would find the locations of the Walmart stores located from fifty to two hundred and fifty miles ahead of my location and plan to stay overnight at them.

Except for the campground at Rocky Mountain National Park, I never stayed in an RV park or paid for camping. I dumped my sewage and filled up with water at major fuel stops. My solar panels kept my batteries topped off. The real expense was the price of fuel. By the time I got to southwestern New Mexico, I was paying almost $5 a gallon. I had the monitor replaced under warranty and headed for Arizona. They were unable to service my broken gears that allowed my slides to extend.

Chip and Annie winter over in Arizona so I planned on stopping and spending time with them. We went out to eat one evening at a Chinese restaurant which was a tradition whenever the three of us got together. It was light when we entered the restaurant but dark when we finished eating.

As I was driving out of the parking lot, I heard an outrageous noise and felt a strange tug on the rear of the RV. When I stopped to investigate, I noticed there was a round, three-foot diameter cement post, two feet high that normally anchored a tall light pole. There was no pole on this cement base. The rear of my passenger side got hung up on this pole-less obstacle and it took a big chunk of my RV as I tried to drive away.

My quarter of a million dollar RV was beginning to look like a piece of junk, and it was now too expensive for me to operate. I started to look for a way to get rid of it.

I think I was just entering Texas when I learned of my good friend Dorian Wright's death by heart attack. He was in his mid-fifties. My dear buddy never got much exercise and when he was not smoking a joint he was smoking a cigarette. I pleaded with him to quit smoking tobacco from the first day I met him at Lincoln School of Law but he couldn't or wouldn't.

Dorian died doing what he loved: he was surrounded by his marijuana harvest, drying his plants and trimming the buds. He would package them for sale by his brother in South Lake Tahoe. I was not able to attend his funeral, but I did send his two children a card expressing to them how much he had loved them.

I would not have wanted to attend the funeral for one reason: his wife Catherine would have pointed me out as a child molester and I did not want that confrontation to detract from Dorian's funeral service.

She had helped to put him in an early grave. Once when I was living in a trailer on their property I overheard an argument between Dorian and her above me on their balcony. Dorian was remembering the anniversary of his father's suicide, when she arrogantly chastised him telling him to get over it. "That was twelve years ago," she screamed at him. She was not a sensitive person. When she was in the process of divorcing Dorian she had burned all of his financial records so he could not prove much of his money was not community property.

I was down to two friends, other than my Russian family and friends: Ray Robinson and John Tramposch, otherwise known by his artist name Chip Fyn.

Another noteworthy tidbit that occurred on my trip was the loss of my house. Although I had obtained the services of a property management firm to rent my house out, those so-called professionals had selected losers for my tenants.

The tenants only paid one month's rent and then complained that the stove did not work. Nick was kind enough to check it out and install a new stove. But that did not get me rent. They came up with a long list of imagined complaints and used that to claim they would not pay the rent, and they would not leave.

I used a credit card to obtain the services of an attorney to evict them. After two weeks, the attorney called me for another $1500 stating that the losers had sub-let the house to a relative and I would have to pay to evict the relative. Instead, I just stopped making payments on the house. I called the city of West Sacramento to shut off the utilities as they were in my name. The city did, but turned them back on the next day when the tenants complained. Nine months later the city's attorney tried collecting six months of utility bills from me but there was no way I would pay for services they rendered to someone other than myself.

I could not afford the $1400 it cost to pay for the RV and the $1300 it cost to pay the mortgage out of my $3100 pension income, so I let the house go into foreclosure. I may have been in the front of the line of the foreclosure mess that is still playing havoc with the economy today, six years later.

While I was visiting Chip in Arizona after my return from the east coast, I found an enterprising guy who was advertising on Craigslist. He was selling RVs to whoever wanted to take over payments. He would get a substantial down payment from them, make sure they insured it and keep the title in the original owner's name until he could get the new owner financing. I contacted him and offered to sell him my Knight. He agreed to give me $2000 for my equity and he would come to Sacramento to pick up the RV in a month. The loan company was reluctant to let me off the hook for the loan, but once they started accepting payments from the new owner, I was de facto off the liability hook.

So now I had very bad credit but no debts. As a resident of Oregon my pension was exempt from collection agencies so I did not even have to file bankruptcy again.

I bought a Dodge truck and a Lance cab-over camper for cash. Although this looked like I was downsizing, in retrospect I should have done this from the beginning. It is a very efficient way to see the country. This setup was getting me 14 miles per gallon of diesel compared to the 7 mpg I was getting with the quarter of a million dollar Monaco Knight. I could remove the cab and would then get 20 mph. Hindsight is always twenty-twenty vision.

My retirement was much as I dreamed. I re-visited the nation's most unique National Park- Yellowstone. Just before I retired at the age of sixty-two I was able to obtain a Golden Age passport for a mere $10. It let me into any National Park free and the cost for campsites were half-price. Many state park systems honor the Golden Age passport so this became an inexpensive way to see God's beauty.

I started to market my photographs and created a website to publicize my work. One page of my website offered a chance for others to become affiliates. For a mere hundred dollars they would have the right to purchase my canvases wholesale, if they bought three at a time, and make a profit.

I spent more time closer to home, which I considered to be Oregon, California and Arizona. I would visit Kathy and Ray in Oregon and make a side trip almost three hundred miles to the east to Christmas Valley. I would also visit Chip and Annie in Arizona, especially when it was too cold in Oregon. And I spent a lot of time with my family, the Klimovs. Visiting them was really like coming home.

One affiliate was from Japan. She quickly bought three of my four-foot wide canvases. But she explained that the Japanese had a hard time pronouncing Panoramagraphs, so I came up with a new name: Vistagraphs. I changed my web address accordingly.

Because I did not want to invest in a $5000 printer, I was having my canvases printed in the Bronx, New York, and they were costing me $10 a square foot plus the cost of shipping them across country. Trying to sell my work for $99 when it was costing me more than seventy bucks was not a good business model if one wanted to make a profit.

One day I received an email from China from a printer who was offering to print on canvas for $2.78 a square foot. Now I could get my eight foot wide canvases, which were about three feet tall, printed for under $75.

As my files were more than a gigabyte in size, I had to put one on a DVD and mail it. The mail to China is not as reliable as it is in the US. Sometimes I would send a DVD with the same file three times because it was never delivered.

It finally dawned on me that although I took the photograph and made the subsequent vistagraphs at 300 dpi, I could reduce the size to 75 dpi in Photoshop, upload it to the server, and have my Chinese printer download it and re-set the dpi to 300 dpi. This solved the postal problem. And it really reduced the turn-around time. I could upload a file and have the canvas in six days.

It was costing about fifty dollars to ship a canvas from China. To get the price down, I would order five canvases at a time and the printer would roll two up and put them inside the tube and roll the next three on the outside of the tube. Now it cost fifty dollars to ship five canvases or only ten dollars each.

I was now paying less than twenty dollars for a four-foot wide vistagraphs and selling it for a seventy nine dollar profit. I even sold a few eight-foot canvases for $275. I was making a profit of almost $200 for my large canvases. Retirement was great. I think I was proving wrong those salesmen who were using fear tactics to hustle people into saving hundreds of thousands of dollars for retirement.

In the beginning of the summer of 2007 I decided to develop my Christmas Valley property. I built an 8x10 feet storage shelter. It only took a few days, so I added a covered "porch" which extended the ten foot side by another six feet. I was gone for a few weeks and when I returned the county building inspector had a note on it that prohibited me from inhabiting the "building". The reason posted was that I did not obtain a building permit. Although a permit is not required for an 8x10 structure, the fact that I added a "porch" was their reason for claiming I was in violation of the building code.

Because the structure was too close to the dirt road and would get covered by dust every time a car drove by, I decided to donate the structure to a local church rather than obtain a permit. As I used screws to assemble the shed, it was easy to disassemble. I required the church member to remove it within forty-eight hours, but I kept the door and window. He did. He left no evidence that there was ever a structure there. I never heard from the building department. Perhaps they could not locate where the violation was. Most lots in Christmas Valley were not developed. Mine was the only one on my block that was different.

The following year I built a 16x12 "shed" about forty feet from the road and did obtain a permit. I used 2x6s and insulated it because the winters get so cold. I did intend to be able to live in it. I would add a liquid propane gas tank and heater later, and use solar panels for lighting and other electrical needs.

I also built another 8x10 shed without a porch and constructed a small 4x4 shed to house my generator.

My plans to put in a septic would wait. I could not justify spending $5,000 when I could just drive my RV over to the local park and dump as well as get a supply of water. I was only spending a few days a year in Christmas Valley so I did not need a septic tank.

In September of 2008 I stopped by Deadwood, Oregon to visit Kathy and Ray. Ray had a problem with his computer. He did not trust his internet provider and insisted they delete all his email and he would keep his email on his computer. That was just Ray being a control freak. He asked me to find out what was wrong with his computer and fix it.

Ray was brilliant in many areas but was absolutely computer illiterate. A few years earlier I had set up a website for him and his railroad. It was very frustrating trying to show him how to maintain his site which consisted of uploading or deleting pictures, and adding or deleting text. I would show him over and over and over. Ray was very talented when it came to artistic activity such as stained glass windows, and he was a whiz at engineering feats as his railroad attested. But when it came to the left side of his brain, he was useless.

So I set out to see what his computer problem was. It turned out much of his hard drive was wiped out by a virus. He had a habit of visiting porn sites and did not bother to install any virus protection. Porn sites are notorious for distributing viruses especially if you visit but do not purchase anything.

I was able to discover and get rid of his virus and spent the next two days re-installing most of his programs. I convinced him that he needed to purchase an external hard drive and to back up all of his emails and other data files if he insisted on managing his own emails. I also let him know that all service providers are required by law to keep copies of everything, and that he should ask his internet provider to get all the email files he believed were lost.

I was very sick during the three days I spent working on his computer problem. When I explained the computer problem to Kathy she understood immediately. Yet she could not convince him that it was a virus. Ray tended to know it all and no one could add to his knowledge base. I headed south to visit with my Klimov family and then as the Christmas season ended, planned to head for Arizona to visit Chip and Annie.

While I was at the Klimov's I received this email from Ray. What he did not realize was that he inadvertently included correspondence to another person in which he made insulting accusations about me.

This was his email to me, and below it was his correspondence to one of his friends.

(email to Steve Mizera From Ray Robinson)
If by some reason you possibly get this message.............
realize you are still my friend and always will be, but never, ever will you be allowed to touch my computer nor even check your email on my or Kathys machine ever again. You fucked me over as no one has done for many, many years. I lost thousands of emails and all information dealing with Lane county. If you do not accept your responsibility in this, then Never, ever visit here again.....................................

Your not quite as stupid friend as you evidently think I am !!!!!

Ray

This is a reply to the original message containing the insult he sent to his mailing list. It also includes Ray's reply.

----- Original Message -----
From: Scouter
To: Ray Robinson
Sent: Tuesday, September 30, 2008 2:10 AM
Subject: RE: Pertinent personal contact info.

Did I read that right, your GOOD friend Steve, (the EXPERT from California)? Begs one to wonder how good of a friend he is now. People I refer to as experts in electronics wouldn't have let that happen. It would have been done with caution and concern, with diligence and deliberation resulting in a safe and a secure data transfer and storage particularly with data of such immense personal importance.

There are professional businesses who can retrieve data from some crashed drives, but it is not cheaply done.

Fred

-----Original Message-----
From: Ray Robinson [mailto:kmr3@pioneer.net]
Sent: Sunday, September 28, 2008 9:48 AM
Subject: Re: Pertinent personal contact info.

I wouldn't feel so bad if it had been some sort of failure. My good friend Steve the expert from California) moved everything over to an external hard drive without saving the existing hard drive and that is where the loss happened. He claimed a virus did it which makes me even madder that he would think I am so stupid as to believe his story because he was in a hurry and never backed up the originals.

Needless to say, he will never touch my computer again....not even to check his emails. I lost over 500 names of people who had visited and ridden over the last 5 years as well as hundreds of letters and documents dealing with he county matters.

Ray

Well I was more than a little pissed off at his email. Had he discussed the issue with me, I would have tried once again to let him know that a virus destroyed his files and not me, but he chose to broadcast his defamatory comments to his entire mailing list.

Actually I was more than pissed. I was angry. It was "you're a dime a dozen" all over again. And I planned to get even. I sent the following email to his entire mailing list:

Friday, October 3, 2008 1:03 PM
From:

"Steve Mizera"

To:

"Barbara" , "Bob and Patsy" , dandyvine@msn.com, "Randall Kathy Johnson" , "Kathy" , "Jody MacDonald" , "Robert MacDonald" , "Greg MacDonald" , "tom and Tina Morgan" , "Randall Kathy Caleb Boaz" , "Ray and Kathy Robinson" , "Steve" ... more

I have not been able to sleep since I received the email below from Ray. As he sent it to many in his address book, including you, I thought I would respond and now I am including you.

Steve

This is my letter to Ray and his mailing list.

Ray,

I am writing only to set the record straight and to deal with your demand that I take responsibility for something you perceive that I did wrong.

When I arrived at your home, you told me you were unable to access your e-mail and you were getting an error message when you tried to use your browser. You blamed it on Peak, your service provider.

(I have not used your computer, or Kathy's computer to check my email for more than four months since Kathy's son Greg installed your network.)

I took a look at your problem and after two hours determined that you had been hit by a virus and that it prevented you from using both your browser and your email (Outlook Express).

I spent a total of seven hours copying ALL of your files to a new external hard drive, and reinstalling your operating system along with Internet Explorer (browser). Unfortunately, because you want to be in control, you kept your email on your computer instead of on your service provider's server. Your files, including your address book, were deleted by the virus.

Nevertheless you sought to tell countless people that I fucked up and was not allowed on your property until I took responsibility. So I have taken the liberty to contact those persons on your undisclosed list and to give them additional facts, less they think I really fucked up as you charged.

Now, here is how I am taking responsibility.

In 1976, when you lived on Ball Way in Sacramento and I lived in east Sacramento, you came by my home and picked up 13-year old Barbara, a runaway staying at my home, and took her to your home. (I fully expect you will deny this happened)

After returning her a day later, you described your experience with her as "having pubic hair just like the silk on freshly harvested corn. You described how "tight" she was, and it was the best virgin you ever screwed. You also mentioned you gave her $5.

Why am I bringing this up now...thirty-two years later?

You went to prison in 1983 for molesting two young girls in Shasta County California. Since that time you have consistently denied your deviant behavior, or have re-stated the facts so they favor you.

For years I keep hearing you tell anyone who will listen how you were not guilty etc, etc. etc.

I cringe every time one of your guests brings their teenage daughters over for a "railroad ride" and somehow you end up taking them for a ride in the all-terrain gator. I can only imagine how many more young girl's lives are being ruined.

Each year when I re-register as a sex offender, I am reminded of my deviant behavior and it acts as a deterrent to my re-offending.

But what, if anything, is detering Railroad Ray from re-offending? I suppose nothing is. If you would register, that might be a way to start, first by getting out of your denial stage and finally into a re-habilitation mode.

Yes, you claim you are NOT required to register with the Sex Offender Registration Unit of the Oregon State Police. (You or anyone receiving this email can check with them at 503-378-3720.) I am sure they will be glad to provide the details from the Oregon Revised Statues 181.595, 181.596 and 181.597 which require lifetime registration for persons who have been convicted, even those who have moved to Oregon. Even if they claim you are exempt from Oregon registration, there are Federal statutes that require you to do so.

In case you were not aware of these provisions of the Oregon Statues, it is a CLASS C FELONY to fail to make an initial report. Or maybe you can get your friends in high places to pass special legislation and exempt you.

You and I have very similar facts that dictate why both of us must register. There are NO exemptions to the registration requirement unless you were convicted by reason of insanity.

So as for taking responsibility, it is still not too late for YOU. First, finally admit to your criminal conduct, then comply with the law and register as a sex offender and finally avoid contact with teenage girls so as not to re-offend.

When you can tell me that you have taken responsibility, I will be glad to visit you again and to re-new our forty year friendship.

Steve Mizera

I received a few emails in response. A few took issue with me and re-affirmed their friendship with Ray, but most did not.

This email I received from Kathy's first husband Robert MacDonald: --- On Sat, 10/4/08, Robert MacDonald wrote:

From: Robert MacDonald

Subject: your email

To: steve_mizera@yahoo.com

Date: Saturday, October 4, 2008, 12:50 PM

Just two weeks ago Greg and I where talking on the phone about Ray's problems with the State and County and I mentioned to him that maybe his history was also causing some of the problems. I told Greg that I didn't think we knew the truth about what had happened, and I was right, I know that now thanks to you.

When Kathy and I were divorced and she and Ray became an item I asked her a lot of questions about Ray knowing that my children would be around him. I don't know if she has ever known the truth, she only told me what Ray told her, I think anyway. It is so ironic that she chose to spend her life with Ray, I don't know what you have been told about our history but we married when we where eighteen, were married for twenty one years.

I'm sure there were a lot of factors for the divorce but the main issue going on at that time was she was in counseling because she had been molested by her father from the age of eight until just before we were married, a fact that I was unaware of for the first ten years of our marriage. She would come home from her sessions with comments like I never loved you I just wanted to get away from my father and later it was she had transferred her feelings about her father to me because I was the next male authority in her life. All these years I have tried to stay neutral because I felt sorry for Kathy and didn't want to try and hurt her relationship with our children.

I will have to admit I have always wondered about you, not that you have ever done anything that I found objectionable but I had no idea about yours and Ray's history. I didn't know how long you had known him and if you knew anything about his history. I have never liked being around Ray but found my short time with you has been enjoyable. Ray just rubs me the wrong way. I was grateful for the revelations in your email but a little concerned about the anger you were feeling. In my opinion Ray is not worth losing sleep over, I hope getting things off your chest brought you some relief. I admire how you admit your own issues and how you try to deal with them and I wish you success.

Bob

And this was my reply to Bob:

Bob,

Thanks for taking the time to write.

I have re-read your email a few times.

Perhaps my empathy is with Kathy because I share a part of the victimization aspect of her life. It would not be fair to blame her for withholding information. Most victims of sexual molestation find it so difficult to discuss.

I was raised from the age of two until I was fourteen in Catholic orphanages. You can use your imagination to fill in the blanks. I ultimately felt much safer and saner living on the streets of Philadelphia from 14 until I was 17.

Most of my visits to Deadwood for the past four years have been to see Kathy and to help her in the limited ways I was able to, specifically in an advisory capacity.

I have been listening to Ray lie and sugar-coat his version of his crimes for so many years and I did not take the responsibility to advise others, especially strangers, to be cautious.

Yes, I was angry in my response to his demand that I take responsibility for screwing up his computer. I am sure by reading his comment about "his server" and Peak's server, you can see just how illiterate he is when it comes to computers. I am not sure anyone could convince him that a virus wiped out both his browser and address book files.

Perhaps I over-reacted and should have ignored his insults but I felt enough was enough.

In his reply to my email he made another mistake and ended with another insult. He will pay for it. In the process, it may just be that it will help Kathy more than it hurts him. Thanks again for taking the time to write.

Steve

Ray had let the malice cat out of the bag and it was too late to re-capture it. I supposed he thought it was ok for him to run me down by telling untruths about me to others. So I felt it was ok for me to tell truths about him to those same others. In one respect I should not have reacted the way I did. But on the other hand, it may have brought a stop to his re-offending, if in fact he was offending. At least it would put others on notice to visit Railroad Ray with caution.

Ray had cultivated friendships and manipulated a lot of those people by using an invitation to his property as bait and by exploiting other's love of trains. He would invite many public officials to his property for camp outs and train rides. And then Ray would brag to his other friends about his friendships with important, powerful people. Of course he never let anyone know the truth about his criminal past, but when some learned of it they bailed out of the relationship with him.

The relationships he engineered and manipulated included the press, both the public TV station and Eugene Oregon's major daily newspaper.

When Ray purchased his property there was a rundown house on it. Within a few years Ray completely rebuilt it, but kept the same footprint the old house had made. He would gladly tell anyone who would listen that he did this so he would not have to pay any increase in property tax. His tax bill was a few hundred dollars for the old house, but would have greatly increased if his tax bill was based on the rebuilt home, valued at a few hundred thousand dollars.

Ray considered himself above the law. Why should he have to pay such high taxes? His behavior reminded me of how I viewed the laws as I was growing up.

In my discussion with Lane County taxing authorities, I inquired about the tax on his property. They told me that the value of his property was scheduled to be re-assessed in the coming year. I suggested they could save a trip to his property by looking at his website which had beautiful photographs of the new house he rebuilt, the new barn he rebuilt, and the miles of railroad he laid, complete with bridges and a tunnel. They thanked me for being a good citizen. Although calls like that were supposed to be confidential, the county notified Ray's county commissioner friends that I tipped them off.

It was not long before the county visited Ray's property anyway and required him to pay his fair share on the newly appraised value. They also passed information over to those folks who are in charge of building permits and they inquired of Ray if he had permits for his railroad. Those folks also passed information along to those government people who are concerned with the environment and noted that his railroad was too close to, and had bridges that crossed over, streams that were protected because they were the habitat of endangered fish.

So Ray was visited and hounded by government official after government official, from the county and the state and the federal governments. They all wanted money for penalties, fines, and taxes. Ray tried to get his public officials to go to bat for him and some did, but most did not.

Even the Eugene Register Guard came to his defense in an editorial. After I read it I wrote to them and suggested they should have all the facts before going out on an editorial limb. They tended to believe Ray and his half-truths because Ray was a master manipulator. They finally did what all good journalists should do: they gathered the facts and verified them. They then had a front page story that was a lot closer to the truth.

This was the story the Eugene Oregon Register-Guard printed.

MODEL RAILROAD OWNER CANNOT ESCAPE CRIMINAL PAST

In 1982, Ray Robinson pleaded guilty and served time in prison for lewd and lascivious conduct with two young girls

By Winston Ross - The Register-Guard

(Appeared in print: Tuesday, May 5, 2009,)

DEADWOOD Twenty-seven years ago, a California man named Johnsey Ray Robinson who had just been named Mount Shasta's Citizen of the Year pleaded guilty to two counts of lewd and lascivious conduct with a minor in Siskiyou and Shasta counties. The charges involved two 10-year-old girls.

The 40-year-old served three years of a six-year prison sentence, then got out early because of work he had performed while incarcerated.

After his release, Robinson sold his house and moved to Eugene, wary of death threats back home. He enrolled in a two-year course for the treatment of sex offenders, which he completed in 1988.

A decade later, Robinson and his second wife, Kathleen, moved to Deadwood, a tiny rural community of about 400 people, on a remote 41 acres one mile from his nearest neighbor. It was on this scenic parcel that Robinson set out to accomplish a lifelong dream: to build a model railroad, complete with 5,000 feet of 18-inch gauge track, four engines and 10 cars.

Now, Robinson invites various groups of people each Sunday to come for a ride on the railroad, free of charge. The visitors, adults and children numbering between four and 30, hear about the project through word-of-mouth or via the spate of media attention Robinson has enjoyed since he started construction.

What they tend not to hear about is Robinsons criminal record, though he says he is open about it when asked and makes no effort to hide the past when confronted with it. Robinson is not required to register as a sex offender here or in California, according to officials with the Oregon State Police, because his conviction predates the existence of registry laws that might prevent him from being near minors or allow parents to consult a list and discover his name on it. He does not have a criminal record in Oregon.

Still, Robinsons past has a way of coming back to haunt him.

In 1986, Robinson tried to persuade the Eugene City Council to let him build a miniature railroad in Alton Baker Park. The project died after opponents threatened to go to the press with a story about sex offender gets to build kiddy ride in local park, Robinson said.

In 2006, Robinson successfully obtained a restraining order against a Deadwood resident named John Dickerson. According to an affidavit Robinson filed in Lane County Circuit Court, the two of them had a dispute about the quality of food at Dickerson's local grocery, and Dickerson decided to post fliers in the area with some accurate and some inaccurate information about Ray's past.

The headline: Warning convicted child molester living in Deadwood, OR.

Robinson told the court he had only a speeding ticket on his record since his time in prison and that he takes great care to ensure that children who visit his property do so only under the close and continual supervision of an adult. This is to ensure that they are safe from injury as well as to protect Robinson, to ensure that I am never in any sort of compromising position and simply cannot be accused of any inappropriate conduct toward any minor.

The fliers Dickerson posted suggested otherwise, according to Robinson. Dickerson could not be reached for comment; he no longer owns the store in Deadwood and has an unlisted telephone number.

It is absolutely untrue that any inappropriate conduct has occurred since my release from prison, Robinson wrote. It is absolutely untrue that any minors are put at risk of sexual molestation by me as a result of visiting the railroad.

A judge agreed and enjoined Dickerson from posting any more fliers. But it wasn't the last time Robinsons past would rear its head.

To keep his followers posted on the railroad projects progress, Robinson sends out regular dispatches via e-mail to a group of about 65 people. Last October, a then-friend of Robinsons sent an e-mail addressed to Ray but including several of the people Robinson regularly e-mails.

In the e-mail, the man accused Robinson of having inappropriate contact with a minor in 1976. The e-mail also stated that Robinson refused to take responsibility for what he had done, and that he should register as a sex offender in order to get out of his denial stage.

"I cringe every time one of your guests brings their teenage daughters over for a railroad ride," the man wrote.

The man, who did not respond to an e-mail request for an interview, also identified himself in that e-mail as a registered sex offender.

Robinson responded angrily.

"You will probably be shocked to know that everyone on this list except four people already knows of my past because, unlike you, I have admitted all and moved on," Robinson wrote.

Beyond those disputes, Robinsons past is not the subject of any public debate. His battles with Lane County over the permits he failed to acquire before building the railroad have become the focus of a fair amount of media attention, but the sex charges aren't part of the land use dialogue.

They do present an ethical conundrum for those who support Robinson's railroad effort. Both Senator Bill Morrisette and Lane County Commissioner Bill Fleenor say they have known for years about Robinsons past conviction, and that they have made conscious decisions not to let that past cloud their choices to try to help Robinson keep the railroad alive.

Fleenor said its about the criminal justice system, which is supposed to rehabilitate people so that they may be released back into society to live normal lives. As far as anybody knows, Fleenor said, that's exactly what happened here.

"He confessed, he did the time, he was released with no strings attached," Fleenor said. "Ray is a changed man. He's happily married, and happens to have a hobby that many Americans would love to have."

Fleenor acknowledges that the issue of whether Ray's past is relevant is a tricky one, given that most parents would probably want to be able to make informed decisions about whether their children should visit his property.

But the courts decided that unnecessary, Fleenor said.

"I do believe our law-and-order criminal justice system serves a function to make people behave right," Fleenor said. "If locking people up doesn't cause people to change their behavior, then we had better stop locking people up."

Morrisette, who introduced a bill in the Legislature that would have exempted Robinson from land use laws for five years, agrees with Fleenor. But Morrisette also said he probably wouldn't have introduced the bill if he'd known that children sometimes frequent the property with adults other than their parents, as part of a group or the like, if only because he wouldn't want to have to answer to upset people about why he advocates for "Railroad Ray."

Morrisette also pointed out that "under today's standards, the law says you need to make people aware you're a sex offender."

Lane County Commissioner Bill Dwyer said the issue is a "precautionary principle," that people should be informed before they send children to Deadwood and make their own choices.

"A guy who turns his life around, I have to commend him for that," Dwyer said. "But for parents to take their kids on railroads, they ought to be aware. I'm not saying it would or wouldn't happen again."

What seems certain to happen again is for Robinsons past to interfere somehow in his present, especially as he continues to make headlines for his battle with the county. He's frustrated by that, he said, but did not react angrily upon learning The Register-Guard would be writing about his history. He said he welcomed the opportunity to set the record straight and has nothing to hide.

"The county picking on my railroad bothers me a hell of a lot more," Robinson said. "I've dealt with this. I spent three years in prison. I had to deal with who I am, all the stuff that happened, to get to a place where I could forgive myself. I have paid for my frickin crime. People just keep coming out of the woods."

So my relationship and friendship with Ray Robinson had come to a dramatic end after forty years. Ray had often told me what goes around comes around. Ray claimed not to be, but he was quite vindictive. I should have been more attentive. I set in motion too many problems he did not have the ability to solve. He could only get even. And he would.

The reason the reporter did not get a reply to his email to me will soon become clear.

Now I was down to one friend, other than my Klimov family and church friends. I was on my way to Arizona after the Christmas holidays in 2008 to visit Chip Fyn, whose real name is John Tramposch, and his wonderful mate Annie, and their neat pups George and Missy.

Chapter Twelve
Return to Grace - 2006

Chronic hostility and hatred are among the most toxic forms of stress. When you are really angry with someone as I was with Ray, you empower that person you hate to make you stressed out or even sick. That is not smart. That was not what I wanted to dwell on. So I spent the next few months with people I love, with the Klimovs, and with my brothers and sisters at Grace Family Church.

Benjamin Kondor is a pastor at Grace Family Church. In my opinion, he is the ideal family man and sets an admirable example for the flock. He is giving and caring. He is intelligent and perceptive. In a conversation with me one day he asked when I was going to be baptized. I pointed out that I was baptized in November, 1940, sixty-eight years ago. I mentioned that I was less than seven weeks old.

Benjamin proceeded to explain the concept of baptism and the beliefs of Baptists in general.

Baptism, commonly referred to as believer's baptism among Baptists and sometimes other groups, is administered by full immersion in water after a person professes Jesus Christ to be Savior. It is seen as an act of obedience to the example and command of Jesus given in the Great Commission (Matthew 28:19-20). It is an outward expression that is symbolic of the inward cleansing or remission of their sins that has already taken place. It is also a public identification of that person with Christianity and with that particular local church.

Baptists believe that Christian baptism is the immersion of a believer in water. It is an act of obedience symbolizing the believer's faith in a crucified, buried, and risen Saviour, the believer's death to sin, the burial of the old life, and the resurrection to walk in newness of life in Jesus Christ.

Baptists, like most other Christians who believe in baptism by total immersion, read Biblical passages to imply that the practice intentionally symbolizes burial and resurrection. Especially when performed before onlookers, the total immersion ceremony depicts a burial (when the person being baptized is submerged under the water, as if buried), and a resurrection (when the person comes up out of the water, as if rising from the grave).

In short it is a "death" and a "burial" to an old way of life focused on sinning, and a "resurrection" to the start of a new life as a Christian focused on God. Christians typically believe that John 3:3-5 also supports this view, with its implication that water baptism symbolizes (but does not produce) a Christian being "born again" spiritually.

This revelation was like a bright light coming on. It was what had been missing in my life. I realized I needed to be baptized. I needed to bury my old way of the life of sin. At the age of sixty-eight, I had such a short period of time left to start a new life as a Christian.

Benjamin further explained that Baptists do not practice infant baptism (pedobaptism) because they believe parents cannot make a decision of salvation for an infant.

Related to this doctrine is the concept, often disputed, of an "age of accountability" when God determines that a mentally capable person is accountable for their sins and eligible for baptism. This is not a specific age, but is based on whether or not the person is mentally capable of knowing right from wrong.

A person with severe mental retardation may never reach this age, and therefore would not be held accountable for sins. The book of Isaiah mentions an age at which a child "shall know to refuse the evil, and choose the good" but does not specify what that age is.

For purposes of accepting transfer of membership from other churches, Baptist churches only recognize baptism by full immersion as being valid. Some Baptist churches will recognize "age of accountability" baptisms by immersion performed in other Christian churches of "like faith and order," while others only recognize baptisms performed in Baptist churches.

Baptists are known for re-baptizing converts to their faith those who were previously baptized as infants or small children. Because of this, the first Baptist congregations were dubbed "Anabaptists", which means re-baptizers.

So I would also be re-baptized. What happened to me at seven weeks of age at St. Ambrose Catholic church in Pennsylvania was not consistent with the Baptist's teachings and beliefs. There was no understanding or accountability when I was baptized within weeks of my birth. There was no immersion, but instead a sprinkling of a few drops of water on my forehead.

During the latter part of the Middle Ages, some people who were studying the Bible became convinced that infant baptism, (i.e. the sprinkling of babies with water by a priest), was unscriptural. As a result, these men began to "re-baptize" each other. These people were called "re"-baptizers by Roman Catholics and Protestants, (because most of these Baptists had already been "sprinkled" by the Roman Catholic Church when they were infants.)

There were millions of such Anabaptists and other early Baptists between the end of the Middle Ages and the early Reformation period.

The Anabaptists (Baptists) based their insistence on the baptism of non-infants who believed on Jesus Christ alone for salvation on three primary arguments: The Bible does not mention any babies or small children being baptized. (There is no record of infants being baptized in the Bible.)

The word for "baptize" in the original Greek means "to immerse" in water.

The Bible says that those who believe may be baptized. Since infants cannot understand, and therefore cannot believe on Jesus Christ, baptism must then be for adults or at least for those old enough to understand. It must not be for infants. Also, Baptists believe that baptism plays no part in salvation itself.

During this period of time, the act of infant baptism was widely practiced throughout Europe. In some places, infant baptism was practically considered to be a part of the rite of citizenship, (almost like a birth certificate is today). Therefore, those rejecting infant baptism were often accused of disloyalty or rebellion against civil government.

These Baptists were also often hated and persecuted by the Roman Catholic Church -- which by this time strongly promoted the practice of infant baptism. (The Roman Catholic Church had originally practiced the immersion of adults, but by this time in history, the sprinkling of adults and then of infants had become its main practice.) Therefore, a rejection by Baptists of infant baptism was often considered to be an attack or subversion against the Roman Catholic Church itself. For this reason, many Popes, and those under them, ordered the persecution of these "rebellious" Baptists.

My resentment of the Catholic Church was based on the beatings in the first orphanage. Now, after researching the relationship between Catholics and Baptist, there also appears to be both an historical and philosophical basis for my rejection of Catholicism as a teenager.

Another reason for the persecution of Baptists was their insistence on "believers only" baptism, which was seen as an attack on the "salvation by works" theology widely taught by the Roman Catholic Church. During this period of time, millions of Baptists and others had their property confiscated and many of them were tortured. Millions of Baptists were killed under direct or indirect influence of the Roman Catholic Church.

The Reformation brought three main groups of Protestants into existence: These were the "Calvinists", founded by John Calvin in Northern Europe; the "Anglicans", (or "Church of England"); and the "Lutherans", (founded in Germany by the former monk, Martin Luther). These three, together with a few other smaller groups, comprised the Protestants.

The Protestants for the most part continued the Roman Catholic medieval practice of infant baptism. Because Baptists rejected such infant baptism, the Baptists were never really considered to be Protestants in the general sense. Also, because of this rejection of infant baptism, Baptists were often persecuted by both Protestants and Roman Catholics alike.

Although I was taught the beliefs of the Catholic Church for most of my first dozen years of life, I had no idea what Catholics believed. So now as I was to be baptized as an adult, I was compelled to research the differences and similarities.

I learned that many Roman Catholic beliefs were different from the Baptist beliefs I was studying. The Roman Catholic Church teaches the doctrine of "salvation by works" -- that one is saved through the use of the sacraments of the Roman Catholic Church, (such as through infant baptism, the "Mass", Communion, etc.).

Catholics believe that by taking part in or participating in these sacraments, salvation is "infused" into a person through these works. (An example of infusion is what happens when a tea bag comes in contact with boiled water. The tea in the teabag infuses into the water, changing the plain hot water into a hot cup of "tea".)

In contrast Baptists believe in salvation by grace alone through faith in Christ, apart from works. My return to Grace would be founded on my belief in eternal salvation by grace rather than by works. I would focus on my faith in Jesus Christ.

The Roman Catholic Church emphasizes the "Mass", which is seen as an act re-sacrificing the actual body and blood of Christ by a priest. Because Baptists believe that Christ is up in Heaven, (and not down on a Communion table), they therefore consider the Mass to be blasphemous.

The primary reason I left the Catholic Church was I rejected their claim to be able to forgive sins in their confessional booth. Baptists believe that Christ died only once, and that this one death by Christ was sufficient to pay for all of the sins of all mankind throughout all history.

Catholics also believe in "Purgatory", a place where men and woman go to be temporarily "purged" by fire for their sins. Baptists teach that the Bible knows nothing of Purgatory. Baptists believe rather that after death, there are only two places where people go: Heaven and Hell. (In other words, there is not a third option, the place that Roman Catholics have devised.

Catholics believe in a Universal (Catholic) Church, which they say was set in place by the Apostle Peter, whom they call the first "Pope" - guardian of the keys to the Gates of Heaven and Hell. Baptists believe in the autonomy and authority of the Local church, that each individual Baptist church is independent from all other human authority and also from all other churches as well.

Catholics believe in offering prayers to Mary and to the Saints. Baptists believe that prayer should only be made to God in the name of Christ.

How many thousands of Hail Marys had I chanted in St. Francis during the afternoon marches through the countryside? For each difference in beliefs I discovered, I was siding totally with the Baptist beliefs.

Is there, as the Catholics claim, salvation in the name of Mary or the Saints? That answer can be found in Acts 4:12 : "...for there is none other name under heaven given among men, whereby we must be saved."

Catholics believe in the authority of the Roman Catholic Bible as well as the authority of the traditions and teachings of the Roman Catholic Church and of the Pope. Baptists believe in the authority of the Bible plus faith - that the Bible alone is a sufficient basis for all faith and practice.

In my opinion the teachings of the Pope are suspect at best because of the world-wide sexual abuse scandal that the last two Popes have ignored or covered up.

The Bible, inspired by God, is the only true authority.

Perhaps the most profound difference and that which turned me against Catholics at the age of twelve was confession. Catholics believe in the mediation of Roman Catholic priests. (What child molested by a Catholic priest could possibly believe that the priest is a mediator with God?) Baptists believe that there is only one mediator between God and man, and that one mediator is "the man Christ Jesus". (I Timothy 2:5) I had personally arrived at this conclusion while rejecting the concept of a mediator between me and my creator at the age of twelve.

Catholics believe in the practice of worshipping icons in the Church. Baptists believe that all such religious icons are idolatrous, and therefore reject their use, both as decorations and as objects of worship. For this reason, Baptist churches generally lack the statues and paintings of saints commonly found in most Roman Catholic churches. Baptist churches tend to be decorated more simply and much less ornately as a result of the views that Baptists hold against icons.

I was sold. I was ready to be baptized, and I would be in mid-March after my visit with Chip and Annie. In late January, 2009, I headed for Apache Junction, Arizona.

Benjamin Kondor loaded me down with a lot of homework that I was eager to complete. Essentially, it was a course of study in what Baptists believed and why they did. There were many references to the Bible.

My trips to Arizona were always a pleasure. I had been making the trip every February for the last ten years while I was working for the state. I would head down Interstate 5 in the afternoon and by evening I would find a rest area in which to overnight, usually a few hundred miles or more south of Sacramento. In the early morning I would head east to Bakersfield and then over the Tehachapi mountains bypassing both the town of Tehachapi and my old alma mater California State Prison at Tehachapi. On a few occasions, there would be snow on the side of the highway but the road was always clear. I usually made it a point to stop at Mojave, California, and get my five mile walk in. The air at the 4000 foot elevation in the desert is so sweet. There was always a rest stop near the Arizona border if I did not want to be in Arizona until the following day. But by early morning I would find myself heading east out of Phoenix on Highway 60 to Apache Junction.

Chip had told me that he was renting space in an RV park and he had made arrangements for me to stay in their parking lot at no charge.

I always had good visits with Chip. He was a brilliant artist and had a great sense of humor. I am always amused when I recall the circumstances under which I first met him in 1975. He was carving life-sized statues of everyone from Charlie Chaplin to Superman out of Ponderosa pine trees. He did a lot of research and had carved and sold many cigar store Indians, his first carvings. I met him when he was putting the finishing touches on an eight-foot Ronald MacDonald holding a hamburger above his head.

After the novelty of making large wooden carvings from pine trees wore off, Chip got into pottery. He would

318

make mug-mugs, or ceramic mugs with caricature faces. Customers would mail him a photograph and he would make a mug with their "mug" on it.

On a visit a few years earlier, I had introduced Chip to the computer age by bringing him a workable desktop unit. The following year it was still sitting on the garage floor where I had delivered it. He had met Annie by then and was living in a house she owned. A few years later Chip did get into computers. Annie bought him a state-of-the-art Apple.

Chip was now doing airplanes. He would research every airplane ever made and make a colorful drawing of it to scale that could be printed onto 5x7 inch cardboard stock. Then by using scissors, a buyer could cut out the various parts and bend and glue tabs together to produce a model of the plane.

He would make an original and have the printer produce thousands that Chip offered for sale at public events where artists sell their crafts.

Finally Chip had such a large collection he bypassed the printer and started offering them on CDs. The customers could do their own printing. There would be a CD for WW1 planes, one for his WWII collection, and one containing every helicopter ever made. He also did dirigibles and other crafts including the plane the Wright brothers made and flew.

Chip is the only person I know that does not have a social security number and he is now 72 years old, two years older than me. On one visit, as a joke, I was with him when he stopped by the social security office in Tempe, Arizona and asked what the balance was on his social security account. The woman could not believe he did not have a number and offered to provide him with one. He declined.

Chip knew how to make a buck other than with his drawings or artistic skills. Even though he and Annie lived full time in an RV for the past ten years, he was able to "earn" about $10,000 annually to pay for the fuel in an interesting manner. He had two puppies: George and Missy. They produced half-dozen pups twice a year and each puppy sold for about $800. They were little white Jack Russell terriers.

Chip had cut a hole in the floor in the RV's bedroom. He then built a walk-up ramp from the storage area in the RV's basement just for the pups. He kept a lamp in the storage space to keep the pups warm and even installed a camera with sound so he would be alerted if there was a problem in his nursery!

We had traveled to so many places together. We often met at different locations for visits and then we would go our separate ways. He had introduced me to the RV lifestyle which I continue to enjoy to this day and do not see myself ever again being any other kind of homeowner.

Annie was a few years older than Chip but absolutely loyal to him. She gave up her home so Chip could get a better RV. She had a good head for business and applied that to Chip's website: Fiddlersgreen.net. That site produced about $400 just from Google ads every month. His CDs provided an untold amount of tax-free cash which Chip kept in hundred dollar bills in the RV's freezer, or his "safe" as Chip referred to it.

Shortly after I met Chip in the mid-70s at the Sacramento K Street mall art exhibit where he was finishing Ronald MacDonald, I moved to Pollock Pines, fifty miles east of Sacramento. Chip had many girlfriends during the few years we spent there. Chip had two of his teenage children living with him: Scott and Jac. Scott later ended up molesting a child when he visited his mom in Tuscon and spent almost twenty years in an Arizona prison. Jac followed in his dad's footprints and learned to make mug-mugs and spent the next twenty years on the Oregon coast making them in his own business.

Chip was living with a beautiful blonde when I went to prison. When I was released I stopped by to visit Chip who was still in Pollock Pines, but the beautiful blonde had taken a fancy for Jac when he was sixteen and she decided she wanted to have him instead of Chip. She was at least twice his age. In California the legal definition of child molestation requires one party to be under eighteen, and the other party to be more than ten years older. By definition she was a child molester.

They eventually got married and their relationship lasted almost fifteen years.

Ironically, when I got out of prison and visited Chip in Pollock Pines, she did not want to have anything to do with me because I was a child molester. I might have suggested to her that people who live in glass houses should not throw stones, but I did not.

She also proclaimed to be a Christian. Perhaps she never learned the words hypocrite or honesty. She was both a hypocrite and dishonest. It is no wonder I cannot remember her name now. That she let me know how she detested child molesters supports the saying: "It takes one to know one."

Chip was only a little annoyed that she snagged his son Jac. Chip has had a number of wives, and other kids, so I guess when it came to women for him it was easy come, easy go.

So I never knew what to expect from Chip during our visits. This visit was different. There was apparently something bothering Chip and I never learned what it was.

The first morning I awoke in the parking spot that Chip claimed he made arrangements for me to stay at no cost.

The park manager was banging on my door asking "what are you doing here?" And "who are you?" She would not accept my answer that I was visiting Chip and he had told me it was ok to be where I was. She demanded $25 a night, and I would have paid her and stayed there but I did not like her attitude so I opted to park on a side street, right across from the park and right across from Chip's rented space. When I brought this to Chip's attention he shrugged it off as it was no big thing. It was to me.

In a day or two Chip asked if we could ride in my truck instead of him having to unhook his RV so we could all go off hiking. Chip and Annie and I headed to a state park to hike. But as I was pulling into a parking lot preparing to make a wide turn so I could back into a space, Chip accused me of trying to run people over and announced he would never go anywhere with me again. Chip was out of character with his anger.

This was not to be a normal visit.

The following morning I dropped in for a cup of coffee as was the tradition for more than a dozen years. Before the water was boiled he proclaimed that I needed to move my truck and camper or else I would get a ticket or be hassled by the local sheriff. The street I was parked on had no traffic. His insistence that I move said much more than I was hearing. I have a long-standing policy with myself that I do not go where I am not welcomed.

Perhaps I over-reacted but I got into my truck and left. It was obvious to me that we could not discuss this incident either. I did not get angry but I had no intention on continuing this visit. I was once again burning a bridge behind me. I did not know why, nor did I want to know.

On an earlier visit to Tempe I had met an 85 year old woman. Helen Schlie, who was a published poet, a dedicated Mormon and a businesswoman who owned a bookstore located just a few miles away. I went to visit her. That was a good visit because it took my mind off my problem with Chip.

She had a lot of art in her store so I asked if I could display one of my vistagraphs of Superstition Mountain. I asked if she would be interested in trying to sell some of her things on eBay. She said she would but had no idea how. So out came my camera, and I made a number of photographs of different items she might be able to sell. I uploaded them to eBay and explained the eBay concept. She was very intelligent and picked up even the smallest details from my explanation.

In particular she had two original Books of Mormon worth many thousands of dollars. She had previously removed a few pages and had each page encased in plastic attached to a solid wood base. I photographed these and uploaded them to eBay.

I also tutored Helen on Craigslist, the world-wide free classified advertising website available on the internet.

Helen's bookstore was in a nice location. I had my trailer behind my truck and camper. She thought it would be a good idea if I tried to sell some vistagraphs from my tent next to her store.

(Almost two years later when Helen learned that I was writing this autobiography, she offered to edit it. So, I made a copy of it and mailed it to her. She emailed back that she cried after the first few chapters. A few weeks later she sent a cryptic email that I could not understand. I think I concluded from it that she became more offended the more she read, especially the research I printed about the Church of Latter Day Saints.)

In my trailer I had about fifty of my vistagraphs, mostly the four foot wide canvases. But I did have a dozen of my eight foot canvases too. One of my favorites is the vistagraph I made of the US hundred dollar bill. Benjamin Franklin is one of two historical figures whose likeness is on

US currency who was never a president. He is my favorite. And when someone sees the eight foot wide hundred, their curiosity gets the best of them and they stop to chat, if not to buy.

Chip stopped by. He also had a small Vespa-like scooter. Strapped to the back was a plastic milk crate and he liked taking the pups for a ride. He had actually made each of them a plastic helmet, even though Arizona is one of the few states remaining that does not require a helmet be worn by motorcycle riders.

But before he could get stopped and start a conversation, I turned and said in disgust, "Oh, it's you."

That was stupid on my part, but it was enough to cause him to leave. We have never seen or talked to each other since. We have not even sent each other an email. I had just erased one of my finest relationships. After sixty-nine years, I still did not know how to make and keep a relationship. And the termination of this relationship was a big loss.

In a few days I headed west on Highway 10, the major route between Phoenix and Los Angeles. Halfway between the two cities is a single lane highway that enters Joshua National Park from the south. I have been to that park at least a dozen times, and it never gets old. I spent a few days camping out. I was somewhat saddened by the loss of my relationship with Chip. And I never got to say goodbye to Annie. That hurt too.

I left the park and traveled north to Barstow, California. About thirty miles south I spotted a small gas station and decided I would top off my tanks as diesel might be more expensive in Barstow.

That was one of those events that changed the course of my history. As I was filling the tank, I became aware that the fuel pump's meter was turning ever so slow. It was cold and windy and I almost stopped pumping. I should have.

About ten miles later on my way to Barstow I glanced at my fuel gauge and notice I was running on empty. I immediately pulled over. How could I be empty when I just filled the tank? I looked under the truck expecting to find it soaked and smelling of diesel fuel. It wasn't. Perhaps, I thought, the gauge just broke. I proceeded to head north to Barstow but the truck was acting very strange. It is an ascent up a long hill as you approach within fifteen miles of Barstow. Although it was a windy day and I was up against a headwind, my truck had eight speeds and a powerful diesel, yet I could not go faster than 35 miles per hour. I stopped and checked under the truck again, but there was not a drop of fluid.

At a repair facility in Barstow I was informed that I must have gotten contaminated fuel and that I would need to change filters and probably the sending unit and maybe a fuel pump. I decided to head for Sacramento and get the repairs done there. It took two more days to finish the next 345 miles to Sacramento.

I stayed with Nick and Marina and looked for a diesel repair facility. It would cost $500 to get me on the road again. I would have to bring the truck in without the camper. So, I removed the camper and set it up in the Klimov backyard. The repair shop said it would take a few days. I told them I was not in a hurry as I was about to be baptized. That would take place on Sunday, March 15, 2009.

I spent the next few weeks with the study materials Benjamin had given me and was ready to become immersed, to become a real Christian, to leave my life of crime behind, just as I had left Ray Robinson and Chip Fyn behind. I was committing to a new life; I would live for Jesus Christ. It felt good to be heading in that direction. Without friends who were not Christian, I would find it easier to return to Grace.

Chapter Thirteen
Priceless - 2011

My baptism at the age of sixty-eight has been the highlight of my life. I don't recall ever taking anything more seriously. I had spent my life breaking just about all of the commandments so frequently, it would be a real challenge to focus on reversing that behavior.

I was one of a dozen who were baptized at Grace Family Church on Sunday, March 15, 2009. The other eleven were all teenagers. We were all dressed in white robes. The regular Sunday service at Grace Family Church was expanded for an extra half hour for the benefit of those being baptized. As is generally the case, the service was conducted in the Russian language. Pastor Benjamin Kondor spoke excellent English and asked me to give a witness or testimony. I had nothing prepared and was very nervous.

Actually, I was very emotional as I started to tell the 350 plus members and guests, how I had led a life of crime for the previous six decades. I was in tears as I told about being convicted and incarcerated in Folsom State Prison. I blurted out how fearful I was and how I cried out to God for help. I admitted I could not make it without Him.

The pastors and those in attendance prayed alone with us as we were about to be immersed in water.

Being totally immersed was for me a "death" and a "burial" of a way of life where my life mostly focused on sinning. As I emerged soaking wet, it was like a "resurrection" to the start of a new life as a Christian but now focused on God. Now I was truly a Christian. I was being born again spiritually.

For the first time, we took of the ceremonial bread and wine in remembrance of Jesus Christ. He sacrificed

His life to erase the sins of my past. I never felt so holy, so clean, so loved.

I had made a big commitment and I had promised to spend the rest of my life walking with Jesus. That was not a light obligation. I welcomed it.

The end of the service was also something I will never forget.

I received a dozen bouquets of flowers. I never knew I had so many friends. I really never knew love could be so profound. The Klimovs took me out for lunch along with about twenty friends. We all returned to Grace for the evening service. I felt like a new man, a complete man, a completely **new** man. Baptism was such an overwhelming and life-changing experience for me. It would be a challenge for me to change my behavior, but I was willing to give one hundred percent.

I had spent the month of March at the Klimov's. It was part of my daily schedule to go to 24 Hour Fitness daily and get four or five miles on the treadmill. Today would be the last time I would do this as I planned to head for Oregon the next day, April 1st. That would also be my retirement anniversary. I had retired five years ago.

As I went to get into my truck, a gray van stopped in front of the Klimov driveway effectively blocking my way as I had to back out into the street.

Two men got out and one asked me if this was my truck. I said it was. He asked if I lived here and I told him I had been here for a while getting my truck repaired but I was heading home tomorrow. He motioned to my camper still set up in the Klimov back yard and asked if that was mine. I assured him it was. I had set up a short clothes line and had a set of my gym clothes airing out. He asked if they were mine. I never got around to asking who he was and what all his questions were about.

The other guy had gone to the Klimov front door and I now noticed him talking to Slava. The fellow questioning me asked if he could look in my trailer. It dawned on me that he had to be a cop, a detective and as I did not have anything to hide I told him he could. He picked up an envelope addressed to me that contained a receipt for Bank of America stock I had purchased.

He said you are under arrest because you are living in California and you have not registered as a sex offender.

He walked me to the side of his van and said he would put the cuffs on here so I wouldn't be embarrassed. By now Marina and Valeriy had come out and were probably as much in shock as I was.

I had never discussed my crime or obligation to register with the Klimovs, although I did mention that I spent time in prison. They never asked for any details and had accepted me for what they knew me to be. So now they would get to know the details of my past.

Being back in the Sacramento County jail was not a fun experience. After being booked and being handed a copy of the booking sheet, I noted that bail was set at $1,000,000. The first time I was arrested, I turned myself in, accompanied by my attorney, and was released on my own recognizance. But that was in 1981, twenty-eight years ago.

Times have changed. I actually was not aware that I had to register in California as I was already registered in Oregon. The Oregon State police had my phone number and if I was ever needed they could call me. When I last registered in West Sacramento five years earlier, I received a small piece of paper that measured 3 inches by 3 inches which was proof of my registration.

What law had I broken? I had not moved to California. I was here because my truck broke down and because I was baptized.

I was able to make a free call from the County jail's holding cell. Fortunately I remembered the Klimov home number. They were totally sympathetic and supportive.

After being stripped and going through the humiliating experience of bending over and spreading the cheeks of my butt, opening my mouth and removing my false teeth, I was held along with a dozen others in a holding tank for the next twenty six hours.

Marina has a younger brother who had a few problems drinking and spent time in the county jail so she knew the procedure for visiting. She and Nick showed up at the first opportunity for an hour and a half visit. Visiting inmates was permitted twice a week and Nick and Marina made sure someone came to visit on every occasion. Pastors from the church came, so did the Klimov boys and Yelena's husband Stas.

Slava became my lifeline providing me with money so I could purchase whatever I needed from the jail canteen. Ultimately, he ordered a bible and books on the Russian language sent to me. Both made life bearable for me.

I was arraigned and assigned legal representation from the public defender's office. I soon learned that Ray Robinson had sent the Sacramento Sheriff's office a letter claiming I moved to Sacramento and was an unregistered sex offender. That is what gave the detectives what they needed to arrest me. What goes around comes around! I had made life difficult for him. Now it was his turn.

I was looking at a sentence of four years if I were found guilty. The charge was simple: failure to register after being in the jurisdiction for five days or longer. I was guilty. The more time you spend in jail the more likely a plea bargain offer comes from the district attorney. I decided to stay for a while.

My biggest concern in the county jail would normally be the reaction of other inmates if and when they found out why I was locked up. It was the biggest and most violent inmates who immediately want to know who is being locked up and for what.

Although as I Christian I should have told the truth that would have created a bigger problem for me. I would have two choices: trying to defend myself from physical violence, or asking to be locked up in solitary confinement to avoid physical harm.

As a diabetic, even a simple injury would take a long time to heal. On top of that there would be constant insults and threats because as a former sex offender, I would be considered the scum of the earth, even though my real crime was committed twenty eight years earlier. Any inmate learning of my charge - failure to register as a sex offender - would demand I lock up or suffer the consequences. There are a number of people who are required to register as a sex offender for life who may have mooned people while intoxicated when they were nineteen years of age. Mooning is where one person pulls down his trousers and points his butt at others. But the reason for registration would make no difference to other inmates.

Although there is a positive side to locking up - no beatings - the downside of going to solitary confinement is twenty-four hours a day in a cell by yourself with absolutely nothing. No visits, no TV, no dayroom, no canteen, no books, no nothing. You do get out twice a week for a shower and a chance to exercise by yourself for an hour. And you get to wear different clothing than the orange outfits the rest of the inmates wore; so that when you went to court your jail uniform announced that you were either a snitch or a coward or a child molester or rapist.

So I created a set of facts where I claimed that I was arrested for fraud. I was quick to follow that up with advice to everyone who asked that I am following the advice of counsel and not discussing my case because there are a lot of snitches who would gladly sell whatever I said to the District Attorney and get me convicted. That held off the nosey and gave me peace of mind. I felt bad and guilty because lying was not Christian. I was sure God would understand.

Being behind bars now was different though. It was because I knew God was in charge of my life. There was a reason I was deprived of my freedom. God works in ways we do not understand.

When Benjamin Kondor visited me I mentioned that right before I was arrested I had prayed to God to help me lose weight. And here I was losing weight. Before my arrest I had weighed 250 pounds and was really beginning to feel unhealthy, in spite of my hours on the treadmill. The food in jail is not of the best quality. I was so depressed the first twenty six hours I did not eat the peanut butter and jelly sandwiches they brought to the holding tank. After that fast, not eating was easy. Ultimately, in thirty days I had lost twenty-five pounds, simply by eating very little.

The DA finally said if I would plead guilty I could go home with a sentence of time served. I had been in the cell for forty-two days so I decided I had enough. I plead guilty. If I had pleaded Not Guilty and gone to trial and won, I would have still lost as they would not have given me back the forty-two days. On the way to the courtroom my public defender handed my a dozen typed pages of a probation report which was a recommendation for the judge. I was given four years probation.

My understanding was that I would be transferred to Oregon and would do probation up there. I was ordered to report to the Sacramento Probation Department within five days of my release. I was also required to pay $450 to the state's Department of Revenue.

I went online to the County Probation website and found their mission statement.

Vision

To be nationally recognized as a leader in the field of probation.

Mission

To ensure the safety of our community by implementing a balanced justice model, which includes:

Community Protection, Victim Restoration, Offender Accountability and Competency

Values

To reach our vision and accomplish our mission, the Department will be guided by the following principles: Integrity, Fairness, Resourcefulness, Professionalism, Excellence

When I showed up at the probation department, a clerk told me to come back in two weeks. I did. When I returned in two weeks I was told to go to a different location, to a unit that handles Inter-State transfers. I showed up there the next day only to learn that it would be difficult to get a transfer because I was required to have made application within seven days of being placed on probation. I suppose this is an example of the Department being guided by integrity, professionalism and excellence.

A probation officer in that unit tried unsuccessfully to get me transferred. He told me he was Sacramento County's expert in the Inter State Compact and if anyone could get me transferred, he could. He appealed and he lost the appeal.

In between his appeal and his losing the appeal, I researched the Interstate Compact. It was clear to me that the law was not being followed. In short Rule 3.101 entitled Mandatory Transfer of Supervision stated that at the discretion of the sending state (California) an offender shall be eligible for transfer of supervision to a receiving state under the Compact and the receiving state shall accept transfer if offender has more than 90 days, has a plan of supervision, is in substantial compliance with terms of supervision in sending state and is a resident of receiving state. How could the Sacramento County Probation Department fail to get me transferred and then lose on appeal? The law was perfectly clear to me. Oregon did not have the discretion to turn down my transfer because I had more than 90 days, there was a plan of supervision, I was in compliance with the terms of supervision and I was a resident of Oregon.

My opinion of the Sacramento County Probation Department was deteriorating. When I asked for the reason Oregon was refusing to follow the Compact I was told that Oregon would not allow registered sex offenders to live in motor homes or trailers. I offered to cement mine to the ground, but that offer was not accepted. I offered to rent an apartment less than one hundred feet from the probation department in Christmas Valley and that was to no avail.

Just like the fox who couldn't reach the grapes in Aesop's Fables, I reasoned that I didn't want to do my probation in Oregon anyway.

I was assigned to Al Thomas. He is the supervising probation officer for any sex offender who is on probation. He is tall and menacing. In our initial interview we were reviewing the terms of my probation. One in particular read that I could not be in the presence of minors without a responsible adult present who was approved by the probation officer. Because attending church meant a lot to me, I asked about being in church where there were a lot of children. Thomas said if one sits next to you get up and leave.

He was quick to let me know he was not interested in questions or conversation so I did not pursue this further. When I went to leave I tried to shake his hand, but he quickly pointed out he does not shake hands with convicts.

I called my public defender to get a clarification. Public Defender Mathew Wise told me he could not prevent me from going to church and that Thomas must have meant get up and move to a different location. That sounded reasonable to me. The church needed someone to make photographs of the speakers and events for their website so I volunteered. This allowed me the opportunity to get up and move if any minor sat close by.

I resigned to do my probation in Sacramento and spend my time living in the Klimov's backyard, helping with yard work, taking care of the garden and the chickens. Making photographs at Grace and preparing them for the church website also would also consume some of my time.

In late October of 2009 there was a sweep conducted in Sacramento County by the probation department. They check the physical location of all registered sex offenders on probation to make sure they are living where their registration states they are. Two probation officers stopped at my address and proceeded to search my trailer.

When on probation, you give up your constitutional rights against unreasonable search and seizure. So they could search me or my home without my permission. They also searched my I-phone and my computer, to make sure I was not visiting porn sites, I assume. They read my emails too. One of the probation officers knocked on the Klimov residence and asked if any minors lived there. Valeriy turned 18 in September so he was no longer a minor.

The officer explained to Marina that a condition of my probation required me not to be in the presence of minors and she explained that she had two grandchildren who visited periodically. He told her that it was ok if I was present, as long as she was too.

They left and were rather civil in the performance of their job.

Within twenty minutes two more probation officers came by. They told me they were checking to make sure I was living at the address I was registered. I mentioned that two other officers had just been by to conduct a search. It was obvious they screwed up and they left. This year the probation department along with most departments in Sacramento County had their budget cut by $800,000. I smiled when I heard that because just maybe the probation department would quit wasting taxpayer money.

Although another term of my probation prohibited me from leaving the state without written permission from the probation office, I did get that permission on three occasions to go back to Christmas Valley and to build a 12 x 16 structure on my property. Actually, I had started the process in between getting out of jail and formally going on probation in June. During two trips I had finished most of the outbuilding. I even obtained a permit. It was the first time in my life I had obtained a permit and I felt so law-abiding. I made a final trip up to install a door and window. The structure would go unused for the four years I would be on probation.

After my next visit with Thomas he assigned me to another probation officer. In the next nine months I had seven different probation officers. Could this be what their mission statement meant by resourcefulness? It certainly was not professionalism.

Living in the Rio Linda area enjoying my relationship with the Klimov family and with my brothers and sisters at Grace Family was not a bad way to spend my probation. Every Sunday I made photographs of whatever was happening at church, and spent the afternoon processing them and posting them to the church's website. I was often asked by members to take family portraits. They offered to pay, but I looked at it as my mission and would not accept money. So I would make family portraits and make prints and deliver them the following Sunday.

Grace Family Church puts on an elaborate Christmas play where about half the membership has an acting role. They are all dressed in very colorful, handmade costumes and do a great job as actors and actresses. At the end of the performance, Pastor Benjamin Kondor's wife asked me to make a group photograph of the cast. There had to be more than a hundred performers so I stood on a pew about twenty five feet from them and made a quick panoramic or vistagraph of them. Later, I made a print on 13 x 19 inch paper to make sure the color was correct and everyone was in focus. I then had a very large 4 foot wide print on canvas made for her.

Although I did not make many more vistagraphs of landscapes other than some in Yosemite, I did make a lot of photographs of the Klimov get-togethers. Sometimes they would have more than twenty relatives and friends in their home, so I felt useful recording the events.

When Stas and Yelena's oldest son Benjamin stood by himself for the first time, I enjoyed making a photograph and print of this milestone. So when Nellie stood up for the first time, I did the same. Her mother Yelena and grandmother Marina were off to the left out of the picture while Nellie stood in front of a rosebush.

When I make prints I usually end up having to correct the color and print a corrected version. I usually save the paper so I can use the other side for making other test prints later.

Christmas came and went and I enjoyed being part of the Klimov family on this holiday. I did miss not going to

Arizona to see Chip and Annie, but I put that relationship into the history book. I substituted going to 24 hour fitness and using the treadmill to keep in shape instead of walking on the bike trail. It had a second advantage in that I used their spa, steam room, sauna and toilet daily so I was not filling my trailer's tanks which are a nuisance to dump.

Spring came and I found another way to keep busy. I decided to try to market my vistagraphs at public events. I bought an easy-up tent that measured 10 feet square. I bought a folding table and a few chairs. I had my printer in China make three eight-foot vistagraphs and ten four footers, half vertical and half horizontal. I framed a few of these. I was ready to meet my public.

I bought another Lance camper with air conditioning and used it exclusively as an office. I had my 12 x 6 foot covered trailer housing my vistagraphs in four homemade wooden boxes with wheels so I could drag them around easily. Now I was in business.

Initially I paid one of the Klimov cousins to accompany me. So it was costing me a hundred dollars to try to sell my prints. No luck. The great recession had emptied out potential buyer's pockets or kept them from spending money for fear their job or house would be gone and they would need their cash.

I managed to set up and take down my displays by myself. It was good for my ego to hear people compliment my work, even if they did not buy anything. I used that time concurrently to continue to write some of this autobiography.

For most of the summer, I set up my vistagraph tent in a Placerville location, which meant an hour's drive twice a day on Saturdays. There were few visitors and no buyers, but it was an ideal situation to write. I even mentioned to the manager that I appreciated the fact that there were very few interruptions by customers as it gave me time to do my writing.

Sloughhouse, about twenty miles east of Sacramento, put on a great arts and crafts, harvest festival for two days. I had lots of visitors, many compliments, but no buyers. This ended the vendor season.

One Saturday morning in late September I was contemplating what I might do during the fall. The tranquility was destroyed by a visit from six cops: two probation officers, two sheriffs, and two guys wearing uniforms indicating they were from a federal agency. They announced they were conducting a sex offender/probation search. After ten minutes they were joined by a detective named Foster, a loud, intimidating guy who appeared to be out for blood. They asked if the other trailer was mine, and I admitted it was.

In a few minutes they showed up with two photographic prints. One was of Nellie standing, and the other was of the participants in the Grace Family Church Christmas pageant. Foster asked me if I took the photographs. I said I did. He was on his cell phone talking to Al Thomas, my original probation officer, the one who did not shake convict hands.

Foster arrested me for probation violation. He said the photos proved I was in the presence of minors. I was placed in the front seat of his car. He went over to talk to Marina and her sons Slava and Valeriy. Stas was also standing with them on the front porch. I could hear Foster screaming at Marina trying to convince her that I was a danger to her grandchildren. She was not buying it because she has known me for a dozen years. This infuriated him.

When we arrived at the county jail, Al Thomas was there. As he removed the handcuffs so I could be booked he stated: "If you don't plead guilty, I won't let you live at the Klimov's." This was extortion, a crime, and he was a law enforcement officer.

California extortion laws are defined in Penal Codes 518 to 527 PC. Penal Code 518 defines extortion (which is commonly referred to as blackmail) as:

1. using force or threats to compel another to give you money or other property,

2. using force of threats to compel a public officer to perform an official act, or

3. being a public official and compelling another to give you money or other property acting under color of official right.

Extortion is typically charged as a felony, punishable by up to four years in the California State Prison and by a maximum $10,000 fine.

Here Thomas was not only acting under the color of a public officer when he threatened to deprive me of the property right to live with the Klimovs, he was also depriving me of due process in the pending litigation.

So I spent the rest of September, and all of October in the county jail. It was my intention to plead not guilty and to fight the charge. The probation term I was being charged with was **being in the presence of minors without a responsible adult** approved by the probation department. The evidence was the two photographs.

My public defender seemed to strongly agree that I did not violate probation. He told me he had an excellent relationship with the district attorney and told me I would be going home soon. We discussed the threat by Al Thomas to deprive me of my due process rights by not allowing me to live on the Klimov property. He agreed it was the felony of extortion.

The days dragged on. I was getting used to jailhouse living. The concern that other inmates would find out my beef - child molestation thirty years ago - and create a problem for me was not much of a concern now. When asked by inmates why I was busted, I would reply: probation violation. And of course they wanted to get down to the nitty gritty and asked why I was on probation. I would explain that I was initially busted for road rage, assault and battery for dragging a teenager out of his car because he cut me off and a sheriff witnessed the incident. One of my probation terms was not to be in the presence of minors. Those white lies seemed to placate those characters waiting to find a target to victimize.

You don't want to go to jail or prison for a sex beef. Life can be unbearable. Having committed murder is socially acceptable behind bars. I have often wondered if the reason so many woman and children, who have been sexually victimized, end up dead is because their murderers would rather have a homicide beef than a sex beef in prison if they get caught.

I had the good fortune to have a pretty good celly. He was Mexican and the complete opposite of the celly I had less than a year earlier when I was busted for failure to register. Manuel Garcia was being held in the county jail on a family, civil matter. His wife wanted sole custody of his two children and he was contesting it. Manuel was finishing a year at Folsom State prison for a parole violation.

One benefit of being in jail again was it gave me an opportunity to lose weight again. I kept to an 800 calorie a day diet and exercised a little every day. I managed a few opportunities to get weighed so I could determine that I was losing two pounds every three days. My size requires about 2400 calories a day. So I was not consuming 1600 needed calories. There are 3,500 calories in a pound. The lack of calories represented almost a pound and a half over three days and the exercise accounted for the rest.

The highlights of my stay this time were again visits from the Grace Family Church pastors and my Klimov family. Slava once again acted as my lifeline, ordering me a bible and a few Russian language books.

On Saturdays, I looked forward to the visits from volunteers who conducted what they called bible study. A one page handout was used and discussed. It was actually also an escape from the cell environment. Being in the presence of other Christians also made this time a treat.

The District Attorney initially indicated that if I plead not guilty I could get a year for the violation. The DA's office was also confronting budget cuts, as was the Sheriff's Office. It cost $2500 a month to house an inmate in the county jail. After forty days she was ready to offer time served, if I plead guilty and gave her passwords to all of my email accounts. So, I agreed to plead guilty to yet another felony.

On the day I went to court to plead guilty, Al Thomas was in the courtroom. He was there requesting permission from the judge to affix a GPS unit to the ankle of another registered sex offender who had a job that took him out of the county on a few occasions. The judge granted him permission.

The judge then directed his attention to me and my charge. When one pleads guilty the judge is required to ask if anyone made any promises or threats to obtain the guilty plea. When he asked me that question I did not answer. I just looked at Robert D. Martin Jr., my public defender. Robert was not paying attention and the judge looked at both of us and asked again but louder. I again looked at Martin who suddenly became aware that it was his turn to talk on my behalf. He told the judge they should go into his chamber. So there was a procession out of the courtroom: the judge, the district attorney, my public defender and Probation Supervisor Al Thomas.

I noted the time on the courtroom clock. It was 5:55 pm. This was night court. It was usually over by six o'clock. The minutes ticked by. At 6:21 they all returned from the judge's chambers. Al Thomas had a shit-eating grin on his face. My attorney was visibly angry. When he stood next to me he said that guy, referring to Thomas, is crazy. He is sick.

I tried to ask what happened but the judge took over and accepted the guilty plea without the usual public disclosure dealing with if anyone made a promise or threat. I never found out what was said in the judge's chambers. It would not have made any difference. I was going home. The problem now was, where was home?

In court my attorney said Thomas won't let you live at the Klimov's because you did not plead guilty a week ago. I told him to go ask Thomas where I was supposed to live. He did. He came back shaking his head and told me: "Thomas said that is your problem." More professionalism and excellence!

The only problem I had in going to jail was in getting out. I got back to my cell before seven, gave away the meal that was saved for me, and packed what little I was going to take with me, giving everything else I had accumulated to Manuel Garcia. He had no visitors, no money, no property so it was like a party getting my coffee, tea, sugars, writing tablets, soap, soap dish, shower clogs etc. This was the easy part. I heard my name on the loudspeaker in the cell: "Mizera, roll it up. You're leaving."

A quick handshake and I was off to the elevator, and the ride to the bottom floor. I was escorted to a holding tank. It was about seven in the evening. There were already eighteen inmates in the holding tank. Some were being released after being picked up drunk only a day ago. You could tell. The vomit was still clinging to their clothing. More joined us and it became more crowded.

The holding tank was "L" shaped. It had three benches that could hold nine persons. There was a toilet in one corner. It was stopped and had overflowed with feces on the floor. Eight square feet had been flooded and was unusable.

I stopped counting when the tank held twenty-three people. I had my two square feet and kept my eyes closed and tried to focus on what it would be like to be released at three a.m.

It wasn't long before you hear your name and get a large paper bag with the clothes you wore when you were arrested. I giggled as I tried to get into the jeans I was wearing. I had lost thirty-two pounds and at least four inches around my waist. I had to find a piece of string to use to hold my pants up.

Finally, everyone leaves the tank, lines up face against the wall until your name is called again. This time you get back your property which was taken when you were booked: I-phone, belt, and the money I had left on the books. The door opened and out I went into the fresh air. I made a quick call to Slava. They knew I was getting out and insisted I call so they could come and get me. The previous time I was released I took a cab which cost $42.

It felt so good to be back home again. Nick and Marina were up and we enjoyed coffee and conversation. It had been forty four days since I had been to Grace Family Church. I missed my families, both of them.

Al Thomas made good on his threat that if I did not plead guilty he would not let me live on the Klimov's property in my camper. I was required to report to the probation department near Rancho Cordova and I did so on November 8th. I learned that Al Thomas was now my probation officer, again, but that he was not in and I should go downtown. I had written Thomas a letter and had the probation office clerk upload it into Al Thomas's file. She did. I also asked her to provide a copy for the Chief of the Probation Department Don L. Meyer. Here is that letter.

November 8, 2010
Al Thomas
Sacramento County Probation Department
3201 Florin-Perkins Road
Sacramento, CA (916) 875-3000
I have been directed by Judge Ben Davidian to report within 48 hours to your office. Because of our interactions on three occasions during the past sixteen months, I feel an obligation to hand-deliver this letter, especially as it relates to the court action that resulted in the requirement that I report to the Probation Department.

As you may recall that as you were removing handcuffs prior to my booking on September 25th, you directed me to plead guilty or you would appear in court and make it difficult for me and that you would not allow me to continue living on the Klimov property.

Because I wanted to continue my living arrangements at the Klimovs, as they are the only persons I know in California, I attempted to follow your directive. Unfortunately, my public defender apparently misunderstood my intention or I did not make myself clear to him. So on October 24th, he denied the violation on my behalf. When I learned that the denial was NOT a guilty plea, I instructed him to admit the violation which he did a week later on the day you were in court on November 4th.

When Judge Ben Davidian asked me if anyone made any promises or threats that caused me to plead guilty, I was unable to answer him truthfully without revealing your directive as stated to me above, so I remained silent. I left it to my attorney to explain my predicament and that resulted in the District Attorney, my Public Defender and you all going into the judge's chamber. You were in there from 5:55 pm until 6:21 pm and it is unclear to me what transpired.

I was told by my public defender that you were not going to let me live on the Klimov property because Marina Klimova was anti-authority. Apparently you based this opinion on a discussion that took place between Marina Klimova and four other family members, and Officer Foster who arrested me. Foster tried to convince Marina that her grandchildren were in jeopardy with me living on their property. The Klimovs tried unsuccessfully to assure Foster that they have known me for twelve years and I was considered a member of their family, and they voiced a collective opinion that they did not believe I was a threat to their children or other relatives visiting their home. I observed this confrontation from the front seat of Foster's car as I was handcuffed and awaiting to be transported to jail.

Al Thomas Page 2   Steve Mizera

I have had a discussion with Marina regarding this matter. She would like to have an opportunity along with her husband Nicolay to meet with you so you can determine for yourself that she is NOT anti-authority, and that she and her husband would both be very responsible supervisors of my conduct whenever minors visit their home. They are both willing to take time off from their respective jobs to meet with you.

You may not know it but the Klimov Family came from Russia a dozen years ago. They are very devout Baptists and my relationship with them has been one reason I was baptized. I have attended Sunday services with them for most of the time they have been in this country. They are serious believers in the bible. At Titus 3:1 it states "Put them in mind to be subject to principalities and powers, to obey magistrates, to be ready to every good work, and to speak evil of no man." The Klimovs adhere strictly to the bible and are teaching me to do so also.

To arbitrarily require me to move from the Klimov property would be unfair to them and to me. I have lived here successfully for the sixteen months of my probation.

You may also not be aware that during the probation sweep in October 2009 I was visited by two sets of probation officers who were determining if I was living at the PC290 address of record and that I was not in violation of the terms of my probation. They asked me if there were any minors living on the property. I told them there was not but that grandchildren visited periodically. They then questioned Marina, as Nicolay was working. They told her that it was ok for me to be in their home when minors were present as long as she was present. No record of these visits was included in my probation records.

My attorney told me that you also stated that Pastor Benjamin Kondor would not make a suitable responsible adult because he would be too busy. Pastor Kondor has indicated that he too would be willing to meet with you to discuss the issue of a responsible adult overseeing my conduct while attending services and other events at Grace Family Church.

As I have told all six of my probation officers during the past fourteen months since you were my first probation office, I only associate with my Klimov family and my brothers and sisters at Grace Family Church. I have made it a point to make this statement and was hoping for a dialogue but none ever resulted. I was only asked for the license plate and description of my truck, which has not changed during my probation period.

You also mentioned that "I should have signed the form." If this meant that there is a form which is used to authorize a supervisory adult as a responsible person so

I could be in compliance with a term of my probation, I have never been told of the

Al Thomas Page 3   *Steve Mizera*

existence or requirement of such a form. I have, as you know, traveled to my home in Oregon on four different occasions. I did obtain the required travel pass each time. Had I known there was a form required for any other reason; I would have certainly complied with that requirement.

I appreciate your taking time to consider what I have written. I have tried to obey the terms of my probation. I am seventy years of age and have serious health issues. All I want is to live my remaining days in peace.

Sincerely

Steve A. Mizera

Cc: Robert Martin Jr. Assistant Public Defender

Of course Al Thomas never acknowledged the letter or responded to it. If the Chief of Sacramento County Probation Department Don L. Meyer received or acted upon my letter, I had no way of knowing. If he did and failed to act he would be covering up a felony. More professionalism and excellence.

While I was at the probation department trying to meet with Al Thomas, he had been visiting the Klimov property and told Marina to tell me I had forty-eight hours to get off their property. He and another probation officer spent time at my truck. I would determine later that they hid a GPS unit on my truck so they would know where I would be spending my time. They did not have authority from a court to do so, as I would have had the right to be present during that hearing.

So here I was, seventy years old and homeless again. But this time I would not have to steal breakfast from porches to survive. I had sufficient funds. I had to register again as a transient, and re-register every month. I started to map out places to stay. As a member of the 24 hour Fitness organization, my shower and toilet needs would be taken care of, as would my daily exercise. Periodically, I parked overnight on their parking lot. But rather than run afoul of the law by staying in the same spot all the time, I drove to the Sutter County border on a levee road. It was quiet there. I was surrounded by rice farms. There was a canal or creek that accepted runoff from the rains. My neighbors would be ducks and beaver and other wildlife. In Sacramento the rains start in November and generally don't finish until April. It was to be a wet, cold winter. It would be expensive too because the price of diesel seemed to increase daily.

When I registered as a transient I gave the levee location as my address. It was seven miles from the fitness center. Diesel was $3.29 in November and due to the problems in the mid-east where everyone wanted to become a democracy, that price shot up to$4.49 by late March 2011.

I had hired an attorney within a few days of my release from jail to protect me from Al Thomas. It would cost me $5,000. I had $2,000 and would pay the rest at $500 a month. My attorney, Steven Plesser, wanted to have a meeting with Al Thomas but Thomas refused to meet with him. Normally someone on probation is required to visit the probation officer at least once a month, but Thomas refused to schedule any meetings with me. He was afraid to meet with my lawyer. I think Thomas was aware that not only did he commit the felony of extortion with me which deprived me of due process for my alleged probation violation, but he had to have done the same thing to other probationers who were busted. I believe his rationale for doing this had to do with the tight budget all county departments had.

It would have been a simple matter for the judge to have both Thomas and me take lie-detector tests and then to question everyone who was busted the previous year who had Thomas as their probation officer to determine if he made a similar threat to them.

When the housing bubble busted and so many people became unemployed, governments just kept on spending and finally found themselves on the verge of bankruptcy. The state of California had a $26 billion dollar deficit, and tried reducing it by not giving counties money, so county departments were trying to come up with reasons their funding should not be reduced.

The general rule of the probation department is that transients must meet with their probation officer once every week. Thomas ignored this rule. It was almost three months before I saw him again. In early January, 2010, I was parked in the Walmart parking lot in a far corner. My truck and camper were not visible from either Watt Avenue or Elverta Road.

Thomas drove his state car up to the rear of my camper and knocked on my door. I opened it and invited him in. He refused to come in but proceeded to have a conversation which consisted mostly of questions about my hiring an attorney.

I asked him again why I could not live on the Klimov property and be gone when their grandchildren visited. Now his answer was "it is a matter of trust," but he refused to explain what he meant by that.

He was also searching for a way to get rid of me. He offered to try to get Oregon to accept a transfer. And he asked questions about who I might know in another county that I could live with. He said he would support a transfer to that county.

I knew he would be unsuccessful in having me transferred to Oregon, but I wanted to see his ego bruised so I encouraged him. I also could have moved to Yolo County where Alex Klimov owned a duplex and he would have let me room with him, but I did not want to disassociate with Thomas. It was my desire and intent to bring his criminal behavior to the attention of authorities, even though Judge Ben Davidian was informed of it in chambers and never did anything. Before the one year statute of limitations would bar me, I wanted to bring Thomas' felony to the attention of the California Attorney General and would ask the American Civil Liberties Union to help me.

As soon as he drove off from this visit, I sent him the following email:

Al Thomas
Sacramento County Probation Department
3201 Florin-Perkins Road
Sacramento, CA (916) 875-3000
via email
First, let me thank you for your efforts in trying to have my probation order transferred to my home in the State of Oregon under the Interstate Compact.

I also appreciate your offer that would permit me to move to another county and transfer my probation to that jurisdiction. Unfortunately, the only people I know in California are the Klimovs, my adopted family, and our mutual friends and members of the Grace Family Church in Carmichael.

During our visit in the Walmart parking lot you brought to my attention that the reason you are preventing me from continuing my living arrangement on the Klimov property was trust. Had it been made clear to me that the probation term prohibiting me from being in the presence of minors meant I could not take photographs of the membership even though you gave me permission to attend church, I would not have taken any photographs. Also, had not there been a conversation during a sweep where Marina Klimova and I were both informed that it was permissible for me to be in her home when her grandchildren were visiting as long as she or Nick were present, I would have not been in their home during such visitations.

Since my release from prison I believe I have lived an exemplary life as my 19 year career with the State Water Resources Control Board will attest. Had I been aware of California's registration requirement while traveling through California from Arizona to Oregon, I would have registered and would not have been arrested, and thus would not have been given the probation order by the court.

As I am seventy years of age and in declining health with diabetes, high blood pressure and recovering from prostate cancer, I am hoping to live out my golden days without further criminal behavior.

I believe I may have a solution to both your problem and mine.

I would like to petition the court to change my probation from formal to informal. I believe this could be accomplished if you would support such a petition.

Perhaps I could then go to Oregon, if that is within the scope of informal probation.

Again, thank you for taking the time to have an honest conversation with me and for your efforts to resolve my dilemma.

Steve A. Mizera

I also sent the following email to my attorney to document this unorthodox visit.

Memo to Plesser

At about 1:30 pm Monday, January 3, there was a knock on my camper. It was Al Thomas. I was in the parking lot at Walmart at the corner of Elkhorn and Watt. As I do not believe he has ever seen my camper, I suspect he must have a GPS on my vehicle and activated it to locate me. When I was in court, he was also there arguing successfully to compel someone else to wear a GPS ankle bracelet because the guy left the county in the course of his job on a few occasions. Nevertheless, we had a long discussion for about thirty minutes. Here is a summary as well as I can recollect our conversation:

1) He said it was not clear that Oregon would not let me return and finish my probation there.

2) He indicated that if I knew anyone in any other county I am free to transfer my probation to that county. (I told him that I only know the Klimov family and members of my church in California.)

3) He asked "what was the chance I could stay with someone from church." I informed him that Russians all have large extended families and all have kids or have people visit who have children, and I did not want any of them subjected to the treatment probation gave the Klimovs when I was arrested,

4) He asked if I could afford to buy a house or mobile home. I explained my financial situations, including the Social Security problem, that fact that I tithe, and that I help to support the Klimov family with 15% of my income, and being homeless now was costing an additional $500 a month for fuel, gas, and propane as well as dump fees. I also answered that I considered it but assumed he would refuse to let me live in a mobile home park because kids reside there. I also mentioned that I had a financial obligation with you and our intent was to go to court to clarify or modify the vague word "presence" in the probation order.

5) I asked him why I couldn't live at the Klimov's he said it was a matter of trust.

6) We re-visited the reason I was arrested: - the photos of the performers in church and the photos of Nellie on

the first day she stood by herself at the Klimov residence - I reiterated that he had given me permission to go to church and that I consulted with my first public defender who advised me that when Thomas said to get up and leave, Thomas couldn't have meant leave the church because I have a constitutional right to attend church. I also told him that during the SAFE sweep of 2009, I was visited by two teams of probation officers within ten minutes of each other and the second team discussed my being in the Klimov home and they said to both Marina and myself that it was permissible for me to be in their home as long as she or her husband was there whenever the grandchildren visited them.

7) We discuss the reason I was initially arrested (enroute from AZ to OR my diesel engine had a problem, and unload the camper in the Klimov backyard, as the repair shop couldn't fix the engine with the camper attached.)

8) I made it clear that because I did not know how to interpret the meaning of "presence" in the probation term, I had hired you to go into court to modify or clarify the term, or to seek informal probation. He said I would never hear from him again if the court granted informal probation. (That might be the way out for everyone. I believe that would even let me go to Oregon.)

9) He said he was going to drive by the mobile home park on Antelope east of Watt to check it out in case I would consider buying a unit there.

10) I informed him that Christmas was a bummer not being with my "family" and that I was very depressed and considered throwing in the towel. Think this covers it all. I am going to delete this message immediately after I send it to you as both the DA and probation have my email addresses and passwords.

Steve in early February I was parked near the corner of Elverta and Walerga, across the street from 24 Hour

Fitness. Again, Thomas drove up. This time he was giving me the bad news. Oregon would not allow me to transfer. He now told me that he would check on me weekly at this location. He departed.

Once again I tried to encourage Al Thomas to appeal Oregon's decision and sent him this email.

Mr. Thomas, I expressed an opinion that differed from your understanding of the Interstate Compact.

This is what I based my opinion on:

Interstate Compact - Rule 3 - 101

Mandatory Transfer of Supervision

At the discretion of the sending state, an offender shall be eligible for transfer of supervision to a receiving state under the Compact, and the receiving state shall accept transfer if offender:

a) has more than 90 days....

b) has a valid plan of supervision

c) is in substantial compliance with terms of supervision in sending state, and

d) is a resident of receiving state.

I meet those four pre-requisites in that I have more than 90 days. I have a valid plan of supervision. I am in total compliance with terms of supervision in California, and I am a resident of Oregon.

In addition, I noted the opinion from ICAOS Advisory Opinions

7-2004 While a sending state controls the decision of whether or not to transfer...receiving state has no discretion.

So if California makes the decision to transfer me, Oregon has no discretion. They have to accept the transfer.

Hope this helps in your quest to have my probation transferred.

Steve Mizera

He actually responded to this email. I believe he knew it was in his best interest to get rid of me.

He called and asked if I had any photos of my Oregon property and to email them to him if I did. I did, so I did.

I was hoping he would succeed because another requirement for a transfer was that I had to agree to the transfer, and that I had to agree to pay a monthly fee to Oregon. Had he succeeded in having Oregon agree to accept me, I would not have signed the transfer and would not have agreed to pay Oregon anything. The dealings I had with Oregon probation made Thomas's behavior, even his felony, look rational. I have to work on my anti-authority behavior. It seems I have had so many reasons to support my position. I believe prayer is the key to success and it will help me change my attitude.

But Thomas did not succeed. He did the next best thing and assigned me to another probation officer: Harry Dayhuff. During my first visit with Dayhuff, I found him to be quite reasonable which was a relief. He did follow the probation department rules and required me to visit his office every Thursday. Diesel was now $4.69 a gallon so I took the train downtown every Thursday.

On a subsequent visit I asked Dayhuff if I could go to the Klimov residence when they were not home so there could be no chance I would be in the presence of the grandchildren. I explained I needed tools and clothing etc. He agreed and granted permission. This is the way the probation department is supposed to act.

While I was in the county jail and although I had not been convicted, Thomas notified Social Security that I was convicted and serving time. This notification prompted the Social Security to stop sending me a check. It would take me six months to set the record straight. They had the right to stop sending a check but only AFTER I was sentenced and spent thirty days. I was sentenced and released on the same date. Christmas was a financial hardship for me because I did not receive a social security check.

In mid-January, 2011, one of the parishioners asked for prayers to help her in her attempt to learn the English language. I finally saw where I had a new mission, now that I was no longer permitted to take photographs for the church. I offered to teach her the English language. But why stop with one? I would organize a class of others Russian immigrants who were interested in learning English. I put together a plan and presented it to Pastor Kondor. He thought it was a great idea.

I would teach the English classes on Monday and Friday evenings from 7 until 9. I was excited about this challenge. At my expense I would provide each student with a binder and make copies of all materials I thought they needed.

On the first Monday of February I started to teach English. I had sixteen students! I had prepared The Lord's Prayer, The ABC's with samples of words for each letter that presented the correct sound. I explained over a few pages what the articles A, AN and THE were, as I knew articles were not used in the Russian language. I had ordered a Pictionary that had categories of great graphics and the words depicting what was in the graphics in both the Russian and English languages. There were categories such as family relationships, parts of the body, vegetables and fruit, etc. I made copies for everyone.

I thought it was necessary to explain the structure of English and did so in diagrams. As an exercise I presented the pangram or sentence: The quick brown fox jumps over the lazy dog, because it contained all letters of the English alphabet. I even provided copies from a dual-language book written from the perspective of an eight year old

Russian orphan who is adopted by an American mom which we would use as a basic reader.

I thought I was ready to teach. Wrong. The look on the student's faces told me my instructions in English were not able to be read by people who only read Russian. Thanks to Google, I was able to provide the instructions in both languages. The class ranged from persons who knew virtually no English, to those who had a basic grasp of English but would benefit from my classes.

On Friday another minor problem presented itself. At least four students were not able to attend a Friday class. I took a quick survey to find that Saturday appeared acceptable to most so I change the schedule. But it ended up that a different set of four students could not make in on Saturdays. So I started teaching the same thing twice. Some students could attend both classes, and all students could attend at least one of the two classes. No one would miss out on anything.

We had a lot of fun. I introduced singing the Alphabet because even those who knew it were not pronouncing all letters correctly. Russians get the Cs mixed up with the Ss, and also have problems mixing up the Es with the Is. Fortunately, my attempt at studying the Russian language seemed to prepare me for a few of these problems.

The church had a lot of faith in me and gave me the keys to the locks and combinations to the alarm system. This also allowed me to fill up with water and use electricity to charge my batteries. Even though I used solar panels, when the sun did not shine for a few days, my batteries got low. I always arrived an hour early to prepare for the class.

As I observed what else needed to be learned, I added it to the curriculum. I took this responsibility very seriously and the students worked very hard. I had a mission and now I was on this mission.

In reviewing my life during the past two years while researching and writing this autobiography, I kept asking the two questions which I hoped to answer: what is the cause of my pedophilia? And what is its cure?

As my first few decades on life indicate, I was physically abused, sexually abused, and deprived of a positive role model. Although I was ostensibly introduced to Christianity, it was done by the abusers which resulted in confusion.

My inability to form basic relationships or friendships was something "mom," "dad," and the nuns had the responsibility to do but failed. My sister bears a little responsibility when she abandoned me. These failures acted as insurmountable barriers and obstacles which I was unable to hurdle.

Our scientists and societal experts uniformly claim they do not know the cause of pedophilia. They hint that it might have a genetic basis and that might be part of the answer. But they also are clear when they state that one's personality is formed by the time they are five years of age.

So I must have begun to become a pedophile by that age. No bonding with mom or dad but a rejection by both had to be the primary factor or cause.

The nightly beatings with the green hickory stick must also have been a significant, contributing factor.

Whelan's criminal conduct had to have re-enforced my confusion and cemented any chance I had to form a normal relationship. In fact it clearly created the anti-authority characteristic I have been burdened with for most of the rest of my life.

Although I tried to escape her hostile environment, another adult, the crazy naked lady who used me as her sex toy, obliterated my future as a normal person. I have intentionally not written about many other times I have suffered sexual abuse, but they too contributed to my dysfunctional behavior.

How many other pedophiles that have gone on to ruin the lives of children as well as their own have had similar obstacles to overcome and failed to develop normally? I cannot imagine anyone who comes from a loving home and who does not suffer physical, emotional and sexual abuse in their formative years will become a pedophile and molest children.

I had a female German Shepherd once, and when she was about six weeks old I took her to the American river on a very hot day. I tossed her in to cool her off. What I did not know was that the runoff from the winter snow had made the water very, very cold. That puppy never would go into water after that. Even when she became an adult, she would not follow other dogs into a river or the ocean. I suppose my stupidity traumatized her and ruined what would have been a pleasurable adult activity.

I am comfortable now in believing that I know the cause of **my pedophilia**. By examining my life through the writing of this autobiography, I have been able to connect the dots. It would only be conjecture to claim other pedophiles have had similar beginnings. Perhaps this writing may encourage them to look at their life and perhaps they might be able to answer that question. The scientific community should leave no stone unturned to find the answer.

When someone is arrested, charged with being a child molester, friends and family are often shocked. They never even suspected that person. They are generally quick to proclaim their support and announce his innocence. Perhaps they need to research the profile of a pedophile first. There are typical characteristics that many pedophiles share.

First, there is not a typical pedophile. They can be young or old, rich or poor, educated or uneducated and of any race. Yes, they can be priests or law enforcement officers. There are certain characteristics that many pedophiles share but these are only indicators that a person may be a pedophile.

Although pedophiles are usually male and over 30, there are female pedophiles too. He is usually single with few friends his age group. He may have unexplained gaps in his employment. Pedophiles are often attractive and well liked by adults and children who are very surprised when the person is identified as a pedophile.

Pedophiles often work with children, either employed or in a voluntary capacity. They like to earn the trust of children and adults and be in a position where they are alone with children. Discovery may come to light only when the abused child grows up and has the courage to report them.

Most pedophiles look for children around puberty. They can target boys, girls or both. They often pay special attention to children who are loners or need extra attention. (Parents, especially where there is only one parent, should make sure their children get all the attention they need)

Sometimes the child will develop feelings for the pedophile. The innocent victim will often lose the ability to tell the difference between good and bad behavior out of compassion and kindness for the predator. The child is rarely forced into sexual activity, but the activity is gained through trust and friendship. Secrecy is often kept by the adult coercing the child into not telling by threatening that something bad will happen.

A pedophile has usually been abused as a child, and a child who is abused will often abuse when they become an adult. They don't believe what they are doing to a child is wrong.

Many people love children and enjoy working with them without being pedophiles. Just be careful leaving your children with other adults. Pedophiles can be friends, neighbors, coaches, teachers or relatives. Be observant and aware of the adults in your child's life.

Again, my examination of my life showed me the cause for MY behavioral problems. I do not mean to imply that the cause is simplistic or the same as I found mine to be. However, the cure as I am about to reveal may be.

Scientists by definition are skeptics. To borrow a little insight from Brian Dunning, a skeptic blogger, *"skepticism is, or should be, an extraordinarily powerful and positive influence on the world. Skepticism is not simply about "debunking" as is commonly charged. Skepticism is about redirecting attention, influence, and funding away from worthless superstitions and toward projects and ideas that are evidenced to be beneficial to humanity and to the world."*

Then why don't scientists direct attention, influence and funding to benefit society's victims of pedophilia by finding the cause?

The scientific method is central to skepticism. The scientific method requires evidence, preferably derived from validated testing. Anecdotal evidence and personal testimonies generally don't meet the qualifications for scientific evidence, and thus won't often be accepted by a responsible skeptic; who often explains why skeptics get such a bad rap for being negative or disbelieving.

So my anecdotal evidence and personal testimony fails because is does not meet the qualifications for scientific evidence. Could this be why our experts have not found either the cause or cure for pedophilia?

Skepticism is an essential and meaningful component of the search for truth, but it should not be the only component. There is room for anecdotal evidence and personal testimony. What would result if there were overwhelming anecdotal evidence and personal testimony obtained from interviewing the many thousands of pedophiles who have been released from prisons? Certainly this autobiography could serve as the beginning of that quest. Interviewing pedophiles who are locked up would be a waste of time. They are not interested in finding or helping to find the answer. They are trying to survive in a hostile environment.

Society's sex registries are approaching a million "known" sexual deviants. That is but a small fraction of reality. How many sex crimes go un-discovered, or un-reported, or un-believed, or un-prosecuted?

If extraordinary claims require extraordinary evidence, then there should be an extraordinary effort to find the cause of pedophilia even if it means modifying the scientific method to do so. Who is interviewing those who register every year? You are correct – no one.

Unfortunately scientists appear to be willing to ignore the challenge for this responsibility, and allow revenge and punishment by the penal system as the only solution while countless victims continue to have their lives ruined.

In California in 1981 at the time I committed my crime, there was an attempt to house pedophiles and other sexual deviates at Atascadero State Prison where such a "scientific inquiry" as to the cause was possible. But that approach was abandoned. As a result child molestation has sky-rocketed and there does not appear to be any relief in sight regardless of the degree of revenge or punishment society imposes.

Society would do well to re-examine its Child Protective Services in order to prevent the creation of sexual deviates or child molesters or predators. If a child is given the right start in life there is no way they will go on to victimize other members of society. There are so many news stories how Child Protective Services dropped their administrative or investigatory ball and learn of their failure only after a child is killed. They have been too busy creating an unstable life for their charges by moving them from one foster home to another.

Had there been a Child Protective Service that, on behalf of the court system that sentenced me at the age of two, monitored the nuns at *St. Francis Orphan Asylum* there would have been no green hickory stick and the resultant damage it caused to society by those at the receiving end of that weapon of ass destruction.

Had there been a Child Protective Service that reviewed the background or credentials and conduct of the laymen hired by the Catholics who had the responsibility to protect their charges at St. Joseph's House for Homeless and Industrious Boys, society would not have had to suffer the consequences. And neither would I have suffered any consequences. Those consequences include countless victims whose lives have been destroyed and the phenomenal expense to house those predators who were caught and imprisoned.

In my opinion the focus should be moved from the end to the beginning. The effort and expense it takes to look at the beginning of a child's development is much less than that required for looking at the end and the resulting damage that is caused.

After a long and objective view of my first few decades through the writing of this work, it is clear to me that my dysfunctional and subsequent deviant behavior was created and caused by adults charged with my care and protection. Society must take responsibility for its failures and not blame it on its victims. Was I supposed to magically become normal when I turned 18 years of age? It is generally believed by society and its experts that one who is molested will go on to molest. That is certainly true in my case. If society does not have the answer to the question: what is the cause of child molestation, then my answer might deserve some serious consideration.

When I write that this is society's responsibility, I also mean it is the responsibility of parents. My victim's mother ignored his needs and care in favor of her need to find an old man. She effectively tossed her son into my web. Every time I see a news report of another molestation I look immediately to the parents. Did they do everything possible to protect their child? Their needs must be second to the needs and protection of their children. They need to team up with their child or children to build a defense using knowledge and warnings that would preclude the child from becoming a victim of a pedophile.

Concurrent with the search for the cause of pedophilia should be the search for the *cure* for pedophilia. I tried to present a summary of the current scientific thoughts and conclusions in researching this autobiography. There were a few tiny nibbles toward that goal by the experts but by and large their answer was loud and clear: there is no cure!

That very well may be the justification for society's revenge and punishment approach to one of society's pressing problems. But it is like using a band aide where a tourniquet is required.

The sex-offender's registration laws are equally ineffective. True, they will let law enforcement know that another attack was made or another murder was committed by a registered sex offender, but the registration laws do not prevent the attack. They are a waste of money. In fact, there is a general opinion forming that concludes more victims of child molestation are also being murdered because the offenders fear they will be caught and believe murder prevents their discovery.

There is no way I can offer what I believe is the universal cure to pedophilia except to look at my life for a cure applicable to me which this autobiography does. So in my opinion the cure I am about to discuss will only be based on the cure of my pedophilia. It is possible that it is also applicable to others, but they will have to make that determination.

Anyone who is in the process of victimizing a child, by thinking about it, by planning it, or by contemplating re-offending, I have this warning for you. Before you think about the cure, think about the consequences of your behavior, and you will not have to worry about a cure. Most persons serving time have failed to think about the consequences of their actions. Child molesters, perhaps, have the most serious consequences to contemplate.

First and foremost you are creating not only a victim by your horrendous act, but your victim is likely to repeat your behavior and victimize others. Almost as important is this advice: think of the consequences of this crime and how it will immediately affect you. **You will be caught and you will not like prison**. The rest of your life will be a stress test that you will fail. You need to ask yourself one question before proceeding: is the self-gratification worth it? But there is one consequence I shall address later which is profound and it will devastate you.

My recommendation is for you to examine what I am revealing as the cure for me. Perhaps it is your cure too.

Skeptics and many scientists look at two of the most mind-boggling questions that can be asked: where did we come from, and where are we going? As to the first question they have devised the Big Bang Theory as the answer.

The Big Bang theory is an effort to explain what happened at the very beginning of our universe.

Discoveries in astronomy and physics have shown beyond a reasonable doubt that our universe did in fact have a beginning. Prior to that moment there was nothing; during and after that moment there was something: our universe.

The big bang theory is an effort to explain what happened during and after that moment.

According to the standard theory, our universe sprang into existence as "singularity" around 13.7 billion years ago. What is a "singularity" and where does it come from? Scientists don't know for sure.

Singularities are zones which defy our current understanding of physics. They are thought to exist at the core of "black holes." Black holes are areas of intense gravitational pressure. The pressure is thought to be so intense that finite matter is actually squished into infinite density (a mathematical concept which truly boggles the mind). These zones of infinite density are called "singularities."

Our universe is thought by the scientific community to have begun as an infinitesimally small, infinitely hot and dense, something - a singularity. Where did it come from? We don't know. Why did it appear? We don't know.

After its initial appearance, it apparently inflated (the "Big Bang"), expanded and cooled, going from very, very small and very, very hot, to the size and temperature of our current universe. It continues to expand and cool to this day and we are inside of it: incredible creatures living on a unique planet, circling a beautiful star clustered together with several hundred billion other stars in a galaxy soaring through the cosmos, along with billions of other galaxies, all of which is inside of an expanding universe that began as an infinitesimal singularity which appeared out of nowhere for reasons unknown. This is the Big Bang theory.

It is no wonder the scientific method is based on skepticism!

Any discussion of the Big Bang theory would be incomplete without asking the question, what about God? This is because cosmogony (the study of the origin of the universe) is an area where science and theology meet. Creation was a supernatural event. That is, it took place outside of the natural realm. This fact begs the question: is there anything else which exists outside of the natural realm? Specifically, is there a master Architect out there? We know that this universe had a beginning. Was God the "First Cause?"

To me the answer is so obvious, but it was not always so. In *St. Francis Orphan Asylum*, we were not permitted to read the Bible. On the very first page is the answer that the skeptics might wish to consider as to how their Big Bang occurred.

In the beginning God created the heaven and the earth.

And the earth was without form, and void; and darkness was upon the face of the deep. And the Spirit of God moved upon the face of the waters.

And God said, Let there be light: and there was light.

And God saw the light, that it was good: and God divided the light from the darkness.

And God called the light Day, and the darkness he called Night. And the evening and the morning were the first day.

And God said, Let there be a firmament in the midst of the waters, and let it divide the waters from the waters.

And God made the firmament, and divided the waters which were under the firmament from the waters which were above the firmament: and it was so.

And God called the firmament Heaven. And the evening and the morning were the second day.

And God said, Let the waters under the heaven be gathered together unto one place, and let the dry land appear: and it was so.

And God called the dry land Earth; and the gathering together of the waters called the Seas: and God saw that it was good.

All of the questions science asks about our beginning can be found in the Bible!

But why should we believe this old book, either its old or new testaments?

Again, a quick look in the new testament at 2 Timothy 3: 16 states: *All scripture is given by inspiration of God, and is profitable for doctrine, for reproof, for correction, for instruction in righteousness.*

In my mind the operable words are "...given by inspiration of God".

The opposite of skepticism might well be faith. Faith can be described as a confident belief in the truth, value, or trustworthiness of a person, idea, or thing. Faith would be a belief that does not rest on logical proof or material evidence. A Christian's faith is a theological virtue defined as secure belief in God and a trusting acceptance of God's will.

Perhaps then, if science does not have the answer to the question – what is a cure for pedophilia – which I sought and found through revealing my life story, perhaps the Bible does. And if it does – and I can attest it did for me – then why not give it a try?

But where in the Bible is the cure?

Since my baptism I have taken to listen to John MacArthur on his radio broadcast **Understanding the Bible, One Verse at a Time**. He has been preaching the bible for 42 years. His **Grace to You** website is an excellent resource for people wishing to understand and then to walk with Christ.

In one particular broadcast he discusses what I believe to be the cure. *A Jewish law expert once asked Jesus, "What is the greatest commandment?" You remember His answer: "You shall love the Lord your God with all your heart, and with all your soul, and with all your mind. This is the great and foremost commandment" (Matt. 22:37-38). Though that seemed to satisfy the question, Jesus wasn't finished. Without taking a breath, He added, "The second is like it, 'You shall love your neighbor as yourself".*

That, to me, is the cure. Because Pastor MacArthur is explaining the bible one verse at a time, let me continue writing what he spoke.

Love for God and love for your neighbor are vitally connected and cannot be separated – you cannot do one without doing the other. How important is this second commandment? James called it the "royal" or sovereign law – it towers over the rest. Paul said if you keep it, you will be fulfilling the demands of the entire Old Testament (Rom. 13:9; Gal. 5:14).

Recognizing the command is one thing – understanding and practicing biblical love is another.

When I first came to Grace Community Church, I wanted badly to love everyone, but I couldn't figure out how to get the emotional feeling I thought was necessary. Some people were kind of irritating, and some even purposely made things difficult for me. I wanted to love them, but I didn't know how. One day I went to a man who was particularly difficult, put my arm around him, and said, "I want you to know something. If there's any way I can ever serve you, I'd sure love to have the opportunity." The opportunity came. My attitude toward him didn't change because of how I felt about him emotionally, but because of how I came to love him by serving him.

Just like the example John Macarthur offers above, the cure for pedophilia has to be the same. Predators in a sick way may feel emotional about their victims, but you love him or her, by serving him or her. Molesting is a tremendous disservice. It is not an act of love.

Loving others is not a question of patting someone on the back and saying, "You're so wonderful, so irresistible. I love you!" You show love by making personal sacrifices to meet someone's need.

The personal sacrifice a predator can show is to make the personal sacrifice of putting a potential victim's need well ahead of his. It is absolutely essential that a predator repress what is seen as his emotional need in favor of the would-be victim's emotional health.

If you still have doubts about what biblical love is, ponder this: Has God ever shouted, "I love you!" from heaven or written it in the sky? No; we see the love of God in Christ laying down His life for us. God put His Son on a cross on our behalf. That is how He expressed His love – through sacrifice. Since Christ "laid down His life for us ... we ought to lay down our lives for the brethren" (1 John 3:16).

There can be no greater sacrifice than the Son of God demonstrated when He laid down His life for all of us.

Is it too much to ask a predator to stop what he intends to do – victimize children – and to sacrifice - what is perceived in error to be - an emotional need he must have satisfied at a child's expense?

This begs the question: can you love your neighbor if you do not love yourself? If because you had a similar upbringing as I have and as a result have such low self-esteem, can you learn how and where to start to love yourself if you believe that is necessary in order to love others the same way?

The Bible says in James 2:8 we are to love our neighbors as we love ourselves." That is a popular concept. But it is not what James 2:8 (or the rest of Scripture) teaches. Psychologists have made a business out of misinterpreting that verse. They say you must learn a "healthy" self-love to gain a good self-image; if you do not have a high regard for yourself, you will never be able to love other people the way God intended.

John Macarthur claims that is a serious misunderstanding.

Those who advocate the saying, "learn to love yourself before you can love others," naively ignore what the Bible teaches about sin – that it is inherently self interested. To teach someone to love themselves is to justify or encourage the consuming sin of pride and to undercut any effort or desire to sacrifice self and love others.

That seems to be a sound answer and it is based on scripture.

So what does it mean to love others as you love yourself? Look at James 2:1: "My brethren, do not hold your faith in our glorious Lord Jesus Christ with an attitude of personal favoritism." The text goes on to give the illustration of a rich man and a poor man visiting a congregation and being treated differently. James is saying that as a Christian you are not to treat certain people with respect while you treat others with indifference. Rather, to fulfill the royal law, you are to treat everyone as you would treat yourself – the assumption is that you are already naturally inclined to treat yourself best. Whatever great sacrifices you make for your own comfort, you should make the same for the comfort of others, without respect to their status in life. It has nothing to do with the importance of loving self; it has to do with your service toward others.

So if the cure is service toward others, how can child molestation be justified? It cannot! It can be terminated and eliminated.

Just stop, for example, and consider the lengths you go to make yourself comfortable. That is the same way you should meet the needs of others. The way you treat your own desires is the way you should treat the desires of others. You should love them in terms of self-sacrificing service, just as you make sacrifices for your own benefit.

It is these two commandments that are the basis for my cure. Serving others is the best explanation of the second greatest commandment. To serve others requires a sacrifice. To stop from becoming a predator requires a sacrifice of what you believe you may enjoy so that another person's basic and realistic needs may be met. **That is loving your neighbor as yourself**.

The words of Jesus are simple, yet penetrating. The command to "Love your neighbor as yourself" is a challenge. Winners in life's race learn to obey the greatest commandment: loving God, and loving our neighbors. This takes supernatural power, since our natural inclination is to love only ourselves.

My 70 year quest for family has come to an end. It is a very happy ending. A dozen years ago God introduced me to the Klimov family. Through God, the Klimov family introduced me to so many brothers and sisters in Grace Family Church.

On March 15, 2009, when I was baptized I became a Child of God. Becoming a Child of God is Priceless!

To a Christian believer, being a child of God means that God the Father, as well as the Son, and the Holy Spirit, are there for them. If we need Him, the Father especially, He is there to answer all of our prayers. Our prayers may not be answered the way we want or even when we want, but He does always answer.

The Father isn't just an Answer Man either, as He is a Person too, and being a Person, and our Foremost Friend, He wants our love, attention, friendship, and devotion and He wants us to give that to Him voluntarily. If a person is truly saved, and walking the right path, his or her heart should be overflowing with these and should love spending their lives with Him, as He has saved their eternal souls, through the death of His Son.

If anyone is contemplating molesting a child, remember that your victim is a child of God and anyone molesting a child of God will suffer **eternal** consequences. Avoid creating a victim, and ruining your life by turning to and trusting in your creator.

I finally got good news from my attorney. He had found a court that would hear my motion. It would not be the original sentencing judge because that judge was a visiting judge. My attorney Steven Plesser was reluctant to bring my case back to Judge Davidian because Davidian, a former prosecutor, appeared to favor the prosecutor's office and had done nothing about Al Thomas's extortion. He had the power to cause an investigation. A lie-detector examination of both Thomas and me would begin to find the truth. An interview with all others arrested for probation violations who Thomas supervised to determine if they were also threatened if they did not plead guilty would establish whether he had committed extortion in their cases too.

My motion to modify probation was asking the court to grant me permission to live at the Klimov residence. It also asked the court to allow me to set up a booth at art shows and festivals so I could sell my vistagraphs. It further asked the court to grant me permission to attend church services and functions.

The most important request in my motion was to ask the court to clarify the probation term preventing me from being in the <u>presence</u> of any minor by changing it to prohibiting me from <u>associating</u> with any minor. And lastly, the court was being asked to reduce formal probation to informal probation. This would allow me to return to Oregon.

The motion was to be heard on April 12, 2011, in Superior Court Department 61.

I let the Klimovs know and brought my problem to the attention of Pastor Benjamin Kondor. At Sunday services on April 10, he asked the parishioners to say a prayer for a successful outcome at the hearing.

Stas Gorobchuk, Nick and Marina's son-in-law, had come to my probation violation sentencing and observed that the Judge took note that the ten people who attended the courtroom on behalf of a defendant who had an alcoholic problem were unprecedented in his courtroom. So Stas set out to ask people to come to my hearing. I assumed Department 61 was in the main courthouse, but Stas had to tell me it was at the jail instead. That would have not gone over well if I had not been there when my motion was to be heard.

I arrived at Department 61 an hour early. Nick and Marina showed up with Marina's two sisters, Alla and Inna. Our good friends Vasily and Ira came. Slava Klimov arrived. Benjamin Kondor and two other pastors Andre and Vasily also came. Nick's brother Leonid, who I had sponsored to come to America showed up with his three sons Roman, Alex and Vitaly. Of course Stas arrived. Six of my students showed up and brought two friends. Two members of Nick's bible study group came as did two young people who I did not know. I was flabbergasted. It was very emotional for me and I held back tears as I thanked each of them. Twenty-seven people took the time to come to the courtroom and support my motion.

The courtroom had seating for forty persons. When we went in there were eleven people sitting. My attorney had given me a little bad news just before we entered. Apparently, the district attorney did not have my case file and the motion could not be heard. The hearing was re-scheduled to April 25 at 8:30 am. My attorney asked the judge to note that I had twenty-seven members of the community in the courtroom.

I would have to wait for two more weeks before learning of my fate.

The two weeks went by fast. I did not want my friends and brothers and sisters from Grace Family Church to take the time to support me in the court proceeding because the judge had already noted that I had community support. On the day of the hearing of my motion, not only did the twenty-seven show up who had been to the previous scheduled hearing, but five more were present for a total of thirty-two.

The bad news this time was that the probation department had not yet submitted their comments and the hearing would have to be postponed again for two more weeks. This might be yet another example of what the probation department's mission statement meant by professionalism and excellence. Although Al Thomas was asked to submit comments for the court, he "delegated" that duty to Dayhuff who was on vacation.

I visited with Dayhuff prior to the next court appearance and he commented that my attorney had done a great job with his petition but that the probation department could not support the request for changing my formal probation to informal. He also said the department would not oppose any of the other requests that I was making.

The primary change I was requesting to the other probation terms was the requirement that I not be in the presence of minor children unless there is also present a responsible adult approved by the probation department. In the court's chambers judge Koller told my attorney that Marina Klimova would be designated as a responsible adult.

In court the judge agreed that it would be impossible for anyone to comply with the requirement "not be in the presence of a minor". She changed the wording to "not to associate with any minor." Although she did not mention "responsible adult" in open court, she did tell my attorney that Marina Klimov would be a responsible adult. Nevertheless she did modify the probation term to state that the defendant may live at the Klimov residence but "if the grandchildren are present, defendant is not to associate with them."

She also amended the probation order to allow me to sell my vistagraphs at art shows, festivals and fairs that are adult oriented. She made it clear that I could attend church services and other functions that were adult oriented.

Life would become somewhat better for me. I now only had to register once a year because I was no longer homeless. I only had to visit with my probation officer every other month instead of once a week.

Although I could live in my trailer in the Klimov backyard, I could not associate with Benjamin or Nellie when they came to visit. I still had two more years of formal probation to serve. With God's help it would go by quickly and there would be no more confrontations with law enforcement or its probation arm.

It is my desire to get back to Christmas Valley with their cool summers, and harsh winters, and to enjoy the rest of my life there. I will, of course, visit the Klimov family and my Grace family periodically, in conjunction with doctor visits or on holidays.

What have I learned in writing my life story? Clearly I have learned and focused on those facts that have contributed to the cause of my pedophilia. I have learned that my minutes of criminal behavior caused my victim a lifetime of harm. And, I have learned that the cure for me includes the support of a loving family and friends. But it is the word of God revealed through the bible that proclaims that we are all children of God. It is this belief that is a guarantee that I will never create another victim.

CPSIA information can be obtained
at www.ICGtesting.com
Printed in the USA
FSHW010727010320
67685FS

9 781463 668068